D0776754

Reading Frames in Modern Fiction

MARY ANN CAWS

Reading Frames
in
Modern Fiction

PRINCETON UNIVERSITY PRESS

PRINCETON NEW JERSEY

Copyright © 1985 by Princeton University Press

Published by Princeton University Press, 41 William Street,
Princeton, New Jersey 08540

In the United Kingdom: Princeton University Press, Guildford, Surrey

All Rights Reserved

Library of Congress Cataloging in Publication Data will be found
on the last printed page of this book

ISBN 0-691-06625-6

This book has been composed in Linotron Galliard
Clothbound editions of Princeton University Press books are printed on
acid-free paper, and binding materials are chosen for strength
and durability

Printed in the United States of America by Princeton University Press,
Princeton, New Jersey

Designed by Laury A. Egan

m.R

If you really want to know, I'll tell you that they were on their way towards . . . yes, why not? . . . towards an immense castle, on the frontispiece of which was written: "I belong to no one and I belong to everyone. You were there before entering, and you will still be there when you come out!"—Did they enter that castle?—No, for the inscription was false, or they were there before entering.—But at least they came out?—No, for the inscription was false, or they were still there when they came out.

    DIDEROT, *Jacques le Fataliste*

Have you ever noticed that a patch of sky, perceived through some vent, or between two chimney-spouts, two rocks, or through an arcade, gives a deeper idea of the infinite than some great panoramic view from a mountain top?

    BAUDELAIRE, letter to Armand Fraisse

I'm fond of representation—the representation of life: I like it better, I think, than the real thing.

    JAMES, *The Tragic Muse*

CONTENTS

PREFACE: READING FRAMES

But this is what I see; this is what I see.

WOOLF, *To the Lighthouse*

The major theses of the following pages are three. First, that often, in the most widely read and enduring narratives, certain passages stand out in relief from the flow of the prose and create, in so standing, different expectations and different effects. We perceive borders as if signaled by alterations of pattern and architectural, verbal, or diegetic clues. In an intensification of focus, the included elements are heightened visually and stressed verbally, as the surroundings are cropped off at the sides. These larger-than-life situations seem to hold the essence of the work, and not infrequently is it remembered by them, each as a metonymy for the larger picture.

Second, these noticeable passages often enable the intrusion of another genre into the narrative text by appropriate means. Passages heavy in repeats, delays, and temporal markings, as in an incantatory or impassioned lyric tone, may be seen as penetrated by musical structure. Static arrests and heavy outlining as well as the description of, or reference to, actual or imagined art objects insist on visual and spatial perception; highly posed scenes, with vivid dialogue and gesture, are felt as calling upon dramatic form. A clearly visible stress in each case upon a density usually absent from the single genre creates a privileged space and a remarkable moment, brief or prolonged, which remains in the mind thereafter.

Third, whereas the passages so marked in "pre-modernist" texts generally call attention to the substance and the field included or stressed, the principal texts of modernism emphasize the very idea of framing as it calls attention, above all, to itself, and to the frames rather than what they include. This change requires in its turn an eventual modification of our own ideas about and methods of framing.

For this volume, the ordering arrangement includes first a general discussion of frames as I mean them here, of their definitions, their techniques, their perception, and their philosophical, psychological, and sociological use.

The main body of the book consists of two major segments and a linking part: first, the pre-modernist writers Austen, Melville, and Hardy, representing, respectively, a framing neat in appearance, but with the extraordinary mental and presentational complexities of *Mansfield Park*; a parody of framing patterns never more disturbing than in *Pierre*; and an obsessive melancholic enclosure responsible for the slow and predictable undoing of both *Tess* and *Jude*. At the center of the body of the text, a study in Poe and Baudelaire dealing with circumspection and circumscription, or looking and writing around, deals with the conjoined problems of crossing and translation, of the mixing of languages and of genres, in a textual portraiture emblematic of this entire study.

Finally, the segment on modernist or high framing treats James (the great ambivalent framer and inspiration for this book), Proust (a conceptual, visual, and metaphysical framer), and Woolf, whose emotional, sensual, and lyric framing in *To the Lighthouse* prepares the way for her high formal masterpiece, *The Waves*.

As for the concentration on fictional and "prose" but often poetic and never prosaic presentations of frames in the works included here, Bernard of the latter volume will speak for the voice speaking in this study: " 'Heaven be praised,' I said, 'we need not whip this prose into poetry. The little language is enough.' "[1]

ACKNOWLEDGMENTS

This work was begun under a Fellowship of the National Endowment for the Humanities, in conjunction with a Faculty Research award from the City University of New York.

The Virginia Woolf chapter appeared, in a slightly different form, in the collage issue of the *New York Literary Forum* in 1982, and the Poe and Baudelaire chapter in the April and May issues of the *French Review* in 1983: to the editors of these journals, my thanks.

Initially, a series of keyhole or preliminary framing chapters on framing in Madame de Lafayette, Hawthorne, Flaubert, Ford Madox Ford, Edith Wharton, Henry Green, Robbe-Grillet, Borges, and Cortázar preceded the body of the volume here: their present ellipsis represents spatial reasons, those of the mind and not of the heart.

Since completing the first version of this work, I have had the privilege of consulting with a number of friends about the topic, each of whom has made valuable suggestions: Yves Bonnefoy, Micheline Braun, Hilary Caws, Ross Chambers, Maurice Charney, Dorritt Cohn, Joan Dayan, L. M. Findlay, Lorand and Jacqueline Gaspar, Alexander Gelley, Claudio Guillén, David Hayman, Judd Hubert, Gerhard Joseph, Sam Levin, Nancy Mellerski, Michael Nimetz, Linda Nochlin, Henri Peyre, Michael Riffaterre, Patricia Terry, Arnold Weinstein, Philip Weinstein, René Wellek, and Sarah Wright. At the Princeton University Press, Jerry Sherwood's encouragement has been warm and unflagging, and Robert Brown's advice, essential.

To my husband, Peter Caws, who has put up with a good deal of talk about Henry James, this book is dedicated.

Reading Frames in Modern Fiction

I / APERTURE

... though the relations of a human figure or a social
occurrence are what make such objects interesting, they also
make them, to the same tune, difficult to isolate, to surround
with the sharp black line, to frame in the square, the circle, the
charming oval, that helps any arrangement of objects to become
a picture.

　　　HENRY JAMES, preface to *The Awkward Age*[1]

STOPPING THE SCENE

This book had its origin in the hypothesis that many readers
recall the same scenes from even the longest novels, that frequently the same passages have stood out from the whole in
successive readings, and are represented in the memory as con-
densations of action and vision. They could be compared to a
static arrest, within the normal flow of the text, for the presentation of a scene whose borders are so marked as to enhance and
enclose its denser, or more "dramatic," more pictorial, or more
musical, or sometimes more "poetic," consistency. The actions
and gestures seem to participate in a space larger than ordinary
narrative space, and yet a heavily bordered one; their importance
seems heightened, the energy unaccustomed, the language more
"meaningful." The elements enclosed within the framed passage
may appear to refer out to the larger or whole text, and the
passage may appear to represent something beyond itself, as if it
were a metonymic indication of some larger significance;[2] at the
same time, the framed passage may seem complete within itself:
thus the fascination with the process and with the effect.

　　To frame in is also to frame out, so that the notions of grid
and selection, of inclusion and exclusion, are constantly in play,
as well as those of border and of centering or focus. Many of the

devices that work so efficaciously upon the imagination in these passages seem to play upon the same motifs and with the same techniques. This study concerns the techniques of bordering that mark such passages for our own arrest: visual, gestural, verbal, and conceptual, as they are contained in works relatively familiar to us all. I have made my own selection from the art of the novel and the tale, with a side excursion into one narrative poem of a heavily framed portrait. Dramatic framing makes its own incursion into the art of James, for example, and in some measure the art of framing is itself a will to the mixing of genres, a point to which I shall return.

The first question to ask is pragmatic: To what extent is the frame useful as a concept? Too elastic in definition, it would enclose too much; too narrow, it would exclude any richness of content. Ruskin's meditation upon the topic of topic itself, as it is problematic and insoluble, opposes inflexibility and encourages fruitful ironies about the very project of investigating any question at all about which we would like to draw simple or simply stated conclusions: "I never met with a question yet, of any importance, which did not need, for the right solution of it, at least one positive and one negative answer, like an equation of the second degree. . . . Mostly, matters of consequence are three-sided, or four-sided, or polygonal; and the trotting around is severe work for people in any way stiff in their opinions."[3]

I take that passage as illustrative of thinking about framing: the frame is valuable as a concept for the imagination, even in its strictest limits, as is the very act of "trotting around" it occasions, plainly self-inclusive and self-framing. The notions presented here and the initial categories of possible techniques that I shall try to establish are in no way to be taken as stiffly opinionated or rigidly "right." They are, like the frames themselves, above all, aids to perception, developed hypothetically in view of a variety of texts.

The topic is further complicated by the observation that, very often, the most interestingly framed passages are to be found in novels and stories in which—as they are offset, inset, and peculiarly visible—they intensify the oddness of the whole. The framed passage, by definition, stands out against the average one, or deep within it. As for oddness, one of the oddest complications of the perception itself is the self-inclusion typical of the topic; given that an observing figure is often included in the passage as framed, the very shiftings of vision by the reader may be controlled by those ascribed to an enclosed figure. *But all frames are constantly open to shift and exchange.*

CONSCRIPTION AND GENRE MIXING

The selective or framing look cuts out, concentrates upon, and centers on whatever is to be emphasized, by a decoupage or circumscription—writing around and about, cutting and cropping—all of which exemplify a technique of limiting with positive aims. A sonnet by Hérédia,[4] to which Philippe Hamon refers in his description of description, showing how it works vertically from head to foot, reveals also a whole universe of action and vision circumscribed in a reduced scene within the queen's eyes.[5] They are not starry but starred with golden flecks, as with time and space gathered within the strictest of possible limits; the severe cropping of everything outside them brightens both the flash of her eyes and the cosmic vision captured there:

Et sur elle courbé, l'ardent imperator
Vit dans ses larges yeux étoilés de points d'or
Toute une mer immense où fuyaient des galères.

And bending over her, the ardent emperor
Saw in her large eyes starred with flecks of gold
A whole immense sea where galleys were fleeing.

This bestarred text offers a privileged and visionary example of the circumspective power, taken within the narrow compass of the eyes themselves, with the gold rendering the vision still more valuable, still more valid. This constrictive art requires, for its recognition, the detection of cut and cropped borders and their visual and verbal emphasis by such procedures as repetition, contrast, reversal, figure change, and patterning around the central focus: of these, repetition is perhaps the simplest to detect, and it or the effect it produces can be stressed as the device most proper to the intensification of those passages we read as deeply poetic. Gerard Manley Hopkins, for instance, presents poetry as what is detached from prose by its frame: "Poetry is speech framed for contemplation of the mind by the way of hearing or speech framed to be heard for its own sake and interest even over and above its interest of meaning. ... If not repetition, oftening, over-and-overing, aftering of the inscape must take place in order to detach it to the mind and in this light poetry is speech which afters and oftens its inscape, speech couched in a repeating figure."[6]

The framed passage "stands by itself": this shape of the texts we contemplate here as framed within the ongoing flow of the narrative, these texts standing out and in, import this technique from poetry to prose, making an arrest of a most exceptional kind, dense, "aftered," and "overed." They also, in other cases, appropriate the techniques of melodrama for the needs of narrative, so that—as critics have pointed out in the case of Henry James particularly—the melodramatic scene occurs within the narrative as a contrast with the picture. Now the inserted picture also, that import from art, is found to make this static arrest— witness the picture described, as in the cases Hamon studies, as well as the inset pictures themselves; the developing power in each case, that of scene and of object, is all the greater for the insertion within the unlike. What is true of the poetically dense moment[7]—or of the dramatically rich moment or of the vividly pictured moment or, again, of the musical moment, which we will study in Proust—within the narrative, is that the contrast of the two genres lends greater force to both.

The framed moment is frequently *the other in the same*: play or poem or artistic or musical pause in the flux and flow of story.

The concentration upon this otherness, with its modern connotations and its ancient reverberations—for instance the *ekphrasis*
of the Greeks, or their inset choruses—is the point of the present
tale. It is this inter-genre impact which my frame circumscribes
and writes about. In these moments of intensified scent and sight
and sound, or of intensified realizations and revelations, the
heightened effect extends beyond the perception of the narrator
out to the reader in an increasing experiential correspondence of
alternate modalities, and of the signs of, or pointers toward, the
inclusion of the other scene, so often stolen from another genre,
and so often worth the steal.

CHANGING FRAMES

The change of genre is always noticeable, for the mode is evident, whether it be lyric, musical, dramatic, or narrative; the particular moments examined here are in general the crossings of
other genres over into the narrative. Of the several techniques
which may mark the limits in which these specific crossings are
situated within the general flow of the text, some are discussed
in the following pages; these borders for the specific passages in
question are the subject of my book. Since the change of genre
is already a breaking of the "frame of expectation" set up by what
precedes the change, these passages so marked are to be read
sometimes as the framed junctures between one frame and expectation and another, and sometimes as framed moments unto
themselves, but almost always of brief duration and bordered in
heavily stressed limits. They can be viewed as the operators of
the narrative text, or the *agents de change*, since they alter the
preceding sight and psychological or mind set, but also as culminations in themselves of the intensive mode characteristic of
genre crossing, in whatever way their own borders are to be
read. The opposite of blank spaces or neutral counters or silences
permitting the interruption of the narrative or discursive flow or
the nondistinctive noise in order to make form and sense, these

highly charged moments or scenes are the bearers of meaning and intensity, the conveyors of revelation and insight. They are themselves what they contain, being the pictures on the wall of the text, the poetic summits of the prose, the tonic highlights of the musical offering, and the dramatic culminations of the play of the text. Giving themselves in particular spectacle, these parts standing for the whole do not just encourage, they force our deeper understanding of the unity and the ultimate meaning of what we are led to contemplate and reflect upon, in a pause or a delay[8] or a tableau, or an interreferential and repeating moment, even as we are swept along in the narrative flow. These are what literature is, for a large part, about.

II / PERCEIVING BORDERS

> Older people tend to overlook the frame, even when they are
> looking right at it, said Thomas. They don't like to think about
> it.
> DONALD BARTHELME, *The Dead Father*

INSETTING, OUTLINING, AND RELATING

Both the simple border separating the enclosed space of the visual object from its backdrop, like the figure cut out or pasted
against it—this border, perceived or not as the isolating element—and the high baroque verbal borders of Henry James state
equally the importance of what they enclose, privileging a re-
stricted area for heightened perception and focus.

In their turn, however, they presuppose other concepts of edging and enable the perception of further edges; borders relate to
other borders, outlines to other outlines. Hierarchic arrangement
in order of difficulty and interest would present first the most
easily perceived architectural outlining, in which the view is set
off by being placed at a certain height, like the scaffold scene in
Hawthorne's *Scarlet Letter* or the figure of Eustachia Vye profiled
high upon the barrow against the sky in Thomas Hardy's *Return
of the Native*, or by backlighting, as in the image of Madame
Arnoux luminously detached, on shipboard in Gustave Flaubert's
Sentimental Education. In the same category is Henry James's
outlining a figure in a door or window as a presentational space:
this often permits the description of the contents of that room
or of that figure. The window permits another level of complication, as the framed picture may be seen from either the viewer's
outlook or inlook, depending on the placement. Some scenes
manage both: for instance, in Hawthorne's *Blithedale Romance*,
Coverdale's framed sight of the leading figures of the utopian

colony, seen out from his boardinghouse window and in through their window.

The visual connects with the conceptual on a level of greater complication, as still another work of art, visual or verbal, included within the larger work to explain and point to parts of it, and deepen its meaning: here I am thinking of the inset play in *Mansfield Park* or the portrait of Mr. Darcy in *Pride and Prejudice*, or the portraits of Charlotte and the Prince in Henry James's *Golden Bowl*. In each case, the smaller work serves as a developing object for the larger one. In an extreme case, the two developments—of the inset picture and the outer one in the entire text—may take place at the same time for a double text-in-process, like a metatext: the inserted story of the oval portrait in Edgar Allan Poe's story of the same name coincides with the narrator's reading of the story of the portrait and with the edge of the story we read as well, just as Lily Briscoe's canvas in Virginia Woolf's *To the Lighthouse* is completed precisely when the narrative of the text itself is completed. The smaller-scale work points to the process and the meaning of the larger or including picture, and indicates its major vector or thrust.

In the general category of formal devices, a verbal border exists where an excess or lack is apparent. A nervous repetition of the same terms, a sustained word play, a noticeable ellipsis or a series of deictic pointers may arrest the scene within the ordinary temporal flow, drawing attention to what is blocked out; here it is, says the frame. These borders mark the most painful and prolonged scenes of James's *Wings of the Dove* and *The Golden Bowl*, of such scenes as the "O sole mio" passage in Proust's *Le Temps retrouvé*, and the natural and italicized borders of Woolf's *Waves*.

The major presentational devices throw into relief the moral and formal issues, for what is set apart as denser in stylistic effect or heightened tension than the rest is read as more significant. The nondescript or emptied-out spatial surround, or the temporal delay as the negative border for the framed passage, serve as well as the highly worked borders to make the essential point: the selective function is of double interest, in the selection itself, and in the ongoing process of how the choice is designated. In the first instance, we are reading what is framed, and in the second, we are reading the frames. The first is characteristic of the earlier works discussed here, and the second is, rather, characteristic of modernism, both of its products and of the way in which we tend to view them. The frames are both perceptual and actual; any consideration of the dissolution of the frame in postmodernism would lie beyond the borders of this study, focussed on the frame itself.

SETTING APART

Philosophical Frames: Handling, Containing, Placing

Frames are ways of handling what we are looking at: a celebrated text on the handle as it makes the juncture between the object and what surrounds it, reaching in and out, may help to get a grip on the frame, as it is always to be read facing in both senses: turned out and in, excluding, including, and focusing. Georg Simmel's essay "The Handle" describes the ideal space of art as it relates to reality, taking as an analogy the vase. Held and used in practical life, it "stands in two worlds at one and the same time" (GS, p. 67), having a dual nature which is often expressed by its handle, projecting artistic form in the real words, constituting a single "aesthetic vision" with the body of the base (GS, p. 68).[1] Its shape harmonizes inside and out, working as tool and hand, life flowing through both: "Thus, a mediating bridge is formed, a pliable joining of hand with bowl, which with a palpable continuity, transmits the impulse of the world into the bowl, into its manipulation. But then, through the reflux of this energy, the bowl is drawn into the circumference of the life of the soul." (GS, pp. 69-70). Utility and beauty are transcended by a higher order to which the handle is a cue, one world reaching into another; *The Golden Bowl*, treated here at length, extends between two worlds in such a manner.

In relation to the bowl, it is valuable to compare Roger Fry's aesthetic viewpoint—as shown in his *Vision and Design* and elsewhere—concerning the removal of art from the grime of everyday by distancing and setting aside. One of his most notable responses is to a T'ang dish with a "swept frame" of bracket-shaped reversed curves, whose frame or rim places this object in the world of art, where it can be handled as such.[2]

The philosophical partisans of this formal setting aside are legion: among them, Georg Mehlis, who claims that in art, as in religion, "detachment means everything." The necessary setting apart of the aesthetic object from the observer in order for it to be aesthetic, may consist of a temporal removal, a perspectival shift within the memory, or simply an attitudinal aloofness on the part of the observer. Intimacy is, he claims, inimical to beauty. Like Roger Fry, he believes that the images of great art should be removed from the dust and trivia of everyday life; this distance is preserved by the framing out of the experience into another realm, that of art.[3]

To enable the reading of what is within the frame, free of context, the borders must function as definitive isolation. Ortega y Gasset, in his *Meditaciones del marco* (Meditations on the Frame), considers in particular how the frame isolates like an island (*insula*), forcing us to make the leap from the surroundings to what is contained, how the gold frame in particular permits no reference outside and so is all the better as an isolating or distancing border[4]; along these lines, Roger Fry, among the champions of the heavily framed, completely self-contained and nonreferential art object removed from the "sphere of possible action" in order to attain the status of art, is the critic whose attitude, unsurprisingly, comes closest to the kind of framing visible in Virginia Woolf. The distancing borders are marked differently in different arts: in his " 'Psychical Distance' as a Factor in Art and an Aesthetic Principle," Edward Bullough discusses the pedestal for sculpture, the stage for drama, and the silence preceding and following a musical work as the elements that set apart the aesthetic object: the "delay" I take up here particularly in James would fall in that category. For the picture to be readable and sufficient in itself, certain criteria must obtain. Referring to Bullough, Monroe Beardsley discusses the essential of the interior space of the picture as it must be *complete* and *coherent*; some of the characteristics of this space will become apparent here.[5]

Louis Marin's *Détruire la peinture* (To Destroy Painting) also discusses the frame as a break in the perceptual continuum which neutralizes the surroundings, to enclose the space of "representation in which the object as a figure, the space as a figurative place can be known and read. The frame thus marks the possibility of accession to the object by the gaze, as a readable object."[6] Poussin already formulated its use for readability: "When you have received your painting," he says "I beg you, if you find it any good, to ornament it with a little section of corniche, because it needs that in order for the eye's gaze, passing over all its parts, to be held and not dispersed outside" (DP, p. 56-57). To contrast this plea with Claudel's observation about the Dutch landscape, a field in which, as it offers no precise horizon lines to the viewer, each viewer is free to "organize his own memory and his imagination,"[7] is to contrast the classic view of framing with the romantic or subjective one; the final pages of this book introduce a modernist view of the frame, different from both.

A well-known recent work on framing, that of Jacques Derrida, *La Vérité en peinture* (Truth in Painting), takes up again the notion of handling and passing, playing upon the idea of the "passe-partout" or the rim linking the outer part of painting to the inner part of the frame, in the problematic space "between the outside and the inside, between the external border and the internal border, the framing and the framed, the figure and the background, the form and the content, the signifier and the signified, and so on for any double-bladed opposition."[8] The question as to where the frame is said to be, and its relation to Hegel's notion of the *parergon*, is of less concern to me here than the effect of the actual passages I read as framed within the texts and the recognition of their borders.

Coming to Our Senses: Psychological and Pictorial Borders

Without a frame there can be no centre. The richer the elements of the
frame, the more the centre will gain in dignity.

     E. H. GOMBRICH, *The Sense of Order*

Perceptual psychologists show how we see and how we frame
what it is we see; J. J. Gibson points out the nervous gathering
of information, both by "successive sampling" and by simultaneous grasping, as we project our wide-angle gaze like an oval
window upon the visual field, from one fixation to the next.[9]
Evidence suggests, says Karl Pribram in his *Languages of the Brain*,
that, although the ways in which we structure our experiences
according to our frames of reference show an optimal simplicity,
the rich configurations of complexity in what surrounds us excite
our receptor surfaces "which must engage some brain mechanism
of equal capacity of richness."[10] Similarly, if we reduce too drastically the categories of our literary analysis, seeing only beginnings and endings, these may in the long run not call forth the
maximum potential of our own reading resources, after we first
detect the passage set in relief.

What we notice above all is any change in pattern, any dis-
crepancy or deviation, as Gibson shows in the *The Perception of
the Visual World* (1950); but, as he said there too, the repetitive
order "is the stimulus for verbal texture" (PV, p. 67). The dy-
namism, then, of the deviant playing against the repetitive prepares the surround for a picture of high relief sufficiently complex to call for the competent reading of frames. The inherent
principle of coherence holding together the selected passage chosen for framing is made available for sight and discussion by the
"affordance" of the frame, in Gibson's term (PV, p. 115).

What Ruskin called the "snap" in the frame summoning our
attention, E. H. Gombrich examines as a pattern break.[11] He
develops among other ideas those of translation from one side
to the other, rotation along a stretch axis, increase or reduction
in scale, branching, permutation, and simple, alternating, or cross-
linked sequences, which the reader of James's *Golden Bowl* will

detect there with no effort (the translation from the Prince's viewpoint to that of the Princess, the increase in the size of the imaged rose, the permutations of the bowl symbol, the sequences of specific images and verbal elements, and so on).

Two other art-historical views of the frame contribute to our own view of it. Meyer Schapiro's article "On Some Problems in the Semiotics of Visual Art: Field and Vehicle in Image-Signs" traces the history of the development of the art object from a time at which there were no set boundaries and no regular field to the moment at which a prepared ground, closed, smooth, and of a distinct color, forms a reserved space with a distinct plane against which to read.[12] The framing border is a late invention, preceded by ground lines or strips that connected figures: not until the second millennium B.C. did anyone think of setting, by its means, "the picture surface back into depth." The frame belongs more to the "space of the observer rather than of the illusory, three-dimensional world disclosed within and behind. It is a finding and focusing device placed between the observer and the image" (MS, p. 227). The picture field, continues Schapiro, corresponds to a segment of space "excerpted from a larger whole," in which the part possesses nevertheless its own balance and coherence.

Rudolf Arnheim's *Art and Visual Perception* shows how the lintels and pilasters that surround the Renaissance altarpieces led to the frame's development, reminding us of the time when it was conceived of as a window looking onto a supposedly limitless space; the frame was seen, not as cutting off the segment, but as masking the continuum.[13] Then it became itself the figure, until finally the picture "began to snatch the contour from the frame" (AVP, p. 31), at which point, the frame became simpler, and narrower strips of wood served to set the picture back into the wall. Its ordinary design in a rectangle or a square draws added stability from the form of the page, as the enclosed pattern, smaller, more variable and continuing the motion, assures that any movement seems to go "from the frame anchor to the free space" (AVP, p. 18); the more oblique the motion, the more dynamic the picture. Art as a dynamic pattern demands concentration: the narrower the stage on which the view is focused and the figures discovered, the faster the motion and the more intense the figures seem.

LITERARY CIRCUMSPECTION: SETTING OUT, CLOSURE, AND SETTING IN

Of framing in literature, the studies have been many: Youri Lotman, in his *Structure of the Artistic Text*, speaks of the frame's impenetrability and of the closure of the framed world into its universality; since the work of art already represents, by metonymy, an unlimited world, it is, although spatially limited, the finite reproduction of entirety even being only one episode.[14] The framed text is also a cultural model, so that the mythological functions of births and of endings give the models or stereotypes for the beginnings and ends of the story: for example, "they lived happily ever after," and other happy ends; or intensifications and prolongations of the sort, "the cold gets colder," opening on to an apparently limitless horizon. It is exactly this kind of neat wrapping up of narration on one hand, and the infinite extension on the other, that is challenged by James's brilliant revolution in the world of framing, leading to the modernist view. Other workers in the field of literary openings and closure—Victor Brombert and Edward Said on incipits and intentions; Frank Kermode, Barbara Herrnstein Smith, Marianna Torgovnick, D. A. Miller, and others on closure—set their own frames of perception around those within and without the text's extreme limits.[15]

As for the studies of interior framing, of what I am calling the *insetting* of text and picture within text as narrated and pictured, Francis Berry, in *The Shakespeare Inset: Word and Picture*, analyzes the process whereby the imagined spectacle about which the audience hears—as the action seen is arrested—is at odds with the actual or seen spectacle, making the same kind of dis-

junction as one would see in a painting containing one foreground and another background scene, framed by an inset window. So the inset disturbs the surface, presenting a contrasting
plane by advance or obtrusion or by recession.[16] Lucien Dällenbach, in his *Récit spéculaire: Essai sur la mise-en-abyme* (Specular
Story: Essay on the Mise-en-Abyme), treats the similarities between the contained and the containing work, between the inserted model and the exterior vessel.[17] Philippe Hamon studies
the redundancy necessary in the inserted description, for instance, of the character ("Le statut sémiologique du personnage,"
The Semiological Status of the Character), as the inserted figures
on a smaller scale, described in terms of oppositions, transformations, and the like, their significance increased by their reference to myth or cliché, reproduce the "global system of the characters of the work as a whole."[18] The work thus closing in upon
itself resembles its own tautology or an anagram of itself, as the
inner and outer texts duplicate each other. What he says of character and its description within the narration might apply to the
use of the framed scene or description as I shall speak of it: "a
system of regulated equivalencies destined to assure the readability of the text" (H, p. 144). The framed portraits by James I
want to consider are considerably clarified by his discussion of
the three kinds of included character: (a) referential-characters,
participating in the "real effect" and referring to culture clichés
or to recognizable phenomena outside the text; (b) shifter-char-
acters, marks of the author's or the reader's presence in the text
or of their substitutes; and (c) anaphoric-characters, who inter-
pret, remind, and predict indications of the past and future action: "By them, the work quotes itself and constructs itself as
tautological" (H, p. 123). In *The Wings of the Dove*, for example,
the lady in the Bronzino portrait functions as an actual recognizable painting; Milly herself acts as the shifter-character, the victim with whom the reader empathizes and around whom everything moves; Lord Mark guides her toward the revelation in its
frame, and implicitly interprets the painting for her, functioning
as a mediating character. In *The Golden Bowl*, the pictures of the

Prince and Charlotte make reference to their real and pictured selves; Maggie is the victim and the increasingly lucid picture by James of the situation, the ego-involved character around whom everything evolves; Fanny Assingham remembers, interprets, and predicts. In both texts, the central image renders the reading of the picture coherent: the dove as Milly, the gentle and self-sacrificing figure at the center of the scene; or the broken and used-up bowl as Maggie's mind, formerly containing what had to be shattered for her future cognition and recognition to take place, and ours along with it.

Hamon's *Introduction au genre descriptif* is of primary importance for the idea of a static arrest and a set frame. As he differentiates description from narration, for example, the serious or reliable view is opposed to the informal recounting at the fireside. He also makes clear how description "saturates the frame," in order to give a feeling of completeness for the describer, who is in the same position as the reader; how a grid is put over the view described to organize the referent and to make it readable—in brief, showing the mapping of the scene, its spatialization and the making of its spectacle; how redundancy, repetitions, and parallelisms are a necessary part of description so that the amount of information is reduced, parallel with an amplification of the text; how the described scene in its pause is at once in a state of "predictive expansion" and "deictic condensation"; how the focalizing observer works in the described scene (we think instantly of James's included observers); and how the competency of the reader is required in order to recognize the whole stock of devices and techniques of such descriptions as they are to be received. Hamon's analyses of Zola, Proust, and in particular, of Maupassant's stories, and the ways doors and windows and signals work in them, are at once rich and to the point. Frames are intended for exhibition and show, as well as for mind sets and mode sets. Exhibitive framing pointedly, repeatedly, and sometimes nakedly sets up or out its display: so the insertion of a finished verse poem into a developing prose poem, timed to coincide with, and be motivated by, a performance and an exhibition of a body whose hair alone is commented on, is at once an inset, an outlining, a crossing of genres, and a disembodiment in the act; such is Mallarmé's "La Déclaration foraine."[19] On the other hand, the exhibition of the head or top stanza of a verse poem within a critical essay throughout which the body thus decapitated is disseminated, as is the case with "Le Pitre châtié" in Jacques Derrida's "La Double séance," in *La Dissémination*, makes its own declaration about the scattering of consciousness when the frame breaks down, or is chastised for its ideality, or is refused closure. Poets and actors, declaimers and critics, clowns and chastisers, we are all framed in, eventually.

SOCIOLOGICAL AND PERCEPTUAL FRAMING

Frames are also provisional representations we are given or give ourselves for dealing with situations. A number of recent and valuable works deal, along lines at once sociological, psychological, and literary, with these representations—how we set them up and how we break them. Frames in this sense can also be regarded as what the psychologist D.W. Winnicott calls "transitional objects," that is, the combined representation by child and parent that enables the child to come, from a subjective state, gradually into contact with the real world by means of a provisional or transitional representation, which can be handled.[20]

Various forms of bracketing and mental framing with their inclusions and exclusions and their levels of codings and relations are studied by Gregory Bateson in his *Steps to an Ecology of Mind*. With the framed section set apart as conveying messages or signifying meaningful actions, the frame has to be read as part of the picture; one might read:

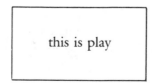

this is play

and the rest is not. The problem arises in the following paradox:

> All statements within
> this frame are untrue.
>
> I love you.
>
> I hate you.

The first statement, itself a contradiction, is false if true and vice versa, whereas the other framed opposing statements depend on it for their validation and interpretation, so that the very notion of "truth" is jeopardized, as it finds inclusion.[21]

Erving Goffman's *Frame Analysis*, which takes Bateson's studies into account, deals with the organization of experience according to the conceiving frameworks available in our society for making sense out of events, including the inevitable question about framing itself.[22] ("And if above I had said: 'What about the ★★★★★★ that divide up and divide off . . .'," FA, p. 11). Signs abound, as sense puts itself in question: "And if it turns out that the preface was written in bad faith, tailored from the beginning to exemplify this use that will have come to be made of it? Will the preface then be retrospectively reframed by the reader into something that isn't a preface at all, but an inappropriately inserted illustration of one?" (FA, p. 17). For no frame, clearly, can frame all the others.[23] In discussing the strips or slices of activity cut out for our recognition by various kinds of keying and scripting of the perceptual game such as matching, exaggeration or expansiveness, repetition, role-switching, and beginning and terminating signs, Goffman shows how the innermost layer of the deep-set game is engrossing, and the outermost fabricated and visible; downkeying shifts the observer to a greater closeness to the activity; upkeying, to a greater distance and to an increased perception of the lamination or levels of framing, as the game is adjusted to its surround. It is this perception and the delight in it which are particularly visible in the late games of modernism, making up the last part of this book.

STRESS, OFFSETTING, AND INCLUSION

To frame is to privilege what is contained within the borders of the picture. The very notion of choice, of electing privileged or "highly placed" scenes, of careful composition, and of arrangement brings into play a series of terms and concepts heavy with implications aesthetic, economic, structural, and psychological. Eisenstein's celebration of the frame as a "dry quadrilateral plunging into the hazards of nature's diffuseness"[24] and James's own work with the isolation of the "sharp black line . . . that helps any arrangement of objects to become a picture" give the same clues to our reading.[25] The focused figure or figures are to be read against the flow of ongoing narration and the dispersion of life narrated and lived; against its unremarkable rhythm, we perceive, in the high picture so highly bordered, a peculiar delay and a singular arrest; against chaos, we perceive a coherent picture. The framed passage is, for everything that is ordinary, dispersed, and unorganized, the other.

My principal concern here is with the techniques enabling a concentration on a specific passage endowed with heightening and intensifying elements within the textual or visual scene; they form a rise in tone, stress, or setting, whether by architectural placing, dramatic lighting, verbal repetition, or other markings, composing finally a distinct and noticeable figure against a less distinctive surround. We are led to expect them, and to remember them, so that their moral impression endures intact within the narrative flux of the whole.

In the subheading I have referred to the various patterns of edges or devices for sharpening the sight and narrowing the focus under the two principal headings of outlining and insetting, that is, the topics of bordering or silhouetting on one hand, and of embedding or boxing inward on the other. Those two categories, like the other subsidiary categories that can be grouped under one or the other for convenience, are not meant to be restrictive or exclusive, but rather suggestive of interpenetration, intermeshing, and continuation. Of the following suggestions, roughly defined and often overlapping, any number may be seen in coincidence: in the major scenes from the authors included here, most occur in some form or other, stressing by rhythm, tone, timbre, and visual devices a picture highly intensified.

They can be grouped by three categories, progressively larger; first *the pictorial or visual*, including the architectural setting; *diegetic or narrative*, including the insetting of tales within other tales, pictures within other pictures, and literary genres within other literary genres; and what we might call *the larger picture*, combining the thematic, the aesthetic, and the moral, where the former purely pictorial or presentational aspects are included in the judgment the reader makes of the willed impact or impacts of the whole, and of the interpretational shifts involved in the rearrangements of readerly frames.

Pictorial Spectacles and Their Focus

ARCHITECTURAL DESIGN

In the most frequent and visible examples, the central figure or action is suddenly placed at an unusual height, dramatically outlined or enclosed in a noticeable set of limits and openings. *The Scarlet Letter*'s famous scaffold scene is placed at just such a height, and the text turns about it as surely as "The Turn of the Screw" turns about its apparitions at windows and on the tower. In James's "Altar of the Dead," the face framed like a memory in the door is caught in the reader's own remembering, like the figure of the author's wife in the door of his "Author of Beltraffio," and like Kate and Milly, Maggie and Charlotte, on the endless balconies, stairs, and at the windows of *The Wings of the Dove* and *The Golden Bowl*; in Proust's great novel, a theatre box sets off a display of costume and aristocratic visage, a half-cracked door gives a sly setting for Charlus, as does a mirror in which he is reflected, whereas the window through which Mademoiselle de Vinteuil and her friend are perceived in the terrible scene with her father's photograph calls still more attention to the narration; the window as the frame for the lighthouse in the leading image of Virginia Woolf's novel of the same name places the emphasis on seeing and on vision, as on symbol.

FOCUS

The centralized gesture, on which the gaze focuses in the more heavily bordered scenes, gives the pictorial clue to the deepest psychological import. The figure of Pierre's mother, in Melville's *Pierre; or, The Ambiguities*, hurling her knife at his picture is all the more centralized as it occurs in the elegant arrangement of the dining room, reflecting what was to be the elegant and neat arrangement of his marriage; Densher's wandering from one park bench to the other, in *The Wings of the Dove*, illustrates his indecisiveness as clearly as Milly's leaning her head on her arms illustrates her discouragement, and, in *The Golden Bowl*, Maggie's burying her head in the cushions of her window seat, or against the Prince's breast, her will not to see; Jinny, in Woolf's *Waves*, lifting her arm over and over, signals her grasping at life in all her energy. The focus upon these figures and their actions is not the architectural one of the scenes first mentioned, but rather an intensified pointing or gesturing of the text toward its own included gesture.

The same remark could be applied to the occasional intensified notice of one specific object. For example, the pink parasol of Madame de Vionnet is seen advancing down the river in James's *Ambassadors* before the identification of the figure itself, like Charlotte's green parasol near the conclusion of *The Golden Bowl*, descending the stair, as it had first been seen against the sky, both times apparent, as a signal of her elegance and her need for self-protection; Densher is perceived tapping his forehead with his handkerchief in *The Wings of the Dove* before his own identification is clear.

Diegetic and Narrative Arrests

TEMPORAL DELAY OR SPATIAL VOID

A noticeable delay in time or an unusually apparent spatial emptiness serves to stress the episode it precedes or follows, or both. The evident and often dramatic slowdown may be made by a drawn-out description or an actual arrest of action or speech, providing the static quality essential to the great framed scenes within the ongoing flux of the narration, where the psychological delay often coincides with a spatial signal. For example, there is a sensible delay by description both before and after the ball scene in *La Princesse de Clèves*, and a temporal slowdown of the rhythm of description and narration in the boat scene of Flaubert's *Sentimental Education*, surrounding the presentation of the figure of Madame Arnoux. In *Pierre*, Pierre's pause at the threshold of Lucy's room as it is fixed all in ruffles and white, indicates both his desire and her innocence, as it puts off the action; the delaying details of the doors and thresholds described in James's "Jolly Corner" intensify the apparition itself, as the Prince's pause in the doorway of his living room after his return from Matcham in *The Golden Bowl*, or in a matching doorway for the actual breaking of the bowl, draw attention to Maggie's interior meditation and exterior action.

VERBAL REPETITION

A set of anaphoric techniques or repetitive statements may form the edges of a framed passage with a deliberately artificial stress, marking, beyond the limits of ordinary expression, an irregularity in the textual surface. The conversations between Densher and Kate in *The Wings of the Dove* form just such a remarkable passage, as do the principal exchanges between Maggie and the Prince or Mrs. Assingham in *The Golden Bowl*. This repetition is frequently associated with a particular choice of perceptual vocabulary, so that the concepts of sight and positioning, of perceiving and knowing, are arranged in cumulative juxtaposition and accelerating rhythm. The all-important verbs "to see" and "to know" and "to find out," terms that James's tale "In the Cage" introduces at the very beginning, mark the high passages of *The Golden Bowl*, whereas in Woolf's *Waves*, the opening scene of the children's relation to the world, the key scene for the impact of the whole work, is entirely phrased in the antiphonal chant of alternate perception: "I see . . . I hear . . ."

DOUBLE INSETTING AND DEVELOPING OBJECT

A framed object in the central episode may serve as a visual focal point: a portrait, a photograph, or a painting, which may itself become the developing or revealing object for the import of the entire scene narrated, as it were, by condensation. So Mr. Darcy's picture in Jane Austen's *Pride and Prejudice*, the father's portrait in *Pierre*, the oval portrait in Poe's tale of the same name, the picture of Jude in Hardy's *Jude the Obscure*, and Lily's canvas in *To the Lighthouse*, are all the focus of a change of realization or the central twist in the plot. James is of course the master of this portait of a tale: the fiancé's photograph in James's "The Friends of the Friends" (or "The Way It Came"); the painting of the clown in his *Sacred Fount*: the photo of the dead friend in *The Altar of the Dead*; the Lambinet painting in Chad's collection of paintings and the imaginary picture of Mademoiselle de Vionnet, both in *The Ambassadors*, or the Bronzino portrait and the photographs in the doctor's office of *The Wings of the Dove*; the photographs of Charlotte and the Prince in the living room of *The Golden Bowl*, and the Florentine portrait representing "some good things" at its conclusion—all are the developing objects for those tales. The development may also be done with mirrors, with a reflection upon reflection, as in the bar scene in *Jude*, where the recognition of Arabella in the mirror behind the bar, seen from behind, hints to the reader about the effective menace; in one of the peculiar mirroring scenes in Proust, the reflection of the Baron de Charlus gives a doubling all the more monstrous to his thus exposed vice, which is also all his glory.

The Larger Picture

METATEXTUAL FOCUS AND INFRAMING IRONY

By its focus on a framed episode related to one central metaphor or symbol heavy with metatextual implications, the text may, in a heightened moment, concentrate upon the entire question of framing itself. These are the privileged passages among the others, as they are typically and inevitably self-referring; they may be seen to make a frame-up of the reader, as of their own textuality, and are thus the signals of the modern reading of the frame.

Often the connection is made between outside and inside, referring us back to the aesthetic and moral implications of the tale itself. Here again, James is the most modern of all; thus, the cage of his "In the Cage," by setting the limits for the girl's sight, sets them, by extension, for that of the reader. Kate's headshake at the conclusion of *The Wings of the Dove* may refer to the entire tale itself, as a refusal. More complex still, *The Golden Bowl* is the container of passion, knowledge, and the past, as well as of the text containing it, and which it itself embodies.[26] James abounds in ironies both of sight and oversight, of mistaken or paradoxical vision and language, as of the encoded telegraphs within "In the Cage," intermeshing with the reader's own deceptive interpretation; his celebrated "Figure in the Carpet" deliberately emphasizes the veiling of vision, as do the horrible, because useless, opera glasses the lovely girl wears after she is blind, responding to the former hideous but useful ones in the story "Glasses"; it leads us to question our own vision, while questioning hers and that of the artist whose story it is.

INSERTED MODEL

The central character is seen to develop by comparison with another literary or artistic model, which clarifies the development of the first in a superliterary vibration. This can also work in relation to an inserted tale, the latter a prediction of the future, whether positive or negative. Thus, in Madame de Lafayette's *La Princesse de Clèves*, it is the husband's tale of the confession on which the heroine then models her own. In Melville's *Pierre* and in Hardy's *Jude*, it is the Laocöon figure, or, also in *Pierre*, Orestes, Hamlet, and Dante. Milly's Lucrezia by Bronzino in *The Wings of the Dove* is perhaps the most famous case, along with the Maeterlinck heroines in slow motion, whose act Kate and Milly are seen to repeat.

INSET TURNS

A sudden change in the central character's consciousness, knowledge, or path of action makes a twist often literally referred to in the text; thus, the "turn" in the situations of "The Jolly Corner," "The Turn of the Screw," and the moral implications about Densher in *The Wings of the Dove* ("his turn was made"), or about Madame de Vionnet in *The Ambassadors*; in the picture Strether sees as the boat rounds or turns the bend, ironically set off by the straightness of the frame that he has transgressed; the central "turn" of Maggie after the episode at Matcham in *The Golden Bowl* is of the same type.

INSET DEVICES FROM OTHER GENRES

The inset tale in the tale, widely commented upon by other framers of narration, is of less interest to me than the insertions and insets of other genres, as if the novel were to profit from the techniques of proscenium staging in its own melodrama, or then, from the framing of the art object. For example, the play in Austen's *Mansfield Park*, the inset drama in Hawthorne's *Blithedale Romance*, the inserted interior monologues in some of Proust's recognition scenes as they are gradually made to recognize each other as well as the self of the narrator, to which they give the clue. Once the reader is accustomed to this inframing, a vibration is set up between what is told and what is seen. The flaws possible in the teller's tale and the seer's sight take on an added fascination from the mixing of genres.[27]

SUPERPOSITIONING

Actual or implied comparisons are often made between two stressed scenes evidently meant to be reconsidered together, with evident reference points: instead of being read in an ordinary linear movement, the episodes are seen to work in cumulative and progressively more significant superpositioning, one scene easily pictured as placed directly above the preceding one, to which it looks back in a retrospective reframing. This is a major frame-within-frame situation, a *mise-en-abyme* by which Proust rivets our attention upon his work as recapture of time and self, and by which James consciously relates scenes, characters, and situations to each other and develops them inward and outward.

I use a metaphor in *The Ambassadors*, the two kinds of passageways—those pictured in Strether's memory, which are characteristic of American architecture in that their doors fold back upon themselves but leave everything open, which make a sharp contrast with the European rooms of Madame de Vionnet, opening one into the other and keeping secrets: we might imagine both these types superpositioned upon each other as the keepers and the openers of the frames we would read with. Thus, the secrets within the very openness and appearance of Densher in Milly's carriage in *The Wings of the Dove* as the picture is superimposed by the reader upon that of Lord Mark in Mrs. Lowder's carriage and that of Dr. Luke Strett in that same carriage, preparing the scene of Densher and Kate in their carriage. Or again, the two heroines of this novel presented upon the balconies or at the windows one after the other, after both the lofty original presentations, Kate at the top of her family's stairs and Milly on the rock overlooking the countryside.

INCLUDED OBSERVATIONS

Finally, the scene may be grasped by its own interior seer. Attention may be focused on the central part of the scene through the eyes of an observer at the edge, or in the center, of the picture; the reader's seeing this observer see adds an included frame for the reading, and clues in the sight to a privileged, if provisional, representation, making an occasionally distorted view. Thus, in *La Princesse de Clèves*, the onlookers at the ball scene, as their glance focuses intently upon the couple, show what the reader is forced to focus upon; later, as the Duc de Nemours listens to the confession scene in hiding, we are given his intensely interested eyes and ears for our own, and still later, as we watch him watching the Princess weave ribbons around his cane and then stare at his picture, we share his knowing perception. As Fanny Assingham watches the Prince and Charlotte go up the stairs, we watch and know with her, as we do with Françoise watching the mother and grandmother walk slowly up the stairs in the annunciatory sequence of death in Proust's great novel. Here we watch too as the waiters in the restaurant watch St.-Loup bring Marcel the vicuna coat by stepping over the red plush dining benches, or as the two rows of observers stand still to frame and to observe the Duchesse de Guermantes walk through them in her resplendent costume, thus doubly resplendent to the view.

These techniques mingle as the text framed refers finally to its own contained models, those texts and pictures so deeply inset within it, as it does also to the page it reflects, and to the larger picture outside, in all its own moral and aesthetic implications, for art and for life. Its high privilege makes a statement of cohesion and coherence against the narrative flux and against the flux of our own time, so that our reading of frames and of the framed passages their perception enables is the model of not just reading, but of what, while reading, we live. This, says the frame, is what matters.

III / PRE-MODERN BORDERS

I must speak within compass.
Mansfield Park[1]

PLAYING AND PERSUADING: JANE AUSTEN

Jane Austen seems to come ready-framed. No space is left too
large to be tamed by civilization: the physical world is tidy, and
only the human element seems in need of bringing back to order.
In this realm of frequent enclosures, salons, parks, gardens, and
forests carefully placed, landscapes and social spaces protected
and mapped in the English style, where clear borders are marked
out, nothing is left to chance. There is no effort to see beyond
the "high walls" and "great gates" of the Squire, or the "compact,
tight parsonage, enclosed in its own neat garden, with a vine and
a pear-tree trained round its casements" (*Persuasion*, p. 64). The
enclosure and the *training* are emphasized as much in the spiritual
and psychological senses as in the physical ones: in the style one
sets oneself to be trained into and by, the boundaries set the
tone. "To the Great House accordingly they went, to sit the full
half hour in the old-fashioned square parlour, with a small carpet
and shining floor" (P, p. 67). Any hint of an "overthrow of all
order and neatness" (P, p. 67), such as may ensue without proper
care, is viewed with alarm; and who is to determine the amount
of irony in this observation? Charlotte Brontë's opinion of *Pride
and Prejudice* proves the relevance of the question: "An accurate
daguerrotyped portrait of a commonplace face; a carefully fenced,
highly cultivated garden, with neat borders and delicate flowers;
but no glance of a bright, vivid physiognomy, no open country,
no fresh air, no blue hill, no bonny beech. I should hardly like
to live with her ladies and gentlemen, in their elegant but con-

fined houses." In a similar vein, Virginia Woolf speaks of Jane Austen's "microscope" which has the power to reduce all extravagance to the proportions of perfection and normality, all chaos to "English parsonage, shrubberies, and lawns."[2] But the relationship of the text to its borders is all the more complex for their apparent simplicity.

Reading Northanger Abbey

This is just like a book.
  Northanger Abbey

Spoofing the sentimental story and the Gothic romance—Mrs. Radcliffe's *Udolpho* acts as the overtly stated referent—Jane Austen's first major novel insets what it sets out to burlesque. Catherine, in training to be a "true quality" heroine, "read all such works as heroines must read to supply their memories with those quotations which are so serviceable and so soothing in the vicissitudes of their eventful lives" (NA, p. 39), and the composite of these works is the self-mocking model for the parallel development and tease of a naive figure whose expectations are exposed and exhausted, along with ours in relation to them.

Black veils and mysteries, doors and cabinets, chests and ciphers—all these containing and cloaking possibilities respond to the architectural features of the castle to which the heroine is invited, materially developing to build-up her dreams and the frame of her hopes: "all the happiness which its walls could supply—the happiness of a progress through a long suite of lofty rooms . . . the happiness of being stopped in their way along narrow, winding vaults, by a low, grated door" (NA, p. 104). Whatever space in her reveries is unfilled by Henry Tilney, the hero thrown in her way, is taken up by her imaginings about the castle and the abbey, and with her delusions from her novel-reading goes our own set of expectations about her set-up and disappointment—for are we not, too, even here, the reader of novels?

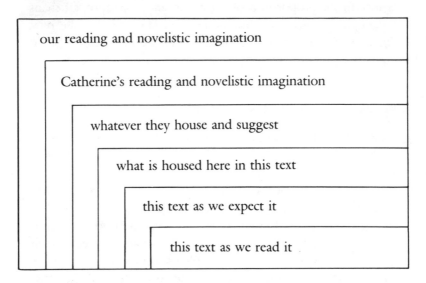

our reading and novelistic imagination

Catherine's reading and novelistic imagination

whatever they house and suggest

what is housed here in this text

this text as we expect it

this text as we read it

As the central scene of the novel is one of exposure and emptiness, our own reactions to it are set out and ironized upon, together with the author's own supposed delight in her own frame of expectation: "A heroine returning, at the close of her career, to her native village . . . is an event on which the pen of the contriver may well delight to dwell" (NA, p. 230). But this heroine returns in disgrace, with her biographer humiliated, her readers disappointed, and her tale rushing to a conclusion. The mocking self-reflection about the "final event" and its noneffect upon us extends to the rhythm of the remaining pages, a metalinguistic close for all the "readers, who will see in the tell-tale compression of the pages before them, that we are all hastening together to perfect felicity" (NA, p. 246). The final judgment is left open in its frame ("Whether the tendency of this work be . . .") and a joyous distancing prevails over involvement. Another step out has been added to the previous set of framing expectations and results:

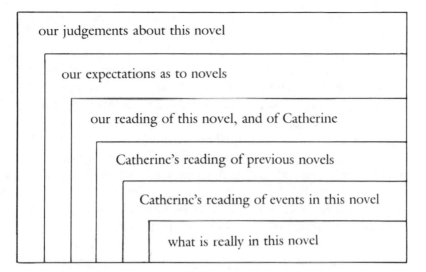

Metanovelistic impulse includes the subjective (what we think and see and judge) and the more objective (what is really in the novel and what it is about) within the field of novelistic reflection on the novel.

Pictures of Pride and Prejudice

Jane Austen's best-known novel could serve, almost in its entirety, as an example of the *co-incidence of frame with substance*, the points of contact ranging from the very simple, formal, and evident, to more subtle enclosure and exposure, that of both Pride and Prejudice, as well as of the principal characters. On the edge of evidence, the ends of chapters can be literally end-stopped, like a line of poetry. For example, "the argument ended only with the visit" (PP, p. 67). Neither of the elements can continue in the reader's mind past the end of that line. Or again, at the conclusion of a later chapter, "the carriage stopped" (PP, p. 127). The cessation of movement is literal as well as textual, the coincidence of frame and imagination complete, in a manner directly opposed to the unfolding of character, which takes place over time.

In a slightly more complex line, the diegetic progression of the action narrated can be conceived of as following a necessarily linear path, in which the sentence "The affair . . . was capable of a turn" presents a possible swerve, the latter focusing the eye and the mind. Set against a background like that of the dialectical debates between abstract qualities common in the eighteenth century (pride against modesty, prejudice against free judgment, and so on),[3] the path and its potential turns are clearly and consciously marked.

The sharpest mental turn is taken by Elizabeth Bennet herself, recognizing her mistake in a sequence singled out within the text by its repetitive devices and by its dramatic potential. A strong repeat, like a verbal breast-beating, sets a metric border for a heightened experience: " 'How despicably have I acted! ' she cried.—'I, who have prided myself on my discernment!—I, who have valued myself on my abilities! . . . How humiliating is this discovery! . . . Till this moment, I never knew myself' " (PP, p. 236).

This turn leads to the obviously centered sequence wherein she discovers Darcy's true character by means of a portrait, and her own with it, moving in from outer to inner knowledge, from nature to art to the human, from the landscape to the house to the portrait to the man represented therein. After a perusal of the grounds—the outer parameter of the story—she is initiated into the gallery by the housekeeper, as if "in quest of the only face whose features would be known to her. At last it arrested her. . . . She stood several minutes before the picture in earnest contemplation, and returned to it again before they quitted the gallery" (PP, p. 271).

When she subsequently encounters Darcy, her arrest is identical to the one she previously made before the picture and his smile; only through the pictured face can she see the real one. Her own blush indicates her self-discovery, so that the exposure and recognition is in fact doubly satisfying. A further detail emphasizes the importance of the scene with its *developing object* in its frame: downstairs, there is only a miniature of the owner, whereas upstairs, in what is presumably the less public part of the house, the larger portrait is exhibited, as if for the more private discoveries. This arrangement, apparently running counter to the ordinary laws of portrait exposure and society, where the more handsome and larger work of art should be on show, is in reality proper to this work, for the larger frame functions to demonstrate in close-up the truth, so that Elizabeth sees in it the answer she needs, writ large.

The other piece of large writing is found at the finale, where the wide scope of the frame enables all to be gathered up in a final union of theme and form, as the quest for self-uncovering, simultaneous with the discovery of the other, concludes in a sweeping convergence: in "gratitude towards the persons who . . . had been the means of uniting them" (PP, p. 396). The final unity satisfies.

Borders in Mansfield Park

VIEW AND BOUNDARIES

The time of the play . . .
    Mansfield Park

Mansfield Park is the most interesting and most complex of Jane Austen's novels, from the standpoint of framing. Exactly in the center of the novel occur the two main pictured sequences, serving as a double hinge for the rest of the action. These scenes relate one condition to another, provide the place and moment of indecision and change, after the initial presentation, and prepare the final outcome. Attention is centered on these two sequences by recognizable stylistic techniques, suspending the narration in a *delay*, both thematic and geographic. Here the grounds of the great house visited form a sort of boundary area, a place of gentlemanly play between garden and terrace and bowling green, between neatly bordered "wilderness" and outlying park, so *the play itself lies outside of real life and lived space*, within another realm altogether.[4] These two times and places are framed differently, set apart within the narrated events.

Mansfield Park as a whole is framed in just the way the central walk at Sotherton is taken, landscaped in just such fashion, with its boundaries also marked as places of passage: doors and steps and walks and windows, the order of a "park" just beyond the chaotic "wilderness" of a life, its dark disorder bounded in turn by the winding terrace, where the walk is planned out.[5] Moving out and in, moving from the space of walk-in-bounds at Sotherton outside, to the space of play-out-of-bounds at Mansfield Park inside, all the intricacies of a social and private life are played out and suffered.

"I must speak within compass," says Mary Crawford, just when she is within the "wilderness" of the walk itself, neatly set between park and house, a little wildness framed. Within the "patronage" of Mansfield Park, and its view on which the novel ends, acts, writings and performance, walks and turns have their prescribed limits, spatial, temporal, and psychological: "that acting week," as Mary says later on, or again, "the time of the play." Acting and being are kept bordered and boundaried, separate from each other: limits enclose every act, serving to intensify what they surround.

On the visual and imaginative frames of Austen's novels this limiting approach has an effect wide-reaching and deepening at once, intense in focus as it is narrow. Since the action is so surely enclosed both socially and spiritually in complete accord with the boundaries of a physical nature—doors, rooms, windows, demarcations always proper—the entire tone of the action can be altered by the most modest voyage to one place from another a half a mile distant: from Mansfield Park to the parsonage, and all is transformed. The displacement to Sotherton, or to Portsmouth, suffices for the most utter change to seem the most natural, in *Mansfield Park*; whereas in *Persuasion*, the displacement from Kellynch-hall to Camden-place, or then the great one to Lyme Regis, where the major alteration takes place, are themselves the "real" fictive equivalent of the personages' mental transport. The reader of Jane Austen is well prepared to experience the mental and physical change of frame typical of the great novels of Henry James, with their incessant switching from one Great House to another in London, and in the countryside, from hotel to apartment in Paris, from house to house in Boston. What goes on here looks different from what goes on there, and the view is often all.

In the visit of Sotherton, one of the purposes for penetrating the park itself is that it includes, as Mr. Rushworth points out, a knoll from which the House at the other end can be seen: thus, the *visual return* toward the point of origin. The novel itself ends with the once-dreaded parsonage becoming in Fanny's eyes, once she is established, just as "perfect . . . as every thing else, within the view and patronage of Mansfield Park, had long been" (MP, p. 457). Here the "bad" object is integrated in the same frame with the good one, in a safe view. The negative power of the other loses its force by its inscription in the familiar view, within the perfection of the *psychological framing* as it is matched to the temporal and situational one. The borders themselves do not alter, but the picture absorbs, little by little, more within itself.

The temporal borders seem particularly well adapted to the slight distancing mode in which the whole is set, or rather, at once distancing and present, owing to the shifter-style beginning: "About thirty years ago . . ." (MP, p. 41). (What reader ever said to himself, "This novel was published in 1814, so 'thirty years ago' is about 1784"? Do we not instinctively place it thirty years before us in time, so that in fact the reading time seems nearer to the narrated time just because of the ploy? We do not, for example, think, "thirty years before 1985"; the very *atemporality* of such temporal frames is paradoxically responsible for their timeliness.) The informality of the opening has the effect of including us within its own frame, controlling our stance, our field of vision coterminal with that of the narrating scope, from "About thirty years ago" to the perfected end "had been," pluperfect in fact. The bottom edge closes up the novel in its boundaries as formally as the beginning is informal, the sense of closure all the more powerful for the initial sense of a slight setback.

ORDERS AND TURNS

. . . as they struck by order into another path.
Mansfield Park

Fanny is the self-ordained onlooker. By a displacement of a few yards, she manages to glimpse the whole group of others, in a "commanding view," ironic in view of her own timidity, and its cheerfulness dreadful in contrast with her unhappiness:

> by walking fifty yards from the hall door, she could look down the park, and command a view of the parsonage and all its demesnes, gently rising beyond the village road; and in Dr Grant's meadow she immediately saw the group— Edmund and Miss Crawford both on horseback, riding side by side, Dr and Mrs Grant, and Mr Crawford with two or three grooms, standing about and looking on. A happy party it appeared to her—all interested in one object—cheerful beyond a doubt, for the sound of merriment ascended even to her. It was a sound which did not make *her* cheerful; she wondered that Edmund should forget her, and felt a pang. She could not turn her eyes from the meadow, she could not help watching all that passed. (MP, pp. 97-98)

Both the seer and the seen are located upon a rise, as if destined for the sight, "rising" and "ascending." The view is *double-framed*, by Fanny within the narration, and by the group she watches as it watches; this is, however, a view that she "commands," and so she is in the ascendant position for the view, even as it gives her pain. The noticeable repetitious border, "she could not turn, she could not help," catches the attention for her lament and centers her "pang" parallel to their "merriment." This exclusion scene is marked by obsessive imaginings, themselves jarring in their repetitious form: "Edmund was close to her, he was speaking to her, he was evidently directing her management

of the bridle, he had hold of her hand; she saw it, or the imagination supplied what the eye could not reach" (MP, p. 98). No
choice is allowed here between the "actual" view and the "imagined" one, as ambiguity is often seen to attach to the passages
concerning sight within the text, their implicit questioning of the
spectacle sighted and recounted. Meanwhile, the multiple images
of *handling* and of *management* and of *direction*, of *holding* and
of *reaching* stress the imagined control outside the scope of what
is actually framed for the heroine's sight as she is set over against
the others, framed against their surround.

Fanny herself might seem to make rather an unexciting picture, as she is unalterably good, sickly, and uncomplaining, except in her inner language: how could such a dull portrait hope
to compete with the other supremely painterly picture of Miss
Crawford in her aesthetic and lively interest, linking event to
event in "a fair train," with her own fair sight giving the apparently proper "order" to the picture? Even the words "scene,"
"frame," and "looking at" remind the reader that indeed this fa-
vorable picture framed so perfectly by a window deserves a prolonged gaze:

> A young woman, pretty, lively, with a harp as elegant as
> herself; and both placed near a window, cut down to the
> ground, and opening on a little lawn, surrounded by shrubs
> in the rich foliage of summer, was enough to catch any man's
> heart. The season, the scene, the air, were all favourable to
> tenderness and sentiment. Mrs Grant and her tambour frame
> were not without their use; it was all in harmony; and as
> every thing will turn to account when love is once set going,
> even the sandwich tray, and Dr Grant doing the honours of
> it, were worth looking at. (MP, p. 96)

In its turn, this picture and the one centered about the couple
on horseback prepare the neatly borded walk at Sotherton in
chapters 10 and 11, and also the extraordinary window scene in
chapter 11, immediately following the central incident of the walk,
where attention focuses once more upon the triangle implied in

the harp scene and visible in the horseback scene. Miss Crawford will always lead the action, Edmund following after, until Fanny will be left behind, at the window, while the others sing their "glee," toward which Edmund makes his "advance," suiting the "advance" of the glee, of which he then suggests a repeat, to Fanny's increased misery, highlighted by the glee itself, to which the others give voice. The desertion of Fanny is double and visibly bordered, set to music even, as before, with the piano replacing the harp of that other window moment:

Mary Crawford & Edmund & Fanny: "at an open window"

Edmund & Fanny at the window: "we must go out"

"turning his back on the window," Edmund "advances"

"Fanny sighed alone at the window"

Between these two parallel situations of Fanny's loneliness, set against the group, framed by windows, and stressed by the emphasis on viewpoints, there is placed a scene of deliberate complication, carefully ordered by landscaping details and degrees of feeling. It plays out an entire range of aspects confronting outside and in, open and closed, wild and tamed, serpentine and straight, disorder of sentiment and encompassing order and border.

The "orders" Edmund is to take, and the orders so pointedly and repeatedly referred to, work to signal each other. Doors and walls, gates and divisions, the ha-ha ditch with its sunken wall and deliberate suprise oppose the visible walls, and neatly designated paths outline the increasing interest in the Great House and the grassy knoll from which it can be seen, itself having "no prospect" to the outside. The whole prospect is included in the rambling walk and its conversation, not all of which we are privileged to hear, but which we suppose in ellipsis, as the landscaped ha-ha indicates a sort of ellipsis in the earth.

The walking passage is led up to by a rise: the stone steps before the entrance to Sotherton. All the different enclosures and walks in the planted garden—on the bowling green leading by the steps to a terrace walk, separated from an adjoining wilderness by a "palisade" with an unusually locked central gate, and by a ha-ha—all the complications permit the two wandering trios or triangles of characters to take devious ways, and the remaining triangle to drag behind. The order of the whole is given by a balance, first of architectural devices and designs, with the symmetries and paradoxes underlining the central equilibrium: if there is "no prospect" from the windows of the rooms in the Great House, all the play there will be paradoxically confined to the outside, whereas in the domain of Mansfield Park, the Park itself will be included in the play being rehearsed inside. This is the overall picture of the order of play.

Verbally, the idea of order or orders is stressed by a triple repetition: Edmund is defined to Miss Crawford as a future clergyman three times, first by Julia ("If Edmund were but in orders!" MP, p. 117), then by Fanny ("My dear Edmund, if you were but in orders now," MP, p. 117), and finally by Edmund himself ("Yes, I shall take orders . . . ," MP, p. 117), these three references following in rapid succession and leading, by a twist of the conversation, to an acceptance of the idea of order itself by Mary, who then "turns" the subject.

That turn then leads immediately to a spatial one "Suppose we turn down there for the present" (MP, p. 118), and to the boundaries gradually traversed, from planted area to bowling green to terrace walk, for the main triangle; and, for the performing couple, to the wilderness: "They were all agreed in turning joyfully" through the unlocked door into the wilderness, a sort of trial darkness where they are plunged as into a disorder, in which Miss Crawford's conversation about the clergy's nonvalue can take place outside the normal bounds of conversation and thought.

Her "nothing," repeated, and taken up again by Edmund, borders the walk as any pattern recurring: "The *nothing* of conversation has its gradations. . . . I cannot call that situation nothing. . . . No one here can call the *office* nothing" (MP, p. 120). This ordered edge contrasts, as borders should, with the center, that walk winding about far from its bright certainty: "We have taken such a very serpentine course. . . . We have been winding in and out," says Miss Crawford (MP, p. 122), and this weaving dialectical motion makes the text, just as it makes the conversation, far from nothing.

As opposed to that textual weaving, the couple plans to go to "one end of it, in the line they were then in" (MP, p. 123), following up on their feeling, and then "turn a little way back" as if for prudence. But the turn planned takes far longer than they pretend to have expected, and Fanny watches them "till they had turned the corner" (MP, p. 125). Now all this repetition of the same terms calls attention, as always, to what is within the neat or obsessive borders: the picture is of a couple "stepping out" together as a trial, beyond the sight of the others, having predicted a straight line and then making "turns" and "turning corners." A rite of passage has led through the wilderness or dark wood of uncertainty, trying out the selves as in a rehearsal of the rehearsal of the play, whose actual performance will, of course, never take place. Its own order is that of trial and passage.

A further symmetrical paradox borders this trial play; from the obligatory wandering in the wilderness the couple is tempted, by the unlocked side gate, toward the apparently orderly "park" (the predictive mirror image of Mansfield Park), before returning all the way through the wilderness to the neat series of steps: the terrace, the green, the cultivation of the garden, and the House, where society rules in clarity, even with no "prospect."

The exploration of the wilderness is a rehearsal and testing of the boundaries of a trial mode of being, a play and an acting out: this serious trial frames a comic one inset within it, with an exaggerated play of key and loss, of delay and "rush" (Mr. Rushworth), of his verbal obsession: "he wished he had brought the key; he had been very near thinking whether he should not bring the key; he was determined he should never come without the key again . . . he would go and fetch the key; he wished he had had the key about him at the time," but dreads the foolishness of "bringing the key for nothing "(MP, pp. 125-26). Order itself—as we would expect, given Austen's frame of reference—turns out to be the key[6] to it all, and only when the couple ordained for each other, Edmund and Fanny, are at last together will the lines seem properly ordered again, will harmony be reestablished, will the frame fit the picture ordained for it. Until then, they walk in their "rambling fancy," until their spirits are "in general exhausted" (MP, p. 133), just in time for the chapter, worn out with rambling, to close.

LEADS

I came to rehearse.
   Mansfield Park

The actual "time of the play" being rehearsed within the novel has itself been rehearsed in the walk at Sotherton, with its setting and orders, its disarrangements and disorder; the order of appearance of the play[7] and its characters is rehearsed by the key image of Fanny not joining in the others' glee, but remaining always on the sidelines. Her own sense of herself is clearly that consonant with her single framing by the window or on the park bench, while the others are grouped about a spectacle or around a piano or somewhere in a circle of consultation:

> 'Ha!' she cried, with instant animation, 'am I here again? The east room. Once only was I in this room before!'—and after stopping to look about her, and seemingly to retrace all that had then passed, she added, 'Once only before. Do you remember it? I came to rehearse. Your cousin came too; and we had a rehearsal. You were our audience and prompter. A delightful rehearsal. I shall never forget it. Here we were, just in this part of the room; here was your cousin, here was

l, here were the chairs.—Oh! Why will such things ever pass away?' (MP, p. 353)

The repetitions: "once only . . . once only," "I came . . . your cousin came," "rehearse . . . rehearsal . . . a delightful rehearsal," "here we were, here was . . . here was," mark the scene vividly for the sight. "Such things" do come to pass, as they are rehearsed for, and then pass, in the rite of the play; Fanny suffers as an outsider before she is integrated into the Park and its view, where the play, even in its repetitions, its rehearsed incidents never to take place, serves as life cannot.

LINKS

She was wanting him to break through.
   Mansfield Park

The time of play and stage is reversed to disorder by an act of stern authoritative disapproval: it is the order of the family "collected" after Sir Thomas's return, which Fanny—still the outsider in life as in play—must confront with all its bright family lighting. Opening the door to the scene after great hesitation, she makes exactly the opposite reflection on her gesture from that of the wandering couple in the gardens at Sotherton, entering the park "to which a side gate, not fastened, had tempted them" (MP, p. 130). For this door offers the contrary of a temptation, rather, a trial: "Too soon did she find herself at the drawing-room door, and after pausing a moment for what she knew would not come, for a courage which the outside of no door had ever supplied her, she turned the lock in desperation, and the lights of the drawing-room and all the collected family were before her" (MP, p. 194). The *delay* before the door works to frame the instant of opening, as does the door itself, and the calling of her name at that instant intensifies the dramatic lighting all the more. As the wandering couple was integrated back into the group at their return from the park, so must she be. Nevertheless, in a later scene framed and prepared by this one, as her uncle enters, she flees out the other dooor, still the prey of "contrary feelings."

	INSIDE					OUTSIDE
SOTHERTON	border of plants	steps to garden	palisade to terrace	gate to wilderness	gate to park	
			———————————→			INSIDE
PARSONAGE	HOUSE · Fanny on watch	Fanny on bench	Fanny at window	Fanny at door	Fanny flees out other door	

Edmund will eventually lead her, oppressed and wearied, "directly into the house" (MP, p. 351), opposing the fleeing and disintegrating impulse, but the real reintegration of the outsider will not take place until Fanny herself admits, from the other point of view on the parsonage, the "perfection" of all that is in the purview of Mansfield Park and its surroundings, the frame into which all the preceding passages have been set.

But to that end, she had to accomplish also the second part of the rite of passage, through the limiting atmosphere of the Portsmouth family, through the "narrow entrance-passage of the house," "the parlour . . . like a passage-room," the "smallness of the house, and thinness of the walls," these preparing her warm thoughts of her "own little attic at Mansfield Park" (MP, pp. 371). Like the constricting corridor of some of the liminal stages of those rites, this had to be passed through in order for the social realization to take place. It is within this Portsmouth passage that her turn against the Crawfords is inserted, her opportunity for refusal, or the definitive breaking of Mr. Crawford's chain metaphorically around her neck; the episode is set apart and stressed by the triple recurrence of the turn itself, as it binds her to Edmund by his simple and neat chain, unlike Mr. Crawford's unwanted one. "She turned away. . . . She began to feel the possibility of his turning out well at last. . . . He . . . turned to Mansfield" (MP, p. 397). But Edmund's final turn is a mirroring of hers, as she returns to that house and its environs, for the conclusive view; she proves herself strong at linking.

In its turn, the metaphor of Edmund's presented chain suggests a verb that keys the scene, as it is first encountered negatively, and in an ambiguous position: "you had not had time to attach yourself." Attachments are made with chains and with human links: Edmund's urging Fanny to keep her own attachment within rational bounds would take her back a step to the enclosures she has already broken through; the novel concerns, in fact, the establishment of the order of communication and thought, after a textual estrangement and a temporary set of turns, taken with a temporary set of characters:

Edmund has to learn to penetrate Fanny's silence just as she pierces her unwanted chains: "a state which he must break through, and which he could easily learn to think she was wanting him to break through" (MP, p. 342).

In the final view, things are established correctly, after the lead is taken from Fanny's "attachment" by Edmund's confession that Miss Crawford had in fact "attached him" (MP, p. 445) and that she "had certainly been more attached to him than could have been expected" (MKP, p. 445), and Fanny's parallel confession that Miss Crawford was in fact interested "in her attachment" to her brother. Another verb controlled by the image of the chain concludes the chapter satisfactorily by another form of clasp and attachment: "Fanny's friendship was all that he had to cling to" (MP, p. 445).

All at last enters, like the picture of the parsonage, into the order of the frame destined from the beginning "as thoroughly perfect in her eyes as every thing else, within the view and patronage of Mansfield Park, had long been" (MP, p. 457). The perfection includes even the pluperfect tense of the verb, gathering up all the action and perception at once and efficaciously, as the frame links grammatical, thematic, and personal observations in its own perfect enclosure.

Returning in Persuasion

TURNS AND BORDERS

Anne's object was not to be in the way of any body.
   Persuasion

The opening of *Persuasion* is neatly marked by the ironic book-in-a-book enclosure, for the self-centered baronet Walter Elliot is reading, about himself, in the Baronetage, a book that always opens at the page including his name. The setting of the book within the book is doubly effective, not only as a textual mirror for the vanity of Sir Walter, looking at himself with the pages, but also because we see there under his title the heroine of these pages, differently entitled.

But the metatextual reference to a "high-class" book in a high-class book leads finally to a wider generalization at the conclusion. After opening with the authorial distance we expect in Jane Austen (like the "Let other pens dwell on guilt and misery. I quit such odious subjects as soon as I can" of *Mansfield Park*, p 446), "Who can be in doubt of what followed? When any two young people take it into their heads to marry" (P, p. 250), the text ends on a rousing salute to wifehood· "that profession which is, if possible, more distinguished in its domestic virtues than in its national importance" (P, p. 254).[8] The boundaries are thus once again clearly signaled, first by the opening into para- and meta-literary suggestions—what, after all, is this book meant to open at?—and last, by its textual closure into an atemporal frame, suggesting yet other questions: Where does this book fit in importance, and what is its scope? Does it aim at domestic virtue and neat gardens enclosed, or for the wider sequence and more open seas in which to set a captain's sail? The view here, with its "quick alarm" as the tax to be paid in this profession, is certainly less calm than that within the park, so *ordered*.

The reader's eye is caught, as in *Mansfield Park*, by a certain sequence of terms and repetitions that border the essential element; as in that novel, the time of Fanny's appearance is put in question, first signaled and then delayed, exactly like her reading of the part, so here the meeting with Captain Wentworth is delayed after initially being put in question. The scene is strongly framed by its obsessive repetition and its drastic heightening of sentiment. After all the buildup, the delay, and the absence, his appearance to her is disappointing; he finds her gravely altered, a term she then obsessively repeats to herself, thus calling attention to the judgment leveled against her, so that we are instantly on her side:

> "You were so altered he should not have known you again."
> . . . "Altered beyond his knowledge!" Anne fully submitted, in silent, deep mortification. Doubtless it was so; and she could take no revenge, for he was not altered, or not for the worse. . . . "So altered that he would not have known her again!" These were words which could not but dwell with her. . . . Frederic Wentworth had used such words. . . . He had thought her wretchedly altered" (P, pp. 85-86)

Her alteration is first aggravated in her mind by the contrast with him, as he is still "the same," both "the same Captain Wentworth" and unaltered or "the same" in his person, whereas she has lost all: him, and her looks. The inset here is itself the same as the one Francis Berry points out and analyzes in his book *The Shakespeare Inset*, to which I have referred in the first chapter. The picture might be framed like this:

Captain Wentworth's view

Anne gravely altered now

she was lovely 9 years ago

But of course this is a shifting perception within a shifting frame; we have no way of knowing, except by the approving glances that Anne will receive from others, to what extent, if at all, we should find her changed.

When Captain Wentworth's original perception is reestablished (she can never have been seen to alter in his eyes, he thinks), even as it blatantly contradicts the facts, his heart is "returned" to her (P, p. 195). Fickleness makes funny frames, for, after all these exterior indications of her never having altered, he too finds her unchanged, at which point it is his own frame of vision that alters:

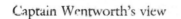

Captain Wentworth's view

she could never change

she was lovely 9 years ago

Another return echoes this one, as they are now "returned" to the past, and thus the picture is turned about. Her memory is put in its proper place after the upsetting and insetting Captain Wentworth's final statement in the penultimate chapter brings the reversals out into the open. As in *Mansfield Park*, following the time of disorder—a wandering in a carefully cultivated wilderness and in a park that is only the smaller and uncapitalized version of the Park—order is restored, so too here. " 'Like other great men under reverses,' he added with a smile, 'I must endeavour to subdue my mind to my fortune. I must learn to brook being happier than I deserve' " (P, p. 249). Until he had recognized her nonalteration, the unchanging situation, he did in fact not deserve the order brought about by his *straightened frame of vision*. The background of order restored then permits the picture to be set at a distance, and leads directly to the opening of the final chapter, already quoted: "Who can be in doubt . . .". Certainty prevails.

EXCURSION AND RECOVERY

. . . as they struck by order into another path.
   Persuasion

As in *Mansfield Park* the walk at Sotherton is placed at the center of the novel's structure and framed by leads in and out, neatly reflecting each other and setting the major scene as it is full of turns, so in *Persuasion* (half the length of the former novel), the equivalent walk—toward the brow of a hill—is centered and framed by just such leads, detectable in the same ways. At Sotherton, the walk includes nine persons, among whom are two important triangles of characters walking and working things out by *trying* them: gates, ways, relationships. In *Persuasion*, six people set out and set off along the fields and narrow paths, forcing frequent separations and divisions, now in twos, now in threes, shifting groups and ways of going.

The "order" they keep to, down and up to the brow of the hill, places Anne and the always complaining Mary on one side, the Captain and Louisa in the hedge-row "behind her, as if making their way back, along the rough, wild sort of channel, down the centre" (P, p. 109). Like the park bordering the wilderness at Sotherton, the paths are parallel, but distinct. The wildness excuses the break in order given by such a flashback as the one Louisa recounts, recounting Anne's refusal, an exposure of the heroine to which she listens. This hearing, an overhearing, and harmless as the talk is flattering, predicts and preframes Captain Wentworth's later overhearing of her conversation with Captain Harville, which determines his own self-exposure to her in the letter of love.

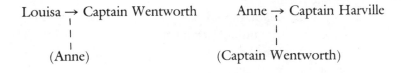

Louisa → Captain Wentworth   Anne → Captain Harville

(Anne)   (Captain Wentworth)

The conversation is full of "turnings back," and of "return-ings," like those windings of the footsteps and of the mind in the landscape framed by literary descriptions of seasons, and, for the reader of *Mansfield Park*, by that other picture and its other view. These returnings lead in turn to Captain Wentworth's re-union with her, that final return which sets the frame to rights, recovering what she had thought lost with the season of youth.

PICTURES

"Here I am, you see, staring at a picture."
   Persuasion

A collective glance cast toward a figure firmly centers that figure as an object of some interest—the gaze of all six people through the window at Lyme Regis directed toward Mr. Elliot confers on him a value at first sight, leading to the look Lady Russell casts at him as interrupted by Anne. The look observed is super-valued, together with the object of the look, and they may both be considered as framed by the intercepted view, a frame-up of a positive sort, enhancing the value of what is framed:

> Anne's eyes had caught the right direction, and distin-guished Captain Wentworth, standing among a cluster of men at a little distance. As her eyes fell on him, his seemed to be withdrawn from her. It had that appearance. It seemed as if she had been one moment too late; and as long as she dared observe, he did not look again: but the performance was re-commencing, and she was forced to seem to restore her attention to the orchestra, and look straight forward.
>
> When she could give another glance, he had moved away. He could not have come nearer to her if he would; she was so surrounded and shut in: but she would rather have caught his eye. (P, p. 197)

The reader applies to this scene a double sense, as is frequent in the highly framed passages. This one has its own border firmly fixed: her "eyes had caught" and "she would rather have caught

his eye"; the chiasmal arrangement catches the reader's eye, and
memory:

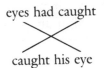

For the reader, this "interval," like the "first act," may carry
further: we suspect this is not just an intermission, but a real
interval before emotions are explained, that this is only the first
act of something which will end differently, and we regard with
amusement the "re-setting" and the "many changes" on the
benches, Anne's "little scheming" to leave herself "much more
within reach of a passer-by," with "a vacant space at hand" until
the exchange of looks just noted. The convergence, stated quickly,
matches her agitation, in a series of fourteen monosyllabic words:
"she saw him not far off; he saw her too; yet he looked grave
. . ." The monosyllabic stress emphasizes the moment of his approach, and the regret at his leaving, tempered by the thought
of his jealousy of Mr. Elliot, is felt by the reader as well as by
the heroine so watched. The reader is pulled into the scene in
this fashion as a result of the strong framing from outside and
inside: outside, by the duration of the concert; inside, by the
verbal and visible borders, and by the lines of sight, toward the
central or vanishing point of the picture, the figure on whom
our eyes, as well as Anne's, are trained. Had the viewpoint flickered between her eyes and his, our own would be unsteady, the
frame less clear; as it stands, this scene, together with the walking
scene, prepare the conclusion of the novel, for the sight as for
the mind.

Frames and Revelations

as soon as the play is over . . .
    Mansfield Park

The framed revelation by letter lies at the heart of *Persuasion* as does the revelation by portrait at the heart of *Pride and Prejudice*, and the trying out by garden and by play at that of *Mansfield Park*. The fact that the latter is rather a trial than a revelation is responsible for the different effect of the more complex novel on reader and critic: it is also differently framed.

Like the picture, the letter is a trace that remains, but unlike it, the letter bears a private address. A pictured exposure, even face to face—Elizabeth Bennet and Darcy's portrait—is in some sense accidental, and could have not come about. The lettered one, Captain Wentworth's self-revelation to Anne, is accidental in no sense. But in *Persuasion* an overhearing determines the letter, for he is not meant to hear the conversation in which she reveals herself, a conversation neatly balanced by her having overheard the revelation to him of her previous offer of marriage. So the accidental and the deliberate are nicely met. On the other hand, Elizabeth's confrontation with the portrait is, like an over-hearing, an intrusion on a certain privacy, although in a portait gallery. The look of the portrait, destined, in a sense, to all comers, is not precisely destined to her, although his smile in the portrait explains by repeating the smile he has had for her on previous occasions: oh, she thinks, he *is* like this. Just so, in Captain Wentworth's letter, he says, more or less, I *am* like this. The exposures in both novels are then framed in a mode of intention and unintention, as the central incidents are led up to and away from. It is clear that in Jane Austen's novels, the framing incidents cannot be placed at the edges, for they need those very enclosures against which Charlotte Brontë reacted so strongly.

In *Mansfield Park* there is a double trial: the temporary couple first wanders in the planned wilderness of Sotherton toward that orderly "park" they are tempted to enter, and which is a mirror image of Mansfield Park, but which they must leave in order to undergo the second step in the ritual passage of the society of the "Park," the trial of rehearsing for a play never to be given. In both these times of trial and play, the insertion of the trial or the play within the borders of park and of house is determining: that trial order overturned, the couple returns to the collective order. Sotherton and its smaller park remain behind, subordinate in the scheme of things to Mansfield Park, the parsonage, and its environs, so that both the excursion and the play serve as only temporary episodes. As the parsonage—once the place housing Fanny's fear—is absorbed within the Park, so that what is over "there" can be seen from "here" in safety, and so that these shifters and deictics settle down to their proper order, all the ordained elements have their reestablished places in the mind as in the actual point of view. The play in rehearsal is, after all, not performance except of the conceptual kind, but only acting and acting out; it is a different order of things tried out and eventually discarded, in favor of what "had always been," a *play frame* or *transitional object* whose memory is nevertheless set within the final outer frame. As the other two novels discussed are implicitly turned toward the future and open out, the world of play and the Park turns, at its close, toward its past and its tradition, so that this frame speaks of the act of closure, as if it were here—as perhaps it is—perfection.

PATTERN'S PARODY: MELVILLE'S *PIERRE*

I write precisely as I please.
  Pierre; or, the Ambiguities[9]

Warning Case

Excess is the key to the fascination of this extreme case of framing as pattern-hunting; this work might well serve as a warning to all would-be perceivers and developers of the framing impulse. *Pierre* disturbs as if its obvious parody were itself to undermine our own studies of parody by an accusation of critical as well as authorial excess, not entirely deliberate. In this sense, the present chapter might well be repositioned at the conclusion of the volume, undermining what has already taken place.

As it stands here, it signals, near the beginning, the danger both of parody and of commentary, of patterns and of their perception.

Hiding and Giving Away

Exaggeration makes here a splendid and terrible parody of the sentimental novel, where every framing device is exacerbated, and stretched to the point of painfulness. The stretching is visible, motivated by the chosen image, itself stretched to breaking: "This history goes forward and goes backward, as occasion calls. Nimble center, circumference elastic you must have" (PA, p. 79)

This odd text is gradually, dreadfully entwined, as if in a dark rope frame, within the long ebony hair of Isabel, until the initial green and golden world is finally wrapped up in the death-black vines of Isabel's crouching figure in the prison cell. This is disquieting enough; disquiet is compounded by the intermingling of conscious melodrama and the alternating images in their crescendo and their decrescendo.

Just as grape-vinegar corrodes copper plates to give verdigris, whose color is "the peculiar signet of all-fertile Nature herself" (PA, p. 29), the corrosion of the gold and the green in their initial purity correspond to the corruption leading toward the final shadows of the text. From the beginning, the open world of a youthful paradise has been presented not only in gold and green, in richness and natural splendor, but in childish pink and white, where Lucy in her "pure pinafore" or her white bed-clothes appears lamblike on consecrated ground, by the door where she is simultaneously blessed by nature and by costume: "the setting sun, streaming through the window, bathed her whole form in golden loveliness and light. . . . Her flowering, white, blue-ribboned dress, fleecily invested her" (PA, p. 83). In this ritual slaughter of the innocent, the telling adverb "fleecily" and the strong verb "invest" clue the reader in to the slow-moving sacrificial rite. The presentation from the sill of Lucy's room of her decor all in innocent white, enhanced by her tiny slippers and her ruffles, has already filled Pierre's eyes with longing because of such innocence, and those of the reader with unease at the clichés and what they must surely prepare, given the parodistic tone and structure. This literally liminal scene opens on a vision of loveliness all white and tiny, encouraging Pierre's reverent awe before this "secret inner shrine," as the ambivalent and ironic phrase sets him up for his own final slaughter, as he irritatingly imitates, here, young purity, and later, the writings of "young America," in its own young purity: "Now, crossing the magic silence of the empty chamber, he caught the snow-white bed reflected in the toilet-glass. This rooted him. . . . Then again his glance fixed itself upon the slender, snow-white, ruffled roll; and he stood as one enchanted. Never precious parchment of the Greek was half so precious in his eyes. Never trembling scholar longed more to unroll the mystic vellum, than Pierre longed to unroll the sacred secrets of that snow-white, ruffled thing" (PA, p. 63).

The reflection and the reemphasized arrest of the observer before it bear reflecting upon. His own metaphor might be considered reversed, upon its liminal standing-point, and framed by its door, for this scholar's trembling ardor before the chosen passage is plainly that of a lover, reading the pages of his desire, far beyond a simple pleasure, to a "jouissance du texte." Pierre will read his world, so framing it as to read it wrongly, including the pretexts of Dante and Shakespeare, as they are stated and implied, and the inscriptions of nature (its stones and trees and vines) as well as of art (the pictures of his father, the *Laocoön*, and the final gallery of portraits), and of the literary and the mystic communities (the pamphlets and the writings), all preparing his misreading of his own hopeless and helpless writing.

Pierre's whole world is backwards, like some baroque vision delighting in its own contraries and its own unease. All the extraordinary fleeciness and ruffliness will lead, characteristically, to just the bareness of "a thing." The very presentation of the opposites—Lucy, fleecy and about to be fleeced, this vapidly sweet and insufferable "little Lucy" in contrast to the basilisk stare of Isabel with her darkly odd face and black dress—forms a tableau protruding in the text by its singularity and its present tense, suddenly inserted in the present as if arrested, in a shrill warning signal, among the past of the narration.

Here Pierre's glance is palely fixed, riveted in a deliberately mannered style by the silent dark girl, whose muteness opposed to the childish prattle of little Lucy is stressed by a sibilant series: "sits steadily sewing. . . . But still, she sideways steals . . ." (PA, p. 71). The presentation is double; his glance and hers meet characteristically in radiant candlelight in the scene marking the contrast of Isabel's instantly and "henceforth immemorial face," which repeatedly looks toward the world of death and the final ebony vining, in the opposite direction from the pink and snowy gaiety of Lucy's life. Pierre vacillates on the threshold between the worlds, neatly framed, caught, and pinned between the paradisiacal green and innocent pink and white, and the mysterious veiling black, like the desiring scholar trembling before two rolls of a different vellum, each with its sacred secret to be unfolded or explicated; one calls for sacrifice, the other for submission.

All the signs and codes contrast; Isabel's hooded messenger in contrast to the "flawless, speechless, fleckless Lucy," who quite dully presents neither mystery, nor menace, nor message. Isabel is progressively identified with the hidden (her father's portrait hidden, her face hidden, her reason for mourning hidden), while Lucy remains naive and candid like the opening Eden so perfectly parodied by the frame and the framed contraries.

Closeting the Ancestors

Within the retrospective inset in the center of the book, the revealing portrait of Pierre's father when young, itself enshrined deep in Pierre's closet and memory, is included by implication in the older portrait of the staid and portly man on show in the drawing room: "Look, again, I am thy father as he more truly was" (PA, p. 109). Hamlet and his ghost of a father haunt this text, whose inset portrait is gradually exposed within its overlay, beginning with a lengthy melodramatic passage, whose key terms are repeated to excruciation by the speaking picture:

> "Consider. Is there no little mystery here? Probe a little, Pierre. . . . Look, do I not smile? yes, and with an unchangeable smile; and thus have I unchangeably smiled for many long years gone by, Pierre. Oh, it is a permanent smile! . . . Consider; for a smile is the chosen vehicle of all ambiguities, Pierre. . . . I once knew a credulous old soul, Pierre. Probe, probe a little—see—there seems one little crack there, Pierre—a wedge, a wedge. Something ever comes of all persistent inquiry; we are not so continually curious for nothing, Pierre." (PA, p. 110)

With its repetitions of the name ad nauseam, and with its summons to sight and its exhortations to "consider," the scene marks Pierre's frequent return to his own closet or inner sanctum, to its shelter, where he can frame his own father, turning his portrait to the wall and then removing it, leaving only a discolored trace, only a smudge where there had been a smile.

Everything about the portraits of Pierre's mother and father, melodramatically bordered, serves to set them at a distance from the reader. The mother's picture is as repetitive in its verbal borders as the father's: "the Infinite Haughtiness had first fashioned her; and then the haughty world had further molded her; now had a haughty Ritual omitted to finish her" (PA, p. 116). A second repetition parallels the above one: "Love me she doth, thought Pierre, but how? Loveth she me with the love past all understanding? that love, which in the loved one's behalf. . . . Loving mother, here have I a loved . . . and if thou lovest me, mother, then thy love will love her, too" (PA, p. 116).

Such bordering language is weighted with sentiment and presentiment of exactly nothing; this portrait of Pierre's mother responds to the earlier portraits of Lucy and of Isabel, as if these initial talky scenes had been placed there for the reader's peripatetic perusal in the gallery as metaphor of the text. In every case, they are held for the glance by the solemnity of the presentation, and distanced from the emotion in being repeated; they are pieces set or set pieces, whose static quality is increased by the adherence to categories, the pigeonholing parodied within the traditional system of social and religious conventions. An included observer thus sees the scene, awful in its cloying and set perfection: "Before him stood united in one person, the most exalted lady and the most storied beauty of all the country round; and the finest, most intellectual, and most congenial youth he knew. Before him also, stood the generous foundress and the untiring patroness. . . . Before him also, stood . . . the same untiring benefactress" (PA, p. 124).

Entwining in the Gallery

The great *developing figure* of the novel, the marble group of Laocoön and his children, "caught in inextricable snarls of snakes," (PA, p. 216), parodies the moral and mortal struggles of the hero against his implacable fate: Pierre remains entwined in and encoiled about by his destiny, ambivalently framed. In the culminating image of the picture gallery where he finally walks between Lucy and Isabel, and between two walls of facing and complementary pictures—light contrasting with dark, just as in the two feminine figures —to the jail cell where his body will rest between them, in a parody of manneristic contrapposto, entwined between the light and the dark, Pierre is still reading the *fiction à trois* he has made of his life. The two ladies, light and dark, represent the two inseparable and inextricable parts of his mental frame, its supreme complex fiction.

Fiction has ever been his familiar frame, fictive characters the revealers of the growing ambiguities of his world: Dante's *Inferno* serves to reveal his future, insetting its unspoken hell within Pierre's erstwhile and free-speaking Eden: " 'Ah! how dost thou change, Agnello! See! thou art not double now, Nor only one!" (PA, p. 111). The lamb implied in the name Agnello, the resonance of the fleecy or lamblike Lucy, and the change in Lucy's own Pierre, shape the double reading of the two texts, as Hamlet shaped the father's portrait and its rediscovery.

In the dramatic burning of the father's portrait with its ambiguous smile, whose "painted *self* seemed the real father of Isabel" (PA, p. 230), retrospective infanticide is already committed against Isabel, as the matrix painting is done away with, ending at once perpetuation and representation. The moment of the crucial action turns abruptly on all sides to the negative, as the fire is diminished, the "gilded but tarnished frame" is detached and dismembered, and the canvas is turned over. Directly in the center of this strong scene, the gaze focuses on one gesture of attempted recovery: on an impulse, Pierre tries to reverse his action as the canvas is reversed, and succeeds only in scorching his hand. "Twice-disinherited Pierre" then casts all his family memorials into the fire until he is "free to do his own self-will and present fancy to whatever end!" Now in a further imbrication of traces, the scorched mark on Pierre's hand makes a Hawthornian transfer to Isabel, the veil of whose hair winds itself about him like Laocoön's entrapment in the coils, toward the silent and yet noisily repeated end: "All profound things, and emotions of things are preceded and attended by Silence. What a silence is that. . . . In silence, too . . . Yea, in silence the child Christ was born into the world. Silence is the general consecration of the universe. Silence is . . . Silence is . . . Silence . . . Silence brooded on the face of the waters" (PA, p. 237). There is anything but quiet in this unquiet text.

Texts and Figures

After the biblical stylization of the outset, the ironic meditations on pamphlets and texts slow down the narrative, and serve again to distance the reading, setting the characters in an outdated style and allegory. The inserted pseudo-learned text, "Chronometricals and Horologicals," insets them in by a metareflexive border, marking their distance from the reader here addressed, teased, and mocked: "At the worst, each person can now skip, or read and rail for himself" (PA, p. 243).

Textual insetting abounds in the latter part of the novel, its tone increasingly negative: Pierre and Glen's exchange of letters, their salutations altered, prefixed, and reinforced, concludes with the final isolated mark upon the letters, the name standing alone, like our hero: "—Pierre." The heavy black line of this abrupt, desperate, and isolated signature protrudes, like death approaching, upon the page and within the text. The loneliness of the name prefigures his exile from society, whose victim he is, among the town's "general gloom," its still deeper gloom beyond, and its "side-glooms." On the stage, whose setting the stagecoach ironically mirrors ("The stage was belated"), Pierre, now an Orestes figure, is beset by whips and lashes, and is compared also to the *Fighting Gladiator* of the Louvre: the uplifting of the hero by mythical doubles refers back to his Laocoön-like struggles and his spiritual pilgrimage accompanied by Dante's figures as well as by Hamlet.

But the heroic is easily undermined by the heavy: sarcasm weighs massively in "Young America in Literature," on the fabric of Pierre's writing as it seeks a cloth and a cover, "coat and fit"; the pamphlet finally undermines the self. Is not the worth of the work in which we are ourselves reading thrown in some question by such pamphleteering? "So that all the time he was hunting for this pamphlet, he himself was wearing the pamphlet. When he brushed past Plinlimmon in the brick corridor, and felt that renewed intense longing for the pamphlet, then his right hand was not two inches from the pamphlet" (PA, p. 333). The ironic insistence—"pamphlet . . . pamphlet . . . pamphlet"—sets off the secret picture profoundly inside the text and its coat and cover ("Deep, deep, and still deep and deeper, must we go," PA, p. 327), but the book, "like the bitter Winter, is yet to be finished" (PA, p. 334).

Easels and Composition

The penultimate reflection is determinedly visual, and self-reflective. Lucy's easel takes up, like Pierre's pamphlet, a major space; Lucy's painful picture of Isabel and Pierre standing embraced looms as large in the reader's mind as the room is small. Between the two women and the two portraits in the painting gallery, where the dark *Stranger's Head* by the Unknown Hand is hung across from Guido's golden-headed *Cenci*, Pierre is stretched and framed forever. In Lucy's canvas, his own figure is a skeleton, sketched by the "marble girl," both skeleton and sketcher fixed in permanence, in a final tableau whose description is reversed in a patterned chiasmus of human figure and surround. The portrait of Pierre is at last composed like a statue, hardened into peace and into its ambiguities; as the stone walls close in, they absorb in themselves the pathos he is hardened to, in the paradoxical frame of the parody of framing: "His immortal, immovable, bleached cheek was dry; but the stone cheeks of the wall were trickling" (PA, p. 402). The whole picture is bordered like a book: "Here, then, is the untimely, timely end;—Life's last chapter well stitched into the middle; Nor book, nor author of the book, hath any sequel, though each hath its last lettering!—It is ambiguous still" (PA, p. 402). The last letter is as unsatisfactory as the first, in this parody of framing and entwining.

THOMAS HARDY: INSCRIBING AND OFFSETTING

The frame is a useful one if you throw out the likeness.
  Jude the Obscure[10]

Portraits

Hardy's attitude to art, he said in 1886, was that of an expressionist, stressing the idiosyncratic view, the distorted angle, like a Bellini or a Crivelli; "Realism," he said in 1890, "is not art."[11] The quirk in the author's "mode of regard" is intensified and quickened by the alternation of the actual or apparent order of things to bring out instead the oddest of juxtapositions.

In his own childhood memory, a skeleton dangles in a shop window before him, while a band plays and some children dance to it, or then again, the ribbons in the hat of a girl in front of him in church are seen superimposed upon the red-robed figures surrounding a stained-glass Christ, so that "the pale crucified figure rises up from a parterre of London bonnets and artificial haircoils."[12] Hardy himself prefers, he says, the late works of a master (late Wagner, late Turner), because their special idiosyncrasies are more clearly evident.[13] So we would expect, in our turn, that *Tess of the d'Urbervilles* and *Jude the Obscure*, Hardy's late novels, would exhibit a set of peculiar idiosyncrasies in narrational and formal devices in relation to his other work. We are in no way disappointed.

But the stacking structures and situations in echo, the linear and figural repetitions that fit together in what Proust called "the stone-cutting geometry" of Hardy's novels[14] engineer all of them. If *The Well-Beloved* shows most clearly the superposition of views, with one heroine replacing the traits of the preceding one, like so many related marble statues, several others show his propensity for the sharp chiseling of one scene as it stands out against the others, or of one profile cut out against the surrounding background. Hardy's conscious outlining is nowhere more visible than in the silhouetted scenes of heroine or hero set over against the landscape. In *The Return of the Native*, Eustachia Vye is profiled against the surroundings with clarity. "The Figure Against the Sky," reads the title of the chapter where we encounter her standing "so singularly," on the top of the barrow: "There she stood still, around her stretching the vast night atmosphere . . . her exceptional position   standing so dead still as the pivot of this circle of heath-country . . . her extraordinary fixity, her conspicuous loneliness . . ."[15] Her description itself pivots around the loneness and exception she makes, around the extraordinary and conspicuous portrait she is, with all the perceptive value placed upon that. The later portrait, as "The Queen of the Night," continues the extraordinary nature of the sight, set against all that is dull and ordinary. If mouths are made for speaking, not so hers; if for love, as one would have thought in a rapid reading, not hers again, by the second sentence, but rather a sentiment that cuts her out clearly as figure against ground: "The mouth seemed formed less to speak than to quiver, less to quiver than to kiss. Some might have added, less to kiss than to curl" (RN, p. 72). The relief of the portrait is heightened by the impersonal beginning of the profile: not "her mouth," but "the mouth."

Then, added to the already lush description of those lips like "fragments of forgotten marbles" on this odd personage who, "when her hair was brushed . . . would instantly sink into stillness and look like the Sphinx" (RN, p. 72), an array of exotic details as far from the surroundings as can be imagined is accumulated to enhance still further the profile of the strange and non-English apparition ("the under lid was much fuller than it usually is with English women" (RN, p. 72). What she brings to mind is the whole baggage of memory, of legend, and of art:

> Her presence brought memories of such things as Bourbon roses, rubies, and tropical midnights; her moods recalled lotus-eaters and the march in Athalie; her motions, the ebb and flow of the sea; her voice, the viola. In a dim light, and with a slight rearrangement of her hair, her general figure might have stood for that of either of the higher female deities. The new moon behind her head, an old helmet upon it, a diadem of accidental dewdrops round her brow, would have been adjuncts sufficient to strike the note of Artemis, Athena, or Hera respectively, with as close an approximation to the antique as that which passes muster on many respected canvases. (RN, p. 172)

Even the "new moon behind her head," here only imagined, is brought in as the pictorial background for this truly pictorial figure, set strongly and heroically against all that is lesser in the surrounding countryside, and given the antiquity and value of art.

Enclosures in Tess of the d'Urbervilles

Fold over simple fold
Binding her head
    Tess[16]

Toward the final dramatic picture of the central figure stretched out, awaiting death under fate's heavy hand, a unique profusion of framing devices work together. All Hardy's exceptionally visual intelligence functions as if Nature itself were bordering, pointing, deforming, directing frame after frame toward that end. To call attention to those frames and thus that end, Hardy's stressed passages include an entire network of oppositions—such as the open to the closed, the free to the imprisoned, and especially light to shadow and its extension in images, such as the positive sparkle of diamonds to the dark glitter of a toad's eye—and a series of visual deformations extraordinarily vivid for all their brevity. Specifically also, his architectural framing, in and through doors, windows, and keyholes, makes heavy use of light as a pointer, the sun's ray, like a finger, often designating the victim about to be sacrificed to society's conforming will.

From the ritual dance of the girls whirling about in their white dresses "in the green enclosure," with their flowers and their suggestive peeled wands, to the remarkable penultimate scene with Tess symbolically sacrificed in the circle of stones at Stonehenge, the ritual circle of a social morality, public code, and folklore slowly closes in upon private values. That first circular enclosure about "the Maiden" is soon recalled by the circle of "opalized light" falling on the three menacing and inebriated female figures dancing or staggering about at the second festival, in mockery of Tess. The dance predicts the final ritual slaughter.

Like the three fates, these ritualized figures, larger than life—The Queen of Diamonds, The Queen of Spades, The Newly Married Woman—prefigure the terrible scene at the end of the Fourth Phase, in which the diamonds that Angel's family has given Tess (seen here as another newly married bride) abruptly change to winking toads' eyes as her white muslin dress becomes a shadow enlarging its menace upon the wall and ceiling, white altered to dark and diamonds altered from precious mineral to loathsome animal. The diamonds, the newlyweds, and the shadow repeat that earlier scene and its elements of diamonds and spaces, in a slowly perceived coherence, for the pattern in all its horror to be worked out.

Already in the initial scene, the singling out of Tess as the one with whom Angel should have danced is repeated by Alec's singling her out and carrying her off into a metaphoric exile from which she will never be reabsorbed into group work or play. The "text" of bad-omen shadowing or painting in Phase Two is also a metatext about the way this text we are reading works; for the words are separated like the moments we retain:

Thy, Damnation, Slumbereth, Not

The text is balanced by another parallel one, incomplete for the insertion of whatever detail will call upon the workings of fate, and the two forming a heavy double line dark with warning:

Thou, Shalt, Not, Commit

Like a natural force, Tess refuses to accept bordering or containing by the social fences on which the texts are painted, but through which she cannot break; text and borders will close in on her like the stones of long standing at Stonehenge, from behind which will emerge the figures wreaking society's final vengeance at the end.

"A field-woman is a portion of the field—; she has somehow lost her own margin" (T, p. 103): in the Third Phase, her picture is distanced, set upon the green enclosure and the marginless field like a far shot: "Not quite sure of her direction, Tess stood still upon the hemmed expanse of verdant flatness, like a fly on a billiard-table of indefinite length and of no more consequence to the surroundings than that fly" (T, p. 121), recalling an intertext from *King Lear*: "As flies to wanton boys, are we to the gods/They kill us for their sport" (act 4, scene 1, line 36). This picture will in turn develop through the multiple later scenes when Tess is seen working in the corn fields harder than all the others, still singled out then, still cornered, still hemmed in.

Once at breakfast, momentary hope outlines her as she is observed by Angel Clare against the light streaming into the mullioned windows, long and wide, so that he senses the purity and the clarity in the figure we have read in the title. *Tess of the d'Urbervilles, a Pure Woman*, as "faithfully presented by Thomas Hardy": according to this faith, the author observes, pictures, judges, and is powerless. So the picture is set up, faithful to its heavy frame, formed by the view of others and the social fate they determine, as the individual is framed by the collective:

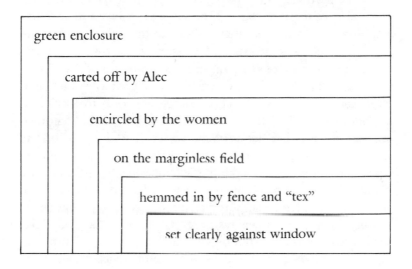

The Fourth Phase begins the series of inset refrains or laments, those ballads and songs that work to undermine the optimistic surface by their pessimistic folk wisdom. The first, sung by Tess in her wedding gown, signals the doom about to descend through her imprudently honest disclosure:

> That never would become that wife
> That had once done amiss   (T, p. 224)

The people's harsh "wisdom" is echoed by the cock crow, by the memory of the haunted coach, and by the refrain Angel sets into the text with his unrighteous self-righteousness:

> The man of upright life, from frailties free,
> Stands not in need of Moorish spear or bow.
>   (T, p. 242)

His refrain opposes hers as it prefigures her actual undoing, prefigured also by the revealing portraits of the d'Urberville ladies literally set into the wall of the ruined house, their hideous and criminal appearance prepicturing Angel's later judgment of Tess as guilty, in contrast to his own upright character. She is pointed to by the portraits, figuratively, and by the sun, visually, as if by some taint of social pressure: "The sun was so low on that short, last afternoon of the year that it shone in through a small opening and formed a golden staff which stretched across to her skirt, where it made a spot like a paint-mark set upon her" (T, p. 235).

"The Woman Pays," in the Fifth Phase: in the scene of firelight shot from close-up, when Tess repeats his words to focus our attention upon the turn of action ("it is not me but another woman like me that he loved, he says," T, p. 246), a sudden noticeable shift in view takes place, with the violent change of scale and proportion marking the emotional transformation. Centered in the frame is not just Angel's face, but the pores of his skin, as one large tear, a revealing, focused, and prefigurative object, slowly rolls down his cheek to magnify the pores like some deformation, functioning "like the object lens of a microscope" (T, p. 247). It is now on the face of Angel, heavily bordered and focused, as on any revealing canvas, that the scene of moral horror and social tragedy is played out, for the sport of Gods and the readers' pity.

Now a third refrain is inset like a tragic chorus to reply to both hers and his, this one chanted impersonally as if by Time, says the text, and the force is greater than that taken to undo one pitiful female figure:

> Behold, when thy face is made bare, he that loved thee shall hate;
> Thy face shall be no more fair at the fall of thy fate.
> (T, p. 248)

When Tess, as if affirming her aesthetic transformation in another's eyes—from the Italian portraits with which Angel at first associated her to the hard portraits of Dutch and Flemish art—snips off her eyebrows and her hair, binding her beauty to set out drably, the scene is abruptly placed at a distance, to emphasize her oneness with the fate of country women, who have neither importance nor any "margin" of freedom for the fates that down them. Kept in focus, her figure is accorded a large, even epic, size, as her suffering deserves: Tess in the field, Tess working and suffering, Tess the image of humankind laboring under odds too heavy. Her transformation into the Picture of a Fieldwoman is set in a lyric mode, in the present, to single it out from the flow of the surrounding text:

> Thus Tess walks on; a figure which is part of the landscape; a field-woman pure and simple. . . . There is no sign of young passion in her now:
>
>> The maiden's mouth is cold
>> . . . .
>> Fold over simple fold
>> Binding her head.
>> (1', p. 298)

Under the surface of this dignified and pictured figure pulses the record of her life and her knowledge: the victim of an unfair fate, she strides tired but heroic through the stubble.

The final social vengeance is already rehearsed in the singular scene of Angel's sleepwalking feat, as he carries Tess's body like a corpse across the river in a striking passage, to lay her in the stone coffin as a preview of the stone slab upon which she will lie at Stonehenge to be sacrificed by her own will. In this moment of reversal and rehearsal for the couple, they retrace their steps by the place they once danced in order, as it were, to undo the dance. Much of the novel thus hinges on repeats and reverses, on prefigurings and rehearsals, the active forms of development of the final picture.

The Sixth Phase thus repeats the warning letters upon the gate, painted by the same hand, but this time they are only mentioned and not quoted directly, as if the inset "tex" were to have been wiped out by the actual flow of the text; the writer is now in Alec's employ, so that all the inset "texes" and refrains are seen as issuing from the persecutor in the narrated melodrama. The unwritten "text" will turn against Tess as surely as do the spoken and written ones: this is the real refrain. The tracing and retracing of steps and texts, the weaving and reweaving of the spoken and written and suggested paths that have led this far work in a way imaged by the spider web focused at the center of the picture made by inner and outer panels of glass at the window, when the rain slides down outside against the tears within, in a coincidence as beautiful as it is suggestive. Tess is hemmed in thereby when the web of that spider is disclosed as it has been caught and drowned, as if she, and we with her, were to drown in tears. This capture in a glass frame is further stressed by the repetitions of paths, sights, memories, and restrictions, all forming the frame of expected doom.

The final phase outlines Angel at last returned, against the light in his parents' doorway, where attention is focused by a detail as sudden and as deforming as the early tear sliding down the pores of the cheek to enlarge them: both details arrest the glance by their oddness, peculiar as the early sights attractive to Hardy: "The new arrival, who was just about to enter, saw their anxious faces in the doorway and the gleam of the west in their spectacles because they confronted the last rays of day; but they could only see his shape against the light" (T, p. 388). The backlighting and the glare within the spectacles delay the sight, retard the revelation, and delight with the paradox: the parents wearing glasses cannot see, blinded by the light itself, whereas Angel sees them and the picture of himself in their spectacles. Like Crivelli's dead Christ he appears, in anguish and in ruined health, and this portrait of him by reference to other portraits equals that of Tess by reference to those of her ancestors set in the wall of the ruined house: ruin echoes ruin.

But the return has its own opposite picture, as Tess herself is outlined in a doorway, wearing her cashmere robe, her "loosely-wrapped" appearance of luxury matching his of anguish, so that the opposite symmetry is maintained. From the doorways the restrictions move in closer and closer, the views progressively more narrow, leading finally to the narrow opening through which Angel will peer out from their hiding place, and to the door opened just a crack, "not more than an inch or two," through which, like a repeat of the landlady's spying upon the couple, the caretaker will look in at them as they take refuge for the last time: "A stream of morning light through the shutter-chink fell upon the faces of the pair, wrapt in profound slumber" (T, p. 412)

All these apertures for looking in and out can be superimposed, and have been themselves pre-viewed by Tess peering through the door's crack at Alec in church. The accumulating references to looking in and out intensify the gradual acceleration of the hunt for fate's victim. Tess's "loosely-wrapped dressing-gown" may have already brought to mind the best sheet in which Angel wrapped her for the coffin, a prefiguring of the winding sheet of the impending death, itself predicted by their double "wrapping" in profound slumber which suggests the lovers Tristan and Iseult asleep and seen as pure.

In response, the morning light shows Tess as pure indeed, despite the closing in of social justice, as landlady and neighbors discover her stabbing of d'Urberville through the murder stain, a blood-red heart design on the ceiling, the developing image for her undying passion.

The last pure sacrifice will be made at Stonehenge by night, upon the slab where Tess chooses to lie as upon an altar, echoing both the coffin that Angel lay her in and the bed they slept on. She selects her final picture: the ritual scene of the borders closing is set in high dramatic relief and in slow motion.

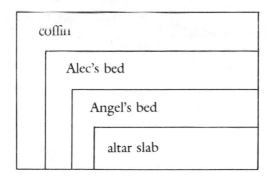

Around the scene a space is marked: the men who have closed in on her from behind the ancient stone pillars stand watching over her sleep, like sixteen guardian angels, with Angel as head of them all. They represent the weight of the past and the pillars of custom, reducing her human size by their ritualized and masked presence, larger than life:

> When they saw where she lay . . . they showed no objection and stood watching her, as still as the pillars around. He went to the stone and bent over her, holding one poor little hand; her breathing now was quick and small, like that of a lesser creature than a woman. All waited in the growing light, their faces and hands as if they were silvered, the remainder of their figures dark, the stones glistening green-grey, the plain still a mass of shade. Soon the light was strong, and a ray shone upon her unconscious form, peering under her eyelids and waking her. (T, p. 417)

In this final picture of the pure woman, the ray of light points, for the last time, at the victim waked for death.

After this massive drama, the last picture itself is narrowed in size, its figures reduced by half: Angel and Tess's sister pass through an opening in the wall, their faces half their normal size, their heads drooping like the two Apostles of Giotto, the final references to the world of art, so that to pagan sacrifice is added all the beauty of another tradition. The closing pattern on this last frame reverses and recalls the milestone "standing whitely on the green margin of the grass," now set as a metonymic border to the picture of the white-clad maidens dancing in the first scene, with Tess in their center:

"white figures in the green enclosure"

"standing whitely on the green margin of the grass"

green-grey circle of Stonehenge

The stone recalls the peeled wand, its vertically suggestive shape replying to that other suggestive shape, recalling also the stones of Stonehenge, themselves standing on the margin of the text.

The cathedral in its rising lines at the last leads the reader's eye to the wall where the wicket is inset, through which the figures pass as if it were a guillotine, repeating the suggested and morbid sense of the tower, where the black flag will be hung to mark the final border. The repeats are both verbal and visual: "viewed from this spot, on its shady side and against the light, it seemed the one blot on the city's beauty. Yet it was with this blot, and not with the beauty, that the two gazers were concerned" (T, p. 419).

The gradual tightening of circles—fenced enclosure to cart to coffin, windowpane to keyhole to shutter-chink—leads to the noose, irrevocably closing in and around. The fly had no importance in the field as pictured expanse, the field-woman no margin, and no freedom apart from her labor; the sport fate takes with Tess is ended. Nevertheless, the last sentence opens and joins with the future, as Tess would have had it continue: after the circle had closed in on the victim sacrificed, her own "pure wish" is carried out beyond it and along: "As soon as they had strength, they arose, joined hands again, and went on" (T, p. 419).

Framing Ironies in Jude the Obscure

LINES, HARROWS, GROOVES

The world is read as particularly flat and framed in *Jude the Obscure*. The "letter" that killeth in Jude is not only the dry texts of Christminster but also the other schoolings-down of the spirit beneath the unbending yoke of learning: those haggard frowning faces in the portraits, and Phillotson's own furrowed brow, are the result. It is also the straight furrows and grooves of any life as it is fallen into, like the harrow-lines into which Jude is soon set, whatever impedes the free progress of the heart and mind. It is above all the redoings and retracings, redoublings, rehearsals, retouchings, which bend the knee and then trace the gestures into *repetitions*. The frame for *Jude* is a severity of line restraining the spontaneity to which Jude is most fitted, the Gothic irregularities in architecture that Ruskin would have approved, and the freestone work he delights in, significantly. In his enthusiasm, Jude would restore freely, joining thus construction and invention, but gradually all the constructive skills of the stonemason are rejected until there is only cemetery inscription, that is, the tracing of lines to death.

Jude's idiosyncrasy is his determination to learn, his fate, the copying of the harrow-lines and grooves, the parallel lines of what has gone before. Initially he takes a path marked by what has been left behind: "a rack of last year's produce," once trodden by numerous members of his own family, now dead: those harrow-lines we now retrace will eventually wipe out the gradations and nuances in Jude's own character, his love, and his ambition.

Such is the frame, and the figure developed in it participates at once in the legend of the Laocoön—writhing in his anguish, always seen *against*, with lines about his mouth and corrugation on his brow—and in that of Samson, deprived of his strength by Woman (of whom both examples here are destructive, one by flesh and one by spirit). Against the tragic power of the Laocoön and his furrowed brow, the reader sets the dead pasteboard figure of Phillotson and the four lines in his forehead.

The set pieces in their distorted angles illustrate those framing lines against which Jude struggles, and the developing figure within it, less and less able to struggle against his fate: not the groove he chooses but the one chosen for him. "The fresh harrow-lines seemed to stretch like the channelings in a piece of new corduroy, lending a meanly utilitarian air to the expanse, taking away its gradations, and depriving it of all history beyond that of the few recent months. . . . Every inch of ground had been the site, first or last, of energy, gaiety, horse play, bickerings, weariness" (J, p. 53).

The flattening out of a mind and a landscape is threatened only implicitly in the expanse of plowed ugliness, at once the past site of "sturdy deeds" and the harnessing of present freedom. As surely as the earth is turned over and its history broken up, Jude's own desperate yearnings are to be undermined, his hopes overturned, his aspirations broken. The harrow-lines are—as if foreseeing that—echoed visually by the *groove* into which Jude yearns to be, always a follower after, never in the lead, never in time, for someone has always been there first. His moment never fits. Even the editions of the classics he consults have already been superseded, have already been used: "already thumbed by hands possibly in the grave" as he "digs" out their thoughts (J, p. 74), his vocabulary already marks his spirit as over-serious, too profound, and even deadly. Lonely, like Hardy's major figures,[17] he represents them all.

But the borders have seemed, for a while, to remain significantly open to the possibility of optimism; as Jude significantly curtains off his bed for study, he proclaims his freedom to himself as to the others in whom he reads: "I have understanding as well as you; I am not inferior to you," he writes on the wall at Christminster with the chalk he carries as a workman—and yet even these words are copied, from Job in his book. The inscription he chooses serves as his own groove to fit into; nothing for him is for the first time. In his work, he repairs cathedrals, rebuilding instead of building anew; in his "free" hours, the models he inserts into the routine of his days come from the ancients and are, being quotations, in no way "free." What Jude seems to long for is yet another way of conforming, since his ambition is directed toward a light already learned. He advances along his harrow-lines, according to the grooves made by the "letter that killeth," advancing directly to his grave before thirty. Not only does he copy to earn his living, but his free time, spent with freestone, is nevertheless concerned with imitation, in mimetically "copying the heads and capitals in his parish church" (J, p. 77). And later, "we must conform," says Sue (J, p. 417).

If *Jude* is seen as the struggle of the free spirit against and within the borders imposed by human conditions, the spirit hemmed in by tradition on one hand and animal instinct on the other, these limits are plainly inescapable and referentially valid: "The frame is a very useful one, if you take out the likeness" (J, p. 119), says the broker about the effects of Jude and Arabella's household. Any individual portrait can be removed to show the social limits; Jude's face can indeed be taken out of that particular frame, but its real destiny is already inserted there: he burns it "frame and all," but likeness is consumed therein. At the novel's tragic conclusion, Arabella's last words hem in the tale, dooming Sue's own free spirit to the same rigid pose of a statue as Jude, "until she's as he is now"; he lies "straight as an arrow," being reduced to "a handsome corpse" (J, p. 490-91), as the final consumption of frames and figures is accomplished in the unforgiving blaze of the book.

PARALLELS AND SEPARATIONS

The terrible irony of Jude is a framing irony, as he and Arabella the pig girl walk in "parallel lines" then, and from then on, with Jude progressively torn apart by the conflicting frames and framing female figures. The piece of barrow pig she throws at him, and the pig grease with which she soils his study books give the image of shame inflicted by the lowly on the less lowly spirit, symbolizing ambition ruined and the free spirit squashed. The developing motif of Samson and Delilah, glimpsed in the tavern amid the strains and traces of drinking, continues the motif of paths already trod, as the scene presages two others, the first where Jude sees the back of Arabella's head reflected in the glass behind the bar—as if in a Manet canvas—and the second where she intoxicates him to pull him along in the accustomed traces. Those traces were marked out even in the beginning, by their footprints in the damp earth as they kissed for the first time, a spot at which Jude sighs and which Arabella passes heedlessly; the picture is again melodramatically revealing, clearly focused, and intensely discomforting.

The bitter repeat of Jude's marriage is set on the stage of decomposition and the uselessness of the "usual" traces, "while they walked up and down over a floor littered with rotten cabbage-leaves, and amid all the usual squalors of decayed vegetable matter and unsalable refuse" (J, p. 221). This scene of memory and hedging in by custom is closely followed by Sue's rehearsal of her marriage, sure to follow in the same traces, to rehearse and repeat the same decay. As Jude now resights the chair Sue had occupied when he first paused before her picture, living but now in its repeat, a living dead moment ("when, leaning over her ecclesiastical scrolls, a hog-hair brush in her hand, her girlish figure had arrested the gaze of his inquiring eyes," J, p. 235), standing precisely in its former spot but empty now, the hog-hair brush recalls for the reader Arabella's hogs, so that the echoes and reflections are, as always here, terrible. The mirrored tavern scene thus reflects more than Arabella, for it reflects too upon the redoubling of all the relations in the novel, and upon its inescapable grooves and repeats and furrows, these harrow-lines not only of age and of concern, but of the helpless repeating into whose reading we are all forced.

Jude's relation with Sue was to have been the "free" one, free of traces and of custom, free of outside measure and painful involvement. Sue explicitly states her repugnance at meeting him at the convergence of two roads, for that cross is *already traced*— all her efforts bend in the direction of freedom. They are nevertheless doomed and framed in, as are Jude's own. Arabella and Cartlett will descend later there as two railways lines converge, and Jude will be swept thus back into that convergence with her, that eventual working out of the once parallel lines, as Sue is swept into the convergence with Phillotson, when her recovery will "set him right. . . . So I may set back in some degree into my old trace." Already the imprints of muddy feet across the steps of the Registrar's Office where she and Jude are to marry have soiled the text, as Jude's own texts were soiled, by the pig grease, image of the initial summoning by the animal and the later revenge of the animal upon the spirit. The notices of previous marriages mark the wall, and the "bare wood floor was, like the doorstep, stained by previous visitors" (J, p. 351). Refusing those marks of other lines and links, Sue refuses the marriage, but human censure will turn out to make more of a stain than that of all those feet, and a more imprisoning frame.

The reframing pattern of the novel is clear. Arabella is at first tied down by her pig-line and her efforts not to let the animal escape, and she will eventually tie Jude down in much the same way. Jude inscribes "Thither" by the road leading to Christminster, that once-original inscription itself a shifter, open to all interpretations, later retraced by his despairing fingers. Retraced, it can only mark discouragement, only repeat what could never be other than a negative result. If Sue is first seen like an angel illuminating an "alleluia," with a hog-brush, she is, as I retrace my steps to say, retracing (through the hog) the Arabella motif, and retracing as well a text already given, even if the expression is meant to signify joy. Like the texts she and Jude recite themselves, these are the repetitions of the already repeated traditions of the same pattern, as her aunt's recounting of her own recounting. Thus also when they repair together and re-illuminate, they are only renewing the letters already given even if they mean to continue the free spirit of the former repairers who left the "nots" out of the commandments in the warning tale the minister tells, enframed and inscribed in this one. In the purity of their impulse and its freshness, Jude and Sue would omit the *knots* or complications, or so an enlightened eye might see it: Jude wants to "cleanse his way" (J, p. 138), in the words the singers give forth in the 119th Psalm ("In quo corriget") but the very parallel is again a dominating frame, as the very church whose monuments he has repaired will act to shut him out even from its repair, and certainly from its salvation.

PICTURES

The lines of separation and fencing in are stressed: Sue and Phillotson seen under the umbrella frame, the glazed partition between Sue and Phillotson in the school, the girls sleeping in their cubicles, Jude's position in the octagonal theatre above the library at Christminster, and above all the "high windowsill" separating Jude and Sue as she stands in a window beneath which he passes,[18] that image then *inverted* a page later in the window of Sue's parlour, a couple of steps below the road outside where he passes, as she contemplates a photograph he hopes is his: this further material picture develops the verbal picture framed.

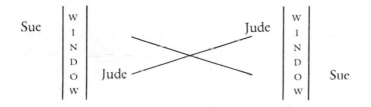

Even that photograph is a *replacement*, since it repeats the picture given to Arabella by Jude on their wedding day, repeating also first the photo Jude sees of Sue, then the one she gives him, itself a duplicate of the one she later gives to Phillotson. As if no picture, sight, thought, were ever to be the first: if the creases across Jude's brow are like those of the struggling Laocoön, it is that no predicament is seen as original. Jerusalem is seen only in a model form; Jude's devotional pictures are seen, and rejected by, Sue, who has already had her phase with them, but who has in any case her own social formulas and fixed opinions. The central figures are hemmed in from all sides and from within, by pictures, texts, and customs, all of which are themselves already *repetitions* (photographs of pictures, models of models, pictures of statues). These repetitions are repeatedly invoked, and led to the final scene of Jude's life, where he is changed to his own statue, as if copied in stone.

Art serves to develop the character's lines, tracing and etching the features. The Samson and Delilah picture is framed in the tap room, empty even of liquor and desolate of customers, in the declining rays and the sharpness of the repeated sibilants and sonorities, pointers for the decline—"on a Sunday evening when the setting sun is slanting in" (J, p. 89)—and directly precedes the unwavering animal trace doubled by the corresponding trace in the human world: "The pig . . . could be seen as a minute speck, following an unerring line towards his old home" (J, p. 96); "[Jude] stood accordingly, placing himself in the direct line of her gaze . . . Jude followed and rejoined her . . . Jude followed her . . ." (J, p. 97). By this gaze, as he follows it and her, like a pet lamb, his own power will be cut off as if the "lamb" were shorn already of his locks.

The predictions and reflections are easily swallowed up in the descending and pessimistic line of the text, but can be shown, when they are pulled forth, to work as Hardy's own Remembrance games, undermining the private hopes by verbal and pictured pre-visions and repeats.

Sue's picture is set—quite unlike that of Delilah—as in engravings from the "paintings of the Spanish School" (J, p. 185); but the training-school subdues and hems her in, almost as if the very term of the Cathedral *Close* were to have linguistically predicted her fate: "Her hair, which formerly she had worn according to the custom of the day, was not twisted up tightly, and she had altogether the air of woman clipped and pruned by severe discipline, an under-brightness shining through from the depths which that discipline had not yet been able to reach" (J, p. 184).

So again the early picture of Sue's passing under the screen in church leads to her separation from the multitude during Jude's public confession at Christminster: "though she stood close to Jude she was screened" (J, p. 399). Screened off from him, as in the scenes of separating sills and stairs, as from those without: the frame works in both directions. Of all the scenic preframings for the major incidents, perhaps the most notable is the series of scenes where Sue wanders among the statues, "reduced copies of ancient marbles"; although they are in *reduction and repetition*, and she is thus retracing her way, these are the mental steps of an attitude described as lively and as vibrant, as luminous: the pagan works comprise "a Venus of standard pattern, a Diana, and, of the other sex, Apollo, Bacchus, and Mars. Though the figures were many yards away from her the southwest sun brought them out so brilliantly against the green herbage that she could discern their contours with luminous distinctness; and being almost in a line between herself and the church towers of the city they awoke in her an oddly foreign and contrasting set of ideas by comparison" (J, pp. 140-41). But the heathen load of two statues remains wrapped in brown paper and covered in deceit, as she describes them as St. Peter and St. Mary Magdalene, when her landlady tears a hole in the paper "to peep in." The white plaster statues unwrapped are framed by a candle on each side and frame, in their turn, a "Gothic-framed Crucifix-picture that was only discernible now as a Latin cross, the figure thereon being obscured by the shades" (J, p. 143). This same Latin cross will mark the deepest *inframed* picture in the novel, that of Sue mourning under the larger Latin cross, as Jude treads his "obscure" and "deadened" path across the church floor toward her black-robed body.

EXTINCTION OF THE TEXT

The book of *Jude the Obscure*, with its intruding texts and messages, is often itself obscured by the shades of system and tradition: the large letters of Jude's one guiding text he himself has inscribed,

THITHER

ITT

J. F.

are covered over by the uncomprehending bustle of set formulas. Sue reads her verse to the end, and then extinguishes, by foretelling its extinction, her own vibrancy:

> Thou hast conquered, O pale Galilean:
> The world has grown grey from thy breath!

> which she read to the end. Presently she put out the candles, undressed, and finally extinguished her own light. (J, p. 143)

The saints are cast in a mold, as if conforming already to a form, just as Sue will be subdued by the training-school, enclosed by borders not of her own choosing. Jude's own hands, rough in comparison to Sue's, are "subdued to what he works in," which is, also, of his own choosing, as are the photographs of the carvings he has executed, exposed in the same room as the "framed photographs of the rectories and deaneries at which his landlady had lived as trusted servant in her time" (J, p. 188). He too will be a servant, and will be framed, by carvings and their traces in photographs, by copies and their copies, and by set pieces, even if in freestone.

FINAL FRAMING

Sue, whose escape from the social and private frames might have been hoped for, given "the elusiveness of her curious double nature" (J, p. 269)—the double nature on which much of the subsequent interest in the book has focused—in fact escapes those framings no more than does Jude. Her self-imprisonment in the little closet to avoid Phillotson's embrace is no more terrible than her laboring on the bed to bring forth yet another corpse of a child after the hanging of the three others. That event is itself the cause of the haunting central picture framed by the cross, as if predicted by the crossroads she had so wanted to avoid:

> High overhead, above the chancel steps, Jude could discern a huge, solidly constructed Latin cross—as large, probably, as the original it was designed to commemorate. It seemed to be suspended in the air by invisible wires; it was set with large jewels, which faintly glimmered in some weak ray caught from outside, as the cross swayed to and fro in a silent and scarcely perceptible motion. Underneath, upon the floor, lay what appeared to be a heap of black clothes, and from this was repeated the sobbing he had heard before. It was his Sue's form, prostrate on the paving. (J, p. 425)

The scene remembers, like the Remembrance game that will set Jude's death, and commemorates an original, a copy but of the same size. As the sobbing repeats, as the cross repeats, as Sue's form is "his," a statement all the more moving in its understatement, his final prostrate form will be hers, and will be, as Arabella says, the only possible model for Sue's own peace. This is the central framing scene, powerful, terrible, and baroque, with its jewels playing against the black clothing, or vestments, as if in a self-priested scene. As the weak ray is caught, so are the figures here imprisoned, taken in the church, their steps "deadened" by the floor-cloth, in preparation for the ghastly end.

The stain she senses from all the deaths will not wash out, as Jude's way will not be cleansed, and Jude's final departure from her as he descends the stairs makes a severe and silent parallel to Phillotson's earlier pause on the stairs with bowed head, and his sighing ascent of them to "his lonely room on the other side of the landing" (J, p. 290). For two beings whose chief aims were purity and free decision, the end is not only terrible, but terribly slow, in its prepicturings like the repetitions previously pointed out, all these scenes framed with noticeable borders.

The final scene of Jude's extinction is framed by three collective scenes of joy, the parade for the new Doctors and the Heads of Houses in their "red and black gowned forms passing across the field of Jude's vision like inaccessible planets across an object glass" (J, p. 400). The glass separating him from them will progressively thicken, marking him as alone away from the general celebration. The procession scene has other observers, who predict death and, with it, Jude's statuesque end: "the quaint and frost-eaten stone busts encircling the building looked with pallid grimness on the proceedings, and in particular at the bedraggled Jude, Sue, and their children, as at ludicrous persons who had no business there" (J, p. 401), and force Jude's realization, "Well— I'm an outsider to the end of my days!" (J, p. 401).

The outsider's lonely death builds up to a climax as, deserted and cold as the statue he will become, he lies, whispering and *quoting* biblical words of doom, against the noisy background of joyous shouts of the University Remembrance games, which indeed he remembers in an ironic antiphony:

> 'Let the day perish wherein I was born . . .'
> ('Hurrah!')
> 'Let that day be darkness . . .'

('Hurrah!')
'Why died I not from the womb? . . .'
('Hurrah!')
'There the prisoners rest together . . .'
(J. pp. 485-86)

The counterpoint is already second-hand—formula against formula with the first voice personal if not original, and the second, collective—and has its equivalent in a novel written almost forty years before. In *Madame Bovary*'s famous counterpointed scene, referred to as the scene of the "comices," Rodolphe courts Emma against the background of the collective celebration in the village outside the window near which they sit. In both, the festivities of the many implicitly undermine and mock the "private" scene within; Rodolphe's words, doubtless often repeated in other situations and in other counterpoints, serve the same formulaic usage as those of Jude: the personal scene is included in the general references to courting traditions and is illuminated in an idiosyncratic light by the collective voice without, in its celebration of the many.

Remembrance is here both private and public, individual and traditional, and the games cast a contrasting somber light upon his obscure death; the prize given to an old peasant woman in *Madame Bovary* is, like the Remembrance games, the ironic double of the scene inside, playing shouts and speeches against whispers. And yet once more, as he lies dying, the crowd on holiday shouts by the river. Each scene is bordered by the other in a double frame.

"The schoolmaster was leaving the village and everyone seemed sorry," *Jude* begins, and Jude's death at the end, like another leaving, stressed by the authorial beginning of the last chapter, closes what that leaving opened. The "seeming" regret at the beginning leads to the words of Arabella at the end, in seeming mourning; all the closing frames fitting into each other at the end are fitted into the bedroom and around Jude's corpse, like a last homage, to the trace of a life in a statue laid out: "the path

'THITHER' has led to this." The last pages to which the chronicle of these lives would ask the reader's attention concern the scene covered with a sheet, and move in and out of Jude's bedroom . . .

> Jude was lying on the bedstead at his lodging straight as an arrow.

> Through the partly opened window the joyous throb of a waltz . . .

> "Yes. He's a handsome corpse," said Arabella.

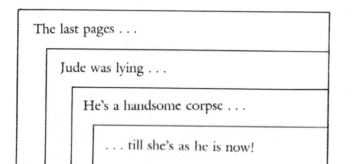

. From Jude's own form, stretched out like a statue, in its noble opposition to the rest—being no longer any copy—to the celebration of Remembrance Day and the crowd's excitement, we make our own remembrance, within this story's borders, and observe there is only a step from one to the other, like the visionary move from the dangling skeleton to the dancing children in front of young Hardy's eyes. That "real" vision and Remembrance frame in with all the resources of art the would-be freedom in this tragic text.

IV / TRANSLATION OF GENRES: CIRCUMSPECTION, CIRCUMSCRIPTION, AND A PORTRAIT IN AN OVAL FRAME

... it has always appeared to me that a close circumscription of space is absolutely necessary to the effect of insulated incident— it has the force of a frame to a picture.
EDGAR ALLAN POE, "The Philosophy of Composition"[1]

INSERTING AND CIRCUMSCRIBING

In the garden variety of narrative frames, a work is simply inserted within another of the same genre and sort: in a Shakespeare play, we see a play; in a James tale, we read a tale; in a Watteau painting, we observe a painting. Narrators and narratees, explicit and implied, present or putative, abound, but the kind of reading competence necessary is of one kind only.

More challenging for the practitioners of narrative voices within voices and texts within texts is the literary hybrid plant: within a play, a tale is recounted; within a novel, a play or a film is described or said to be acted out or shot; within a poem or a tale, a painting, invented or real, is "shown." The picture I want to get in focus here is a double hybrid, being the translation of a tale by a celebrated translator and poet, the leftovers of whose translation can be seen, in one light and with a properly obsessed observation, to make a poem whose very topos is that of the painting recounted and inserted in the primary tale. The painting thus becomes the visual developing object verbally recounted at successive distances, in all these three texts, so that it is triply translated: translated from the original language to the second one, from the second language to a third text, and from its visual impact to a verbal one. The complex tale tells both loss and gain, as a gradual owning and disowning are worked out, through the roles of the painting and narrating subjects and their painted object, whose own subject loses, one after the other, her tongue, her reality, and her life, in order to gain the "lifelikeliness" bestowed upon her in translation, the act of possession and dispossession.

Around a picture included in a text, the metaphor of circumscription can picture itself in a fitting sense. To write about or around a text—to circumscribe it—is in a sense to frame its likeness. It is at once set in relation to the other pictures in the place it is found, and "insulated" as Poe would have it (and Ortega after him, comparing as he does in *Meditaciones del marco*, the frame to an isolating border). Texts translated or shifted sideways may be considered, to that extent, resketched or reframed, reset in a new isolation, which may be the life or the death of the picture.

As a double illustration of that pictorial metaphor, I will take not just an ordinary picture inside a text, but a portrait inside a text it entitles and gives life to, together with the poetic translation of that picture-in-a-text and the text-around-a-picture, to show in what sense its nonliterality is both murderous and creative. The slippage within the translation, or what it does not manage to or want to possess in the text, is itself the creator of another text whose portrait is verbally and ardently framed.

My deliberately obsessed and obsessive reframing or circumscribing of this object made by the translator of the portrait and the text—in this case Baudelaire the poet as translator of Poe the poet and taleteller—attempts to account for the partially suppressive translation. It is haunted, or marked, rather, by a passionate adherence to both the subject and a supposition about the translation, its suppressions, and its own haunted quality; this obsession in turn occasions a circular or repetitive style, that of the circumscription which is the real frame around this tale.

Finally, across from the ardent and enrapturing portrait I have set a landscape of snow and ice, painted and translated by the same four hands, those of Poe and Baudelaire, concerning a different adventure, although no less passionate. The pictures are set ready for the oblique look with which the tale ends, a cooling indirection after so much direct onslaught upon the senses.

The following meditation, then, looks at the substance of Baudelaire's sighting of Poe, in its losses and profits, returns to its pointers and its obsessions, and takes its own form from the oblique look, the oval shape, and the circular or framing scription—the circumscription—of the included portrait, unforgettable as the foreground of the other landscape. It is intended to exemplify a way of reading certain texts, both obsessed and oblique, circular and passionate, destructive of linearity and logic, but in its response to both the death and life-giving forces of the translating impulse, pictorially creative.

TELLING AND RETELLING

Poe's tale *"The Oval Portrait"* forces a deliberately circumscribed focus on the reading of its inserted and principal object. The reader's gaze is trained in the same way as that of the narrator, within a range progressively narrower, from dark corridors to dark room to dark-curtained bed, the latter providing an imaginatively perfect if gloomy position from which to contemplate the portrait of the young bride upon the wall. In that bed is found, providentially placed upon the pillow, the explanatory tale for the portrait. Placed there "by chance," the written counterpart to the visual object determines a simultaneous and parallel reading between a portrait that catches the light and its own verbal enlightenment, the text in the volume. What is pictured is in fact loss, while it speaks of life. The painter of the elaborately framed portrait is the lady's husband, so loving and so much an artist that his admiring brush has stripped the real bride of her color to place the color on the canvas, life upon the wall, and death within his bed. The inserted tale ends there, with no return to the outside frame for the narrator, as if the recounted drama of the exchange of life for truth in representation were in fact to operate in much the same way within the text of the tale itself.

But the story is far from stopping there. In Baudelaire's translation of the text,[2] what seem to be small losses will make in fact a major gain. Moreover, the very embedding or insertion of the portrait in the tale and the subsequent embedding, or framing, of the tale in Baudelaire's rendering at once covers and reveals it. The whole process calls into question our previous assumptions about translation as a sort of inferior and horizontal *a* to *b* reading, and about framing as reading-in-depth, whereby the most central object is the most deeply set into the background. I think we can detect here a more subtle correspondence than a one-to-one, *a* to *b*, or horizontally situated relation, exactly in this text so heavily, and literally, *embedded*.

Baudelaire takes full possession of this text and this reading is equivalent to a reframing. The encounter between Poe's story and its French rendering suggests some instructive relations between reading, retelling, and representation, about translating and framing.

In a Gothic castle "one of those piles of commingled gloom and grandeur" fancied by Mrs. Radcliffe, deep within the enclosure, in a small apartment within a remote turret—whose walls are hung with many "very spirited modern paintings in frames of rich golden arabesque"—a wounded man in a delirious fever seeks refuge. Bidding his servant to close the shutters and throw open the heavy black velvet curtains around his bed, he contemplates the pictures; reads a small volume, left providentially upon his pillow, which tells their stories; and moves the candelabrum, whose position displeases him. The beam of light falls on the portrait of a maiden, so full of "life-likeness" that had it not been for the peculiar style of vignetting, as of a Sully portrait, and the frame, "oval, richly gilded and filigreed in Moresque," he would have mistaken it for the maiden herself. He places the candelabrum back where it was, thus throwing the portrait again into the shadow, and takes up the volume to read the story of that painting, couched in "vague and quaint words" within the written text, so that the narration has two levels of discourse and two styles: the "ordinary" or extraordinary style of Poe, and then this inserted "other style," for tale and portrait, thus set. The setting is meant to be permanent: from this told story there is no exit, nor from the bed, nor from the castle.

Of this intensely claustrophobic atmosphere Baudelaire renders a French version, but the original tale is, like the portrait, so "very spirited" that what is left over from the supposed correspondence of translation remains in supplement, its spirit returning two years later in the framing of another text. The translation is in fact already a framing of the doubly framed initial text, so deeply inset in its heavily marked contours: within the typical Radcliffean Gothic universe, within the thick castle walls, within the room so remote, within the heavy-curtained bed, within the ornate frame, within the volume, within the tale as told within the volume.

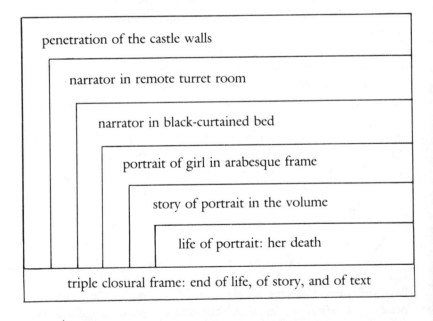

penetration of the castle walls

narrator in remote turret room

narrator in black-curtained bed

portrait of girl in arabesque frame

story of portrait in the volume

life of portrait: her death

triple closural frame: end of life, of story, and of text

Baudelaire's representation of the Poe tale and portrait sets it still further in, or at a further remove. The peculiarity not just of

Poe's design, but of Baudelaire's redesigning of the textual picture, has, quite like the inserted vignette, a force of circumscription and constriction sufficient to set it apart from "real life," but also from "ordinary art." The story so written around or circumscribed, so framed, has all the strength of the "insulated incident" Poe wanted in his close "circumscription of space": the vignette is preserved living even as life is lost.

Baudelaire's own art of translation can be seen, strangely, to take the colors from the cheeks of Poe's own portrait and enframing text, to reframe the story and the model, and eventually to make yet another lifelike canvas, in a future poem.

LYING AND LIVING: EMBEDDING THE PORTRAIT

But what of the portrait? Baudelaire's poem "Un Fantôme"[3] seems to include what his translation of Poe's tale excluded, as if, in fact, his rendering or reframing were to have drained off the lifeblood of the tale for his own purpose. Translation is in no sense here any effort at mimesis, but is rather a circumspection of the text, which then results in circumscribing it, reframing it as object come to death, or then to life. As Poe has translated the oval portrait into words, and the enframed painter before him has translated the live girl into death and the dead painting into life, giving life to his text by recounting the life-draining of another act, so Baudelaire in his turn drains Poe's text for his own obsessive engulfing of both objects; visual and lifelike, verbal and deathlike, embedding and enframing them in this parallel translation as a steal. Then, as a guilt working itself out, he recounts his own story of frame and dying-into-life and only later translates the story of the process of embedding itself: "So much depends on lying close" (PCT, p. 781).[4] From this the text is engendered in intimacy and in a possessive and obsessive double-crossing of genres and figures.

The relation between translation and framing finds a peculiar example in the encounter between Poe's "Oval Portrait" and

Baudelaire's rendering of it. After all, the violent obsession with reading and visual and verbal portraits, on the part of the narrator so feverishly embedded and curtained in, entails the entire question not just of language but of gaze; in opening and shutting his eyes upon the oval portrait, which is the focus of the tale, the speaker, who is also the reader, gains time for thought and manages to fix his contemplation upon exterior appearance, as in the portrait, and interior reality, as of the life. At the same time, he gives the impulse to the alternating rhythm, which will be the characteristic of Poe's most hallucinatory *Tales of the Grotesque and Arabesque*.

But the most singular atmosphere of the tale is lent it by the embedding of the narrator and of the narration: even the illumination of the portrait is elaborately interwoven thereby with the story of the marriage and of this very textual marriage bed, so that the narrator becomes the second painter of the tale, and Baudelaire becomes the third. The displacement and replacement of the lighting agent is intimately involved with the scene of the portrait itself, illumination and desire commingling like the gloom and grandeur of the castle enframing the entire reading. If the portrait is suddenly lit up by the beam of the candelabrum and by the gaze of the delirious reader of both texts, it was originally "thrown into deep shade by one of the bed-posts," that description already tracing a dark line from bed to painting, erotic and deadly in the same moment. The theatre box of the bed is curtained, as if there, too, the presentation of the pictured scene were also to be a representation of the reading and interpretation, bordered in black, like the deadly double of the gilt-framed portrait. As unfolding the visual text, the written tale of the marriage lies upon the very pillow, bringing death for the sake of art into the bed, the presumed source of life, mingling the notion of the corpse with that of creation, and making the bed the reliable viewpoint for the tale within the tale. It is there that this text itself also expires, as if this lushly embedded tale claimed for itself an ultimate privacy, leaving no trace.

TRANSLATION AS OBSESSION

Baudelaire's rendering of the English text, faithful to the apparently essential, in fact blocks just the details which, upon a re-reading, become significant, starting with the indications of ardent speech and deliberate closing-off, and the folding into itself of privacy: these themes intercross in their relation to the bed and the embedded portrait: "I bade Pedro to close the heavy shutters of the room—since it was already night—to light the tongues of a tall candelabrum which stood by the head of my bed, and to throw open far and wide the fringed curtains of black velvet which enveloped the bed itself" (PSW, p. 250). The closing of the heavy shutters prepares the lighting of the inflamed tongues in an expectation of some ardent word, while the pulling back of the shadowy folds which enclose the bed explicates or unfolds it, as the origin for the interpretation of what is to follow and what has passed. But none of this meaningful frame to the tale is translated into Baudelaire's version, only into his mind for a later product: the candelabrum loses its explicit "tongues" in the other tongue, the bed, its "envelope" and almost its whole message. The passionate letter of the English text arrives in another French form altogether; the metaphor of tongues for speech as well as light is carried over to that of a tree, and mere multiplicity of nature, while the metaphor of the envelope and the letter is simply changed to one of surrounding: "j'ordonnai à Pedro de fermer les lourds volets de la chambre—puisqu'il faisait déjà nuit—d'allumer un grand candelabre à plusieurs branches placé près de mon chevet, et d'ouvrir tout grands les rideaux de velours noir garnis de crépines qui entouraient le lit" (OC, p. 553).

The many tongues of fire illuminate the text as well as the reader in the English, and the message arrives on the black-curtained scene, or in it, properly and dramatically represented. The function of the bed as matrix is scarcely to be overlooked in the repetition of the moral text, where the insetting technique is genially increased by its staging within this embedded creation depending as much on the death of the original model as does death upon original creation. The black curtains around the reading crop out the inessential from the page or the wall to be read, so that "reality" is framed out and art is framed in. Yet another formal border is made here by the repeated phrases focusing on focus itself, riveting the attention, centrally: "Long—long I read—and devoutly, devotedly I gazed" (PSW, p. 250). This first repeat and second near-repeat invite us to reread the sentence as the edge of an interior text, heavily boxed in, in an essential airlessness.[5] Baudelaire lightens the second repeat by a sound change, which takes away from the heavily ornate quality of the edge: "Je lus longtemps—longtemps—je contemplai religieusement, dévotement" (B, p. 553).[6]

This is not the only loss, or the gravest one: in the Poe original, the interior crescendo leads to a secret suddenly wakened in the place of sleep and of creation: "At length, satisfied with the true secret of its effect, I fell back within the bed. I had found the spell of the picture in an absolute *life-likeliness* of expression, which at first startling, finally confounded, subdued, and appalled me" (PSW, p. 251). The crescendo and the darkening of the visual text as read determine the key word here, which functions, at least in my reframing or translation of it, as the second true secret, revealed as the narrator takes a fall toward the bed of his creative interpretation in its deathly perfume. The second secret, implied in the word "appalled," mingles death—as in a pall, a pall-bearer, and to cast a pall—not over "real" life only as prediction, but also its visual semblance: "life-likeliness."

But in the Baudelaire translation, in the place of this "life-likeliness," this term subtly expressing the very contrary of a real vitality, being artifice itself, we read another adequacy entirely, and all the more appalling: "A la longue, ayant découvert le vrai secret de son effet, je me laissai retomber sur le lit. J'avais deviné que le charme de la peinture était une expression vitale absolument adéquate à la vie elle-même, qui d'abord m'avait fait tressaillir, et finalement m'avait confondu, subjugé, épouvanté" (B, p. 554). The "vrai secret" of this translation or reframing is, I think, that the gentleman protests too much in attempting to reassure us about the equality of the terms in the first representation: the adequacy replaces the life. Moreover, the impressive prediction of the pall of death disappears in the final word of the French frame, as "épouvanté" in the place of the key term "appalled" suppresses the entire and double sense both of "pall" and also of the "pale" implicit there,[7] exactly what the picture becomes in its fading, the model in her dying, the Poe text in its framing. We have only to examine some criticism about the term "appalled" in Blake's poem "London"[8] to perceive that this word already carries in itself a long shadow, not a shade of which is to be found in the translation either of that first portrait or of its second or narrative frame.

It is, says Poe, in closing the eyes that the gaze learns to veil over and frame out what is irrelevant. Poe's "more sober and more certain gaze," however, implies only the subduing of the fancy, and a steadying of the look; Poe's gaze remains nevertheless tipsy, when it is contrasted with Baudelaire's narrator's gaze "plus froide et plus sûre," which suggests not just sober, as the opposite of the poetic drunkenness to which he so often exhorts us, but also the strong feeling of "cold" as an opposition for the delirious ardor to be found in Poe's characterization of the artist's fervor, as if it had been communicated to the narrator: it has been, of course, yet it is in Baudelaire quite as surely a displacement of the rigors of death found toward the beginning of the story. Here, by substitution, the proper sense is of the "pall" in "appalled," now restored.

And in this exact moment the narrator or first reader of the visual and verbal texts replaces the candelabrum, turning toward the written commentary on the portraits as it reposes on his pillow, directed toward his ear as are the portraits toward his eye. The perspective and lighting change; in Poe the words framing this all-important turn of the text are stressed in the repetition of the words "long, long," and the "devoutly, devotedly" quasi-repetition. All of these, being insistent verbal markings of the act of reading and interpretation, serve as border words to focus the gaze upon the proper place for obsession. The parallel acts of generation and degeneration in the inside story call for a somber isolation of the subject or model and for a focus upon the darkest edge of closure: "With deep and reverent awe I replaced the candelabrum in its former position. The cause of my deep agitation being thus shut from view . . ." (PSW, pp. 251-52). Here the translation conveys, surprisingly, no shutting out, but rather a concealment or a burial at a great depth: for "shut," Baudelaire uses simply a term for taking away or hiding: "dérobé," losing the sense of closure and replacing the narrator as an agent of the act of hiding, an agency Poe had deliberately transferred to the candelabrum itself ("being shut from my view"), separating the cause of closure from the awe of the spectator. Baudelaire's "terreur" gives a darker color to the awe: "Avec une terreur profonde et respectueuse, je remplaçais le candelabre dans sa position première. . . . Ayant ainsi dérobé à ma vue la cause de ma profonde agitation" (B, p. 554).

Now there are in the original two gestures of closure, first, the removal of the source of light, second, the closing of the eyelids: both shuttings-out or croppings-off work like a severe frame, serving a clearer inner sight. The English text accentuates the closure heavily by a triple use of the terse and striking term "shut" in a brief space of text: "while my lids remained thus shut, I ran over in my mind my reason for so shutting them. . . . The cause of my deep agitation being thus shut from view, I sought . . ." (PSW, pp. 251-52). The equilibrium thus established between the monosyllabic brevity and the initial as well as the terminal alliteration of "shut" and of "sought" stresses, quite like the regularity of some decorative border for a picture, some exotic entwining of a serpentine figure *S*, this closure of the text swinging upon its own mortal gates, whereas in the translation, the repetition is rendered totally invisible by the double avoidance of the one identical word in English. The "shut" is, as it were, shut away: "Mais, pendant que mes paupières restaient closes, j'analysai rapidement la raison qui me les faisait fermer ainsi. . . . Ayant

ainsi dérobé à ma vue la cause de ma profonde agitation, je cher-
chai" (B, pp. 554-55)

As the light is now replaced where it had been at the start of
the tale, its beam removed from the portrait like a blinding of
the canvas, the transferred illumination opens the textual or second portrait while closing off the "real" or painted original copy
of the model: life is brought to the word, and death to the lifelike
image upon the wall, the most living thing about the once-living
maiden, become the bride only of art. Poe's setting exudes mor-
bidity: "the light dripped upon the pale canvas . . . the light which
fell so ghastlily" (PSW, pp. 250-51), as if dripping blood, lugu-
brious and slow, upon the pale canvas, raking up that pall once
more. Its lack in the translation marks an emptiness in the text,
not unlike the other murder committed by art. But in the French,
the dripping ("s'égoutter," had Baudelaire so wished) becomes a
simple filtering, liquid but without the menace of the English:
"la lumière filtrait sur la pâle toile . . ." (OC, p. 555). The original force itself pales, but the painter and the narratee also choose
not to see the pall of the genial narration, hiding what it purports
to reveal, replacing light by closure of light.

The repetition of the painter's refusal—"so that he *would* not
see that the light which fell so ghastlily . . . And he *would* not see
that the tints . . ." (PSW, p. 252)—as an open confession of the
willful blindness, is rendered double in the second version, couched
in the bed of the French. The framing repetitions of the central
murder, in both the tale and the rendition, are stressed still more
by the double echo of "the light which fell so ghastlily . . ." and
the end, juxtaposing the pale and the ghastly: "he grew tremu-
lous and very pallid, and aghast," which sets off the final cry,
"This is indeed *Life* itself," just at the moment when the text will
close upon the words "She was dead!" for a final frame, bordering in contrast and in finality what the painter's brush has sketched.
From the beginning, after all, the young bride is pictured as
"dreading only the pallet and brushes and other untoward instruments which deprived her of the countenance of her lover."
Here already are the pall and the brush of the wing of death,

with the deprivation of life assumed in that of love: from these untoward instruments the deadly portrait in its present appalling "reality" (this is "Life" itself) is made, draining the once-true colors of the past for the future fiction.

The ardent and perverse pleasure taken by painter and poet in their own reading, which recreates death in creating the work, motivates not only the replacement of the candelabrum, but also of the *tongues* which might have said too much, by the mortal and deadly brush.[9] The colors dripping upon this work are drawn from the girl's features, *drawn* as the reader draws the curtains back or around his book, drawn as one's features are drawn by sickness, drawn, finally, as a secret sense is drawn from the neutral vocabulary of a translation, already or then, as blood is drawn, for the features of another portrait of a phantom, which will itself in turn be drawn from this very portrait and its life, into *lifelikeliness*. But the phantom is still to come.

These concluding touches given to the portrait touch up at the same time the linguistic and repeating pattern within the frame: "one brush upon the mouth and one tint upon the eye . . the brush was given, and then the tint was placed" (PSW, p. 253). Already the portrait is mortuary in kind, in the word "brush," as if the wing of death were to brush repeatedly before our eyes. And before this deathly gaze, the spirit that first haunted the purloined text, "very spirited" as it was, trembles: "her spirit again flickered up as the flame within the socket of the lamp" (PSW, p. 253), "l'esprit de la dame palpita, encore comme la flamme dans le bec d'une lampe" (B, p. 555). Not only does the original return us to the triumphal paintings of ghosts, those future phantoms, but the flame in its own ardor adds to the cold look of the narrator/narratee of the French version a retrospective passion; the third mortal allusion bears a still longer shadow, within the word "socket," which goes far past the signifying system of the lamp, however clear that is, to remind the Anglo-Saxon reader, whether he will or no, of the eye, especially of a corpse's eye-socket. This eye, which wanted to close and to be closed—like Poe's old man's eye in *The Tell-Tale Heart*, already glimpsed—has opened, and the tongues that it tried to replace have begun to murmur once more, and the shadow that he wanted to negate casts its obscurity upon the final lucidity, which there is no escaping: "he grew very pallid." How much stronger is that than the simple "il devint tres pâle" of the French, precisely by the expression to which the expression returns us: "pallid as a . . . corpse." Here at last is the phantomatic spirit of the word "appall," closing off the text and the gaze, in this brusque turn: "He turned suddenly to regard his beloved . . ." This final gaze kills with certainty and love, like the look cast by Orpheus upon his wife: *"She was dead!"*

Death or the dead figure is found exactly at the center of the egg as the image of renaissance borne implicitly by the oval portrait,[10] so carefully framed in its repeating and opposed patterns, far from the "real life" or the lifelikeliness, nearer, however, to the "true secret" within, like the equally morbid secret of the *Oblong Box*, this tale's mirror image.[11]

RECUPERATION AND REFRAMING

When Poe's "Oval Portrait" as translated by Baudelaire finds a reframing two years later in Baudelaire's poem "Un Fantôme," which explicitly includes its own frame, "Le Cadre," the four parts function like the four corners of the frame for the larger picture.[12] Between the two points, Poe's tale and the tale recounted from Poe by Baudelaire, we have seen a slippage, genial and textually productive: the reframing or translating process works toward a positive end, in spite of the subject on which the texts focus, being the death of the living model for the life of art. What is lost in the translations of the tale seems to be recuperated in the poem as the return of the "phantom." Baudelaire creates "Un Fantôme" quite as Poe creates the tale, and both already imitate the creation-as-murder theme of the framed topic: the intensity of the look is creative as it is macabre, and Baudelaire's recreation doubly so. The rectangular frame as coffin is implied, like another sort of "Oblong Box," but the form is highly worked. This is, on Baudelaire's part, a literary borrowing, we might say euphemistically for what is, consciously or not, a sort of purloined letter, or just a Big Steal.

In this perspective, with the shift of this other candelabrum, we begin to reread the paintings that Poe calls "very spirited," marveling at Baudelaire's devivifying rendering: "pleines de style" or full of style. Styled, indeed, but it is simultaneously the elimination of Poe's strong and deliberately significant expression "highly spirited" in all its ambivalence. This was to prepare the despiriting of the actual maiden, and its own despiriting prepares instead the inspiriting of Baudelaire's own phantom, both dark and luminous, like some incarnation of an oxymoronic baroque figure in its "dazzling darkness." The Moorish frame is replaced around the Creole Jeanne, who was, at the time Baudelaire wrote "Un Fantôme," an invalid, so that her presence in memory is all the more voluptuous for its lack of actual presence. When Baudelaire remodels the text, the spirits echoed in Poe's words will hover over the text as the eventual denial of life and over his poem, born from the difference between the original text and its rendering, in the bed of the spectator-reader, as on the later page.

The poem, now including the phantom, will absorb the Moorish frame within its model and within its own luxurious framework, keeping the pale tints within its odd outline half-effaced by the wing of time, applying them to a bedding of satin and lace, not unlike a winding sheet. Baudelaire will recuperate the textual difference in his translation and the original in order to revivify a ghostly portrait, in a literary vampirism which needs no conscious gaze to stand aghast: he too "would not see that the light which fell so ghastlily in that lone turret withered the health and the spirits of his bride." This second erotic brush, creative and murderous, of the translator's pen and the poet's own desire, stealing in order to live, makes a plumed pennant to sign away the "life-likeliness" of its model, within the curtains framing and the embedded sight. If the initial glance of the late-come reader is drawn first to the portrait of life as death, it may end by perceiving in the oval frame the possibility of an egg-shaped rebirth, at least of a spirit, in the life of the poem.

UN FANTÔME

I
LES TÉNÈBRES

Dans les caveaux d'insondable tristesse
Où le Destin m'a déjà relégué;
Où jamais n'entre un rayon rose et gai;
Où, seul avec la Nuit, maussade hôtesse,

Je suis comme un peintre qu'un Dieu moqueur
Condamne à peindre, hélas! sur les ténèbres;
Où, cuisinier aux appétits funèbres,
Je fais bouillir et je mange mon coeur,

Par instants brille, et s'allonge, et s'étale
Un spectre fait de grâce et de splendeur.
A sa rêveuse allure orientale,

Quand il atteint sa totale grandeur,
Je reconnais ma belle visiteuse:
C'est Elle! noire et pourtant lumineuse.

II
LE PARFUM

Lecteur, as-tu quelquefois respiré
Avec ivresse et lente gourmandise
Ce grain d'encens qui remplit une église,
Ou d'un sachet le musc invétéré?

Charme profond, magique, dont nous grise
Dans le présent le passé restauré!
Ainsi l'amant sur un corps adoré
Du souvenir cueille la fleur exquise.

De ses cheveux élastiques et lourds,
Vivant sachet, encensoir de l'alcôve,
Une senteur montait, sauvage et fauve,

Et des habits, mousseline ou velours,
Tout imprégnés de sa jeunesse pure,
Se dégageait un parfum de fourrure.

III
LE CADRE

Comme un beau cadre ajoute à la peinture,
Bien qu'elle soit d'un pinceau très-vanté,
Je ne sais quoi d'étrange et d'enchanté
En l'isolant de l'immense nature,

Ainsi bijoux, meubles, métaux, dorure,
S'adaptaient juste à sa rare beauté;
Rien n'offusquait sa parfaite clarté,
Et tout semblait lui servir de bordure.

Même on eût dit parfois qu'elle croyait
Que tout voulait l'aimer; elle noyait
Sa nudité voluptueusement

Dans les baisers du satin et du linge,
Et, lente ou brusque, à chaque mouvement
Montrait la grâce enfantine du singe.

IV
LE PORTRAIT

La Maladie et la Mort font des cendres
De tout le feu qui pour nous flamboya.
De ces grands yeux si fervents et si tendres,
De cette bouche où mon coeur se noya,

De ces baisers puissants comme un dictame,
De ces transports plus vifs que des rayons,
Que reste-t-il? C'est affreux, ô mon âme!
Rien qu'un dessin fort pâle, aux trois crayons,

Qui, comme moi, meurt dans la solitude,
Et que le Temps, injurieux vieillard,
Chaque jour frotte avec son aile rude . . .

Noir assassin de la Vie et de l'Art,
Tu ne tueras jamais dans ma mémoire
Celle qui fut mon plaisir et ma gloire!

A PHANTOM
I
THE SHADOWS

In the caves of deepest gloom
Where I am already cast by Fate;
Bare of any joyful rosy ray
Alone with my grim hostess, Night,

I am like a painter a mocking God
Condemns to paint, alas! on shadows;
Cooking with funereal greed,
I am to boil and eat my heart.

Sometimes a graceful splendid specter
Shines, and stretches out at ease.
By her dreamy oriental charm,

When she is full-length
I recognize my lovely visitor at last:
Black, yet luminous, she appears.

II
THE PERFUME

Reader, have you ever breathed in
With drunken rapture slow
This incense wafting through a church,
Or musk in its fullest scent?

Deep magic spell the past restored
Enchants us with at present!
Thus lover plucks from body loved
The exquisite bloom of memory.

From her resilient heavy tresses,
Live censer scenting the alcove,
Animal and wild a fragrance rose,

And from her muslin and velvet dress
All steeped in her pure youth,
A fur perfume is released.

III
THE FRAME

As a lovely frame adds to a canvas,
Even from a well-known brush,
Something enchanting strange
Setting it off from nature vast,

So jewels, trunks, metals, gilt,
Were made to suit her rare beauty.
No shadow on her perfect clarity,
And all seemed to fit her as a frame.

You might even say she thought
All tried to love her; voluptuous
She drowned her nudity

In a satin and linen kiss
And, slow or rapid, with each gesture,
Showed a childish simian grace.

IV
THE PORTRAIT

Death and sickness turn into ash
All the fire that flamed for us.
From those large eyes of tender fervour,
From that mouth my heart plunged into,

From those kisses potent as a balm,
Those raptures live as light, what
Can remain? Dreadful, oh my soul!
Only a pale sketch, in three shades,

Dying, like me, alone,
Brushed every day by the cruel
Brusque wing of Time . . .

Dark assassin of Life and Art,
In my memory you can never kill
The one who was my pleasure and my pride!

(literal translation M.A.C.)

Baudelaire's "Fantôme" may be seen as a double phantom, coming back in two stages, in the poem itself explicitly, and then coming from the remains of the Poe story implicitly, thus, framed within that story in its French rendering. It is, like the original story, inserted and buried at the beginning within a somber niche, within the "caves of unfathomable sadness" where the canvas of the poet-as-painter is composed solely of shadows. The gloomy hostess prepares for this new cave man a collation exactly appropriate to funeral appetites: the dark background of the painting in "Les Ténèbres" is stretched out horizontally like a black table-cloth to receive the macabre feast of boiled heart, that traditional romantic dish of poets: "he will eat his heart out." The painting prepared for the self by Fate as the hostess, but also self-prepared ("I am like a painter") is to be read as black on black, the gruesome dish predicting the mortal fading from one sonnet to the next in the four sections where life seeps away, and the verbs progressively lose their energy.

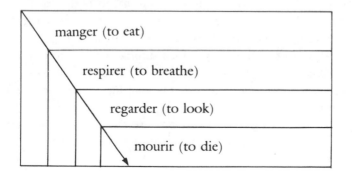

manger (to eat)

respirer (to breathe)

regarder (to look)

mourir (to die)

From the initial dark caverns to the alcove and the altar of "Le Portrait" and its erotic secret places, like some amatory church where the censer spreads out the heavy fragrance ("Le Parfum") upon a perfumed fur, "Le Parfum" is itself protected by a heavy frame as ornate as the Moorish one of Poe's own making. The poem, like the portrait, is bordered in filigree at once to isolate the scene in sanctity for the ritual worship and to ensure the private value. The exquisite black flower will bloom only once in this place so set aside, in this radiance so ephemeral, where "pure youth," in all its paradoxical lush secrecy, will have quickly perished amid the deep velvet and upon the redolent fur outspread as on some couch, this rebedding blasphemously and wonderfully lit by a torch, as by the former candelabrum, near the altar of a wild passion. It is just this outspoken and secret contrariness that gives this portrait its feverish exaltation, in these stanzas, like the model, at once "black and luminous."[13] The model herself is dressed in contraries, both in muslin and in velvet, the pure muslin of youthful innocence and the deeply dark velvet plushness of the siren, a costumed incorporation of the double postulation characteristic of Baudelaire. The model's figure, reeling with the dizzying incense and the intoxication of desire, will sink gradually into a deadly calm in the imperfect tense, drenched in satin kisses: all this within the third part, upon which the gaze is concentrated by its explicit Frame. Again, key words opposed here are "kiss" and "drowning," amatory and morbid, recurring in the last part of "The Portrait" to take on there a negative sense. The identification of love with death is intensified in this moment, before this altar for synesthesia, in both senses of the senses, so that death is reframed and retouched—touched up as a painting is touched up, or as death touches up the colors of life—toward this rereading which summons us, as toward an altar: "Lecteur, as-tu quelquefois . . . ," "Reader, have you . . . ," forming an inclusive frame for the painting, fully mortal as it is human.

"Le Cadre" of the third part now isolates the painting, setting apart the model from the actual mistress, bedecked in fittings most strange. This isolated space retains the precious image jealously guarded among the riches thrown in a heap: "jewels, furniture, metals, gilt," everything together as if Poe's "Philosophy of Furniture" were to cast an odd light upon this former "perfect clarity," placed from the beginning against a shadowy backdrop, deadly in its infolding of implication. Before this new philosopher in his bedroom, the perfume of lovely youth, as well as of the pure naked flower surrounded by this Creole's hair, are already teased by the "grâce enfantine du singe," undermined by the imitation of some bare Venus[14] bedecked with supplementary jewels echoing her natural ones with art. As she is bordered or edged in by the frame, within her gilded couch, the shadow of another verb, "bordée" or tucked in, adds for the obsessed reader the hint of another bedding altogether. With the "very celebrated" brush of painter and poet, the intense voluptuousness of the painting takes no verbal embroidery, no poetic jewels, for the model is sufficiently bedecked and bejewelled as she is embedded in the poem.

After the altar of passion, which is inflamed and ablaze against the shadows and the frame as of gold around a madonna, set around the picture, this last section of "Le Portrait" portrays a night- and death-watch, a double vigil at the bed of Love's prisoner, who will be the prisoner of Death as soon as her portrait is finished. The blaze dies down to ashes, as the reversal is made: the one who was, says the painter, "my pleasure and my glory," will bring death to the painter himself. Like the loving husband-artist with his brush in the Poe story, the poet-artist devours his model for his art and kills himself in turn with the sacrifice of his love. The flowering love for the model-mistress will be cut off in order to nourish the life of the art-in-flower, that is, transformed into a memory before its own altar. The model wins out over the woman, and the poet-artist over the lover-husband, as the heavy baroque colors, black and red and gold, become less vivid in this three-colored pale sketch, "ce dessin fort pâle, aux trois crayons," as if the three spindles of the fates were to have replaced the unique and famed brush of the painter, instilling not just a pastel but a deathly pallor. The painter will be remembered for his celebrated and secret portrait of this model, who came here upon the scene as a black and luminous visitor, a phantom from another highly spirited text, already a spectre, to remain as an effigy. In this other "Harmonie du soir" with its censer, its altar, and its monstrance, all wrapped in a vertiginous perfumed spell of twilight, the initial pleasure gives way to death, and death to memory in its isolated performance set in the borders of ritual and in the frame of art.

ADDITION AS SUBTRACTION

The paradox is terrible in what it so clearly implies: indeed the frame adds to the painting, but by setting it apart, and, finally, by killing its model. This isolation of the third part of Baudelaire's picture, where the Frame is openly the entitled subject, is, in the fourth part or Portrait itself in summation, the gravest of solitudes, where death does its own framing in the greatest possible bareness of design. To preserve her from death, the painter or poet, the one always as the other now, circumscribes the model by "lifelike" artifice, but the vital lines that stretch from the real woman to the surroundings are cropped off, exactly as curtains are pulled back so that the drama may be seen, or then the curtains around the couch of dream and narration so that the tale may be recounted. What the passionate glance of the artist-in-love obscures by its very ardor is the fact that these presentational curtains stifle the movements of the reader so embedded in the narration just as surely as the ornate frame stifles the model so enframed in the picture, cutting her off from the flux of life itself. So outlined, so lifelike-seeming, the severed object perishes.

The "beau cadre" adding its funeral framing edges to protect the beauty of the living portrait of this Venus checks any movement of the model, thus rigidly fixed in her limits at once enchanted and nonetheless normal (the mistress of the poet or artist is, after all, the model by rights). Before the painter's gaze and that of the loyal reader or narrator of the double canvas, both visual and textual, and now before that of all others, the living portrait grows pale, as she is now triply enframed. By the canvas, by the text, and by the bedding, this lectural or Frenchified *lit*eral frame (bed = "lit"), the model in her gold and jewels and arty finery is transfixed, impotent against the representation of the wing of time, that *aile* in language and in art arising from the very mention of herself the first time, *Elle*, and in the very moment when the poet and the painter (ironically in the case of Baudelaire, the celebrator of "the painter of modern life") is putting his last mortal touches on the exquisite flower imprisoned in her luxurious frame. Of all this black and luminous radiance there will remain only the perfumed memory and her halo in the secretly illuminated niche for a saint more voluptuous than saintly, whose brilliance dies within this poem. Circumspection or the roundabout gaze leads for the reader and writer, as for the poet and painter, to circumscription or writing around this framing outline: so the look cast upon the translation itself has permitted a longer look at a supplemental study of the experiment of translation as frame, and as final frame-up.

TARN AND TUNNEL: FALLING INTO TEXT

As a companion picture for the highly wrought frame or circumscription of such an Oval Portrait in "circumspect" Baudelairean translation, and including the same significant references to arabesque contour, Poe's "Fall of the House of Usher" presents itself as already bearing an ambivalent and androgynous trace even in its self-naming (Us and Her, leading to his—Poe's own—Hys-teria in the place set apart and underlined by him; a gloomy *STUDY*). The study, it is clear, should be, yet again, our own.

Studied from the visual point of view, the "Fall of the House of Usher" is a scene, a landscape, and a painting, easily modifiable by "a mere different arrangement of the particulars of the scene, of the details of the picture" (ST, p. 165). In such a personalized scene, an intense visual consciousness is responsible for the abstract design of the downward lines in formal parallel to the thick atmospheric touches of the gloom descending, the evening hanging densely, the torches smothering, and the Lady Madeline succumbing. The study slants down, and inward, inframing the readerly consciousness.

The pronominal eroticization—"us" being the feminized audience for "her" tale and "his" corresponding hysteria—of its explicitly decadent or falling story is reflected not in the polished surface of some table or tale but, by a baroque doubling and inversion, in the tarn-ished waters preparing the fall ("the precipitous brink of a black and lurid tarn that lay in unruffled luster by the dwelling," ST, p. 165), indwelling already in the tale.

At the core of the erotic correspondences reside the paintings Usher meditates upon and whose images "he" communicates to the narrator, who would in vain erase their accumulation, showing the text as faulted, in its lack as in its excess. Usher paints "his" idea, casting shadows and lights on the canvas in an abstraction even more vivid than Fuseli's "too concrete reveries"; here the painter's occupations "shadowed forth . . . in words" include a small picture of the interior of a tunnel flooded by radiation, which the narrator finds inappropriately splendid, for no outlet is observed, and no inlet for light. The tunnel shape includes and encloses, like an optical illusion turning inside and out, writing in and writing out, tunneling and traveling faster and faster, to guarantee "the success" of the design. This design has encompassed the fragments of the remainder of the construction, from the initial fissure to the closing waters, over the inner and outer walls as they merge, drunk in or devoured:

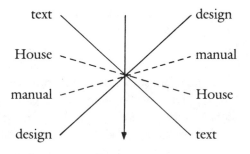

But who has designs upon this dwelling, and whose design leads to the downward plunge of the matter of house and text? What correspondence is there between reading and design and designation, between painting and arrangement and textural terror, not to say truth?

In the indwelling *study*, in the inserted ballad, an abandoned place is crowded with pale forms and time entombed; this *inset* shadows forth in its depth the fate of the falling house. But here too the gray stones, the fog, and the decaying trees make an arrangement then duplicated and repeated in the waters of the tarn, like a still life, still more impressive with all the linguistic force of a "nature morte," a nature dead already in its expression, however natural the expression.

The coffin will enframe yet another "nature morte," in the sense of a life stilled as well as a still life: "the mockery of a faint blush upon the bosom and the face, and that suspiciously lingering smile upon the lip which is so terrible in death" (ST, p. 189). The lid is screwed down, but the sight served as the border for future ones, as the outer or framing narrative suddenly converges with the narrative enframed, for instance, in Ethelred's gaunt hand tearing down the door during the reading of the story itself.

The whole text, "branching" out from the "stem" of the Usher race, inframes its two included tonts, in poetry and in prose, and inframes its own paintings, those bizarre imaginings of Fuseli, parallel to the more sober sights of the Sully version of the "Oval Portrait": these developing objects cannot stem the falling tide. But the latter tale reads its own story through its embedded and incurtained reader, with its speaking picture illuminated by the candelabrum with its speaking tongues, with its verbal and bookish text already pillowed. The *Usher* tale, a feminized tale as I read it, is remarkably unseen, at least initially, before its inversion and reversion in the more liquid and mirroring eye of the tarn, as it is originally and in the English, vacated twice from the inside out by its own sightless openings, by these "vacant and eyelike windows," I-like indeed, but unseeing all the more in the French, which offers only "des fenêtres semblables à des yeux distraits," "des fenêtres semblâbles à des yeux sans pensée" (ST, pp. 162-64). The very vacancy is suppressed in the French sight, as we might have predicted from Baudelaire's bloodless rendering of "The Oval Portrait," with the parallel absence of the telltale eye sockets and especially of the tongues to tell the tale.

The eye is emptied out then from the Poe story, but seen by other indwelling eyes, inframed by those very pictures caressed by Usher (whose ruin is already predicted by his "cadaverous" appearance) and inscribed or ingrooved by his "fantasmagoric" image of the highly eroticized, smooth-walled tunnel, that feminine space, that invaulted private part, womb- and tomblike, which we can scarcely vault over (as it is so "small, damp, and entirely without means of admission for light"). Here the Lady Madeline will be buried: presumably, this place for textual and twinned burial can admit only the light we bring, unreadable to those vacant eyes which are that other's self, that us and her, and not yet him. The French admits an ambivalence the English might have welcomed, even in that lightless place, as it "n'offrait aucune voie à la lumière du jour" (ST, p. 186), which is to say, no "voix" or Voice and no *admission* of that light or any other dreaded lucidity or presumed crime. To stop the admission of the text itself, the two narrators ("us," still, in some sense) "replaced and screwed down the lid" (ST, p. 189), where, again in the French, the eye is suppressed with its lid, becoming just a "couvercle" and losing its eyes thereby. As for the I regarding the tale, included always by the metonymy of its own "lid," and as for the "us," the look cannot stand the maidenly, un-a-wed character of the twinned and incestuously loved textual sister: "Our glances . . . rested not long upon the dead—for we could not regard her unawed" (ST, p. 189).

Only when those material and quite unsubtle sides of the frame, those "huge antique panels to which the speaker pointed" (ST, p. 201), are pointed to by this undesignated speaker does the whole design become clear in its fragments, as the silence swallows up the text. The import of Usher's words was "drunk in" in the English and, with more gourmandise, devoured in the French ("je dévorai l'horrible signification de ses paroles," p. 198). But the words, written or said, are not yet dead, are rather buried living, and then devoured on the rise.

As the Oval Portrait itself became the speaking picture for the engendering textual act, from which there was no outcome except the vampirism of death into life, that is, a Fall into art, here again the Fall is made into the mirroring or inversion of a real if webbed and fungused building, into a tarnished image, previewed triply, by painting and twinned texts and vaulting imagery, transforming finally the text of the first Us and Her into the text of Hysteria, which is our own if we in turn I the text, which had been only gifted with the vacant eyes. Linguistically and visually framed up and out and in by a self-conscious translator of a highly self-conscious text and commentator, Baudelaire's translation, emptied-out of the essential, leads Us as Her in turn to see, as if indeed the speaker were pointing at this very text.

The downward sloping lines, leading inward, predict in their intense hysteria, in their violent provocation, our own embedding within the design formed less by our choosing than by our irrepressible seeing. The scene had originally been rendered as a "tableau," a picture made already, and keeping still. But later, and finally, "I might well have congratulated myself upon the success of my design" (ST p. 195); the design might have been the killing off of the feminine twin, in order for hysteria to reign unabated, and then to cause the fall. But alas, in French, the design of death and authorial dominion is dissembled under another and simpler technique, working out well as the "succès de ma ruse." Even the specific design and designation of the text give way to what seems far more trivial, the purposeful narratorial plotting of the speaker, by his or Her own design: just a ruse, of whatever gender and however it is engendered.

In the emptiness of the eyeless windows, the design is deconstructed: Baudelaire has undone not just a portrait, but this time

the text Poe as Her gave Us, engendered doubly and incestuously in his own Hysteria. From this castle too, even in ruin,
there is no exit.

WRITING AND THE SIDEWAYS LOOK

A year after *Les Fleurs du mal*, Baudelaire's translation of Poe's
Narrative of Arthur Gordon Pym appears, whose preface warns of
the difficulty in writing an account of adventures "so minute and
connected as to have the *appearance* of that truth it would really
possess" (PCT, p. 748). Yet in French the statement is quite a
different one: "pour avoir toute la physionomie de la vérité—
dont il serait cependant l'expression réelle." Now the altered terms
"physionomie" and "expression" circumscribe the adventure within
the realm of the portrait, reminding us of Baudelaire's constant
representational obsession, whereas in the original there is no
trace of a portrait but just of a neutral appearance, and only the
question of representational truth. In fact, the balance between
seeming and having is the focus of these linguistic adventures as
translating the imagined ones they represent.

Baudelaire's pen attributes the preface to Arthur Gordon Pym,
assuring us there will be no difficulty in determining where the
few pages of this tale, written by Mr. Poe, give way to his own
tale and his own voice: "it will be unnecessary to point out where
his portion ends and my own commences; the difference in point
of style will be readily perceived" (PCT, p. 749). That suffices
to complicate the relations between appearance and real physiognomy: more than a stylistic difference is at stake. From Poe's
style, "serré et concaténé" as Baudelaire describes it, tightened as
in a vise, closely linked as in a concentrated space, as in a frame,
Baudelaire makes a better tale than any other translator could;
the loss and the profit will bear progeny.

From the incipit-as-lie: "My name is Arthur Gordon Pym,"
and its exact double, doubly a lie: "Mon nom est Arthur Gordon
Pym," until the inconclusive conclusion, two or three chapters

are lost—so we are told—and the tale is in lack. To discover the true text, then, we should perhaps follow the same procedure as the narrator-adventurer holed up in his hiding place, or "in the hold" of another force, within another space than the normal one to which we are assigned. His effort to read a little slip of paper as message is successful only when his gaze makes itself oblique, when he sees it *askance*; it is, moreover, a gaze reversed, for the written words give him, precisely, the *slip*, when he neglects to look at the other side. "The other, or under side, then, was that on which lay the writing, if writing there should finally prove to be" (PCT, p. 770). When, in the light of the phosphorus, he reads the seven concluding words already quoted, *"blood—your life depends upon lying close"* (PCT, p. 770), he learns what we learn as readers: to be possessed is "to lie close," suggesting already the embrace of something or someone, supposing already an erotic sense, and possession itself, in some obsessive "hold" or "grip" we should not loose. This is the major lesson of a passionate reading.

But in the Baudelaire version, it is a matter simply of lying hidden in one's hiding place: the original is indeed in its hiding place within the French version: *"sang—restez caché, votre vie en dépend"* (B. p. 595). All the terms of the original document, those terms on which, I think, we should take the text, focus on the same subject, that of possession—that subject is what my text means to frame. That is what seclusion imposes, remaining hidden within that other face of Poe's own painting, and life drains it to nourish something else. That physiognomy perceived in Baudelaire's version is precisely not "l'expression réelle," that *expression* itself invented by Baudelaire; that lack and that lie are the source for still another possession, that of the translation of the second text.

If the Baudelairean grip on the English-language reader takes hold of us in fact, it is in the fashion of the *incitamentum* or the little detail that incites Poe to discover his own *incipit*. Of a wonderful set of teeth, for instance, as in *Bérénice*, we feel the hold and the bite, like that of the dog menacing the narrator in Pym:

the *incitamentum* could be defined as something which grabs you in its teeth, getting a grip upon you as circumscription with a vengeance, all the more incisive.

DECIPHERING

As the narrator, like the narrator-reader of "The Oval Portrait," incites us to read also this fragment "slightly askance," let the reader so reread this text of possession and erotic deciphering. When the lost fragment of the tale is juxtaposed with the other text, this bloody bit scratched and scribbled in red will urge the substance from its ink, the red trace italicized from its tale: "*I have scrawled this with blood—your life depends upon lying close*" (PCT, p. 781). And that continues to remain hidden in the Baudelairean hold taken of the matter, life having passed into the other text, a translation of spirit into letter.

Might not the possessive embrace of the hide-out and the reader—"the hold it has over him"—return us to the bed of the narrator-reader of "The Oval Portrait," like a theater box surrounded with black velvet curtains, which we might, were our imagination ardent enough, see now as red? Might not this embedded reading as baroque or mannerist imitation, yielding the painting with its traits stolen from life, itself be read as a double transformation of the Dracula legend, as a bloody and textual execution in the flickering light of the candles with their "tongues" of flame well hidden by the cover of the second tongue? If these two tales took proper possession of the reader's spirit as it is impaired and embraced, might the weakened narrator framed within his own curtains[15] not be seen to suffer the same fate as the girl whose virgin blood is drawn by the monster, in a scene where it would be impossible to distinguish one from the other bedridden desire? Sickness, transfusion of blood and of tongues, baroque intertwining of life and art, of death and love: as Baudelaire points out, all Poe's arrows "fly toward the same end" (B, p. 1268). They obey the language of submission and sex: pens and feathers—as in the double sense of *plume*—have been seen to fly also, sometimes for the benefit of the reader, in the embedded hide-out. The portrait of Poe, and of Poe's Pym, is set by Baudelaire within a new oval frame: this strange embrace is productive, for the egg of the oval is hatched within. But the text, like the slip of paper, can only be read askance: the oval leaves room for an imperfect form of reading, not a circle, but an ellipsis, when the reading itself is forced to become elliptical, circumspect like the circumscription.

There follows then the period of gestation and disguise-as-death: the narrator, taking on the physiognomy of death, looks at himself only in a fragment or mirror, to mirror the preceding fragments of text. All the arrows continue to fly toward the same goal: disguise, fragment, looks set aslant, elliptical reading. The episode of the mysterious ship contains its own reserve of sense, its hidden meaning. How could we know, without comparing the two versions, what the following sentence hides beneath its apparent simplicity? "Le navire en vue était un grand brick-goelette" (B, p. 651). For the translation has once more effaced the key term, covering it over or rather translating it into a different form: "The vessel in sight was a large hermaphrodite brig . . ." (PCT, p. 808).[16] The black steamer with its figurehead gilded and highly visible is thus the bearer of a heavy meaning, like the haunting embrace of two unlike forms within a key figure. The French version, like some *thyrse*, translates the embrace of the male term with female term, but once more the underlying female figure is at least partially effaced, in the picture of the phantom ship, outlined between black borders tinged with gold. The representation of the object focused upon is once again assured as deceptive, as was the original "life-likeliness" of that first portrait, to the end: "I relate these things and circumstances minutely, and I relate them, it must be understood, precisely as they *appeared* to us" (PCT, p. 809). Appearance seems to be the guarantee of the rightness of the narration, the truth of the story, in all its proper seeming.

The appearance, however, both embraces and hides. The enormous seagull devouring the face of the man on board, until only his set of very white teeth appear in view, incites to wonder, like the teeth of the cadaver in *Bérénice*: for the toothy sparkle strikes the sight of the reader, sharing the place of the narrator, just as it is perceived that the eyes above them are pecked out. At this point the tongue ceases in prudence to recount ("This the—but I forbear," PCT, p. 810). The figure is shrouded in the English, and explicitly circumspect, whereas the French stops short, as if the translation were from a dead man's tongue: "mais je m'arrête" (B, p. 654).

The picture is red, but all trace of blood will disappear from the conclusion in white on white: the original closes by the repetition of the segments of a measured sentence: "of . . . of . . . of . . . of," marking the solemn blows as if to salute the apparition of a great human figure: "And the hue of the skin of the figure was of the perfect whiteness of the snow" (PCT, p. 882). Like the blows upon the coffin of Baudelaire's own "Chant d'automne," where the rhythm spells out the hammerings of time upon the self, the Poe original here is marked by its very repeats, a perfect border for the conclusion of the story. The figure is shrouded as if in death; but in the translated version, reframed, the French reader sees only a "veiled" form, where the winding sheet remains unspoken, and thus unseen. The mortuary shadows disappear, and the sentence ends only with three dots, suspending the French version of sight in the snow: "Et la couleur de la peau de l'homme était de la blancheur parfaite de la neige . . ." (B, p. 759). Unlike the heavy curtains corresponding to the final borders of death in "The Oval Portrait," where the implicit red of the lifeblood plays against the black shadows and against the pallor and illumination in the baroque or mannerist scene, this picture remains ambivalent and almost unreadable in the snow, leaving exposed against and upon the white background the odd lyricism of the white letter inscribed, opposed to the shadowy being, in a white on white and a white on dark from which the red has gone.

Deeply inset into the text that frames it, the figure Poe paints encircles a womblike space, as if to embed some secret of generation (fig. 1). The translating reader reads into it also the picture of an L or a wing ("aile") and an *Elle* reappearing; translation is repicturing, in another frame.

Fig. 1

The final "windings," like an implicit winding up of the original, close the text over its own inscription traced in the dust and the rock, inscribed as a response to the blood-red text previously scrawled on or engraved in the slip of paper recrossing the reader's mind; they are sinuous, like Baudelaire's rendering "sinuosités," but the original word "winding" spirals too about other gestures, as of the winding up of a clock, or of a tale, where every trace of blood as the basic sign of life has been liquidated from the shadowy background of some monumental and murderous monstrance, some frame black against the white of snow and the pallor of death.

PASSION AND PALLOR

Finally, what is translated is also framed; the spendid isolation conferred upon the picture by the second brush may be heavily or lightly penned in. Genius uses what it betrays, and well: Baudelaire's supplement adds richly to our own seeing.

In that alcove which he opens for us within his dark caverns containing heavy-laden tables and their terrible feast, the focus is upon his secret painting whose goal is the restoration of the past within the present. Here the flower of a youth perfumed and perishing upon some scented fur is sensed once more, but within a black-edged frame, which has absorbed and is absorbed within the rich gilt frames of Moorish design. The gold halos projected about the head of painter as of poet, and the vignetting technique of his recreated Oval Portrait, whose figure can be assured not to fade, take the original and lifelike obsession with a legend into a second rendering with all the added riches and the productive losses, constructing thus a double frame about the inner figure upon the wall or page. This is a work for and of passionate circumspection and circumscription, and demands a response no less passionate in its look, in its text, and in its own translation. Thus the critic is called upon in turn to treat the topic and the sight in a limited or circumscribed space, to insulate the incident and to add "the force of a frame to the picture," arresting the flux of reasonable reading by an ardent enclosure.

Against this shadowy background of a murderous and paralyzing hue, some readers may have perceived, in the brush of the painter and the pen of the poet, the feathers of some other wing, brushing by the text, already sensed in Poe's seagull as a relation of some Baudelairean albatross or as the prediction of some Mallarmean swan, so far inscribed only in a white writing upon the snow as upon a future lake,[17] as the phantom ship finds its doom within this adventuresome but incomplete text, at once circumspect and circumscribed within its own figures. Of this portrait and its end, there is perhaps no original; it might be then a picture of representation, with no model, or a model already pallid in its frame. As translation sets frame across from frame, and within it, so the readings and rereadings, mixing genres, languages, and sights, keep their odd faith with passion as with pallor.

V / HIGH MODERNIST FRAMING

... though the relations of a human figure or a social
occurrence are what make such objects interesting, they also
make them, to the same tune, difficult to isolate, to surround
with the sharp black line, to frame in the square, the circle, the
charming oval, that helps any arrangement of objects to become
a picture.
       Preface to Henry James *The Awkward Age*[1]

FRAMING IN THE LATER JAMES

Reflecting and Constraining

We know that Henry James's original ambition was, like that of
his brother William, to be a painter; he never ceases to stress the
metaphors and vocabulary of the painter's craft, especially in the
prefaces to the New York Edition of *The Novels and Tales of
Henry James*, filled with "brushstrokes," "foreshortening," "impressions," "imposition," "form," and the like, betraying a
painter's passion for perception and transcription, and for econ
omy of expression.

If Proust has a strongly temporal sense of setting and over-
setting or superpositioning, James demonstrates a strong spatial sense. Capital scenes in the texts are treated, and literally
described, as pictures to be varnished and hung; "real" works of
art are often inserted in them as touchstones, distances are mapped
out, the figures are set in surrounding doors and windows, deliberately confined for the optimal sharpness of impression essential to James's "little constituted dramas." Because of the very
limitation, a high intensity is trained upon the "set and lighted
scene, to hold the play." The holding of a play is a particularly
fortunate image for James's later style, whose peculiarities, ques-

tions of ambivalence, obsessions, covering over, and misinterpretations are repeatedly brought before the eyes; it is their play that must be focused.

In *A Small Boy and Others*, James describes his first visits to the Louvre's Great Gallery, whose "golden riot and relief figured and flourished in perpetual revolution, breaking into great high-hung circles and symmetries of squandered picture, opening into deep outward embrasures that threw off the rest of monumental Paris somehow as a told story, a sort of wrought effect or bold ambiguity for a vista, and yet held it there, at every point, as a vast bright gage."[2] More pertinent still is his early fascination with the "prodigious tube or tunnel" of the Galerie d'Apollon, like a cylinder through which to focus on the scene, where he "inhaled little by little, that is again and again, a general sense of glory." The interest of the central subject is heightened by the narrowing channel through which it is glimpsed, this exterior constriction or visual telescoping enabling the observer to concentrate on the privileged view.

James's own "intense perceivers" in the fiction act in the same way, channeling the reader's view toward what is supposedly central in the text: "that provision of interest which consists in placing advantageously, placing right in the middle of the light, the most polished of possible mirrors of the subject." They serve as models of our sighting of the situation, ambivalent as it is. The side edges to their view make what I call here framing devices. "Really, universally, relations stop nowhere, and the exquisite problem of the artist is eternally but to draw, by a geometry of his own, the circle in which they shall happily appear to do so."[3] This study aims at the examination of some of these circles and the ways in which they are perceived.

It is fitting that James be the model framer of the frame, for complexity is part of what he termed "that masterly and magnificent indirectness" he so cherished. The art of seeing "through" one thing to the next, and to the next, is an art of endless vistas inserted each within the following, guiding the gaze toward a center which, if empty, has as its own substance that of its being framed.

Parallel to that inframing for the visual and the conceptual presentation are frames used on the verbal level, where, grammatically, the elements are embedded and boxed within the sentence, and where, narrationally, the stories are inserted within each other. Tzvetan Todorov, pointing out the various devices, reminds us that James was after the vertical exploration of an event as opposed to a horizontal knowledge of its unfolding.[4]

A further packing in of elements on the vertical axis has to do with the infinitely worked doubling of concepts, and words, the displacements of perspective from which the reader must constantly view what is to be looked at. A French critic has compared this to the technique of anamorphosis, in which the drastic foreshortening of the object in view works directly against the traditional forms of mimesis or imitation of "reality," so that the correct position from which to see is an abnormal one.[5] I would accept the parallel except that in the case of James, since there is, strictly speaking, no object in view at all, there is only what we think we might be seeing from where at various points in our reading, we think we should be placed. The shifts occasioned by the reading process itself are the very joy of James, but precisely, there is no correct stance, as there is no central object, only a foreshortening of things surrounding the empty middle.

But then, the wary reader might ask, why all the fuss, made by James himself, in the preface to *The Wings of the Dove*, for example, about the canny alternation between picture and scene or action, the pictures without dialogue, carrying the narrative forward (if you consider that it moves that way) and the scenes providing the keys for understanding the characters and their relation to each other? Charles Anderson underlines, speaking of this same preface, James's comment about his own "odd insistency with which picture . . . is jealous of drama, and drama . . . suspicious of picture," and discusses at some length, as does Viola Hopkins Winner, the role the specific pictures and telescopings of pictures play in this novel. Tintoretto, the great mannerist, is of course, the model for James, and, I think, the indirect reason for the enduring fascination of the spectator. Another model too: "I felt," says James, "pictorially, the great, beautiful, terrible spectacle of human life very much as Shakespeare felt it poetically. . . . I'd give a great deal to be able to fling down a dozen of his pictures into prose of corresponding force and colour."[6]

Of all the commentators on James, one of the most lucid and highly styled—an important factor in the appreciation of the James case—is Lawrence Bedwell Holland. In his *Expense of Vision: Essays on the Craft of Henry James*,[7] he celebrates the marriage of form and vision in these texts, where the characters remain costumed, and where the form itself creates the moral issues. Of *The Sacred Fount*, he says it has more structure than representation, showing how its great "palace of thought," with its empty paths, long corridors, deserted rooms, and repeated pictures of the void, creates the perfect setting for the story of the mask "smothering life in artifice," just as in *The Wings of the Dove*, the novel perhaps most involved with economy in all its senses, the appearance of Milly herself mingles art with death. As for its art, the novel sets its own frame, as Kate's family opens and closes it, and as the figures frame and betray Milly; beyond that, the novel makes its own "anguished withdrawal from Milly's agony . . . and pays tribute to what it leaves behind." We can scarcely fail to notice that here James himself is set at a distance, and the novel takes over, bearing its own burden, economic, artistic, and moral, and bears it in parallel with its author. This criticism itself is brilliantly economic in its means, and all the more persuasive: "The novel's action spends itself, as the form completes itself, in the consuming passion with all its waste which James found life and art to be" (EV, p. 327).

The melodramatic aspect of this novel, and I am picking up the term here from Leo Levy in his *Versions of Melodrama*,[8] depends at least in part on its having been conceived first in scenario form; to Milly Theale's situation, James applies the terms of staged tragedy: it is "the soul of drama—which is the portrayal, as we know, of a catastrophe determined in spite of oppositions." All the drama comes in the cross-relations of characters, as in a formal ballet, with no exterior reference, with interapplication tied to "things exactly on the same plane of exhibition with themselves . . . relations all within the action itself; no part of which is related to anything but some other part . . ." Once they are inserted in the novel, becoming its high points, such "action" and "scenes," to use James's terms, lend "mimetic value" to this nondramatic genre, providing the immediacy of drama. James's passion for moral issues inclines him to melodrama, "an essential Jamesian mode of perceiving and organizing moral experience," which "insists upon the ultimate goodness of man; its single dramatic aim is to demonstrate the triumph of good over evil." Melodrama, Levy continues, arouses the feelings tragedy arouses, but it "evades catharsis by its refusal to permit evil to become part of the internalized experience of the good." It is, he says, a mock tragedy, in which virtue escapes free and intact. This explains, I think, the reader's uncomfortable reaction to the novel, where the good suffer and die, thereby saving others, where the very bad, like Kate, inevitably lose out in the long run, and where only to the in-betweens, like Densher, does any question as to a future good or bad fate apply.

The intricate beauty of *The Golden Bowl*, as one might expect, draws forth from all the Jamesians their full measure. Ruth Yeazell makes an excellent study of the seeing and knowing metaphors around which it turns; Quentin Anderson makes an equally convincing one of the Bowl as "The Great Containing Vessel," with Charlotte's comparison to a silk purse opening out like a flower neatly tied to the proverbial "love of money is the root of all evil," with the Prince himself compared to the ultimate bowl, "complete, polished, and round," and with the breaking of the bowl, presented by a Jew, compared to the breaking of the Old Law to permit the final "chamber of the soul" to house the infinite human possibilities, while Adam, as God, hymns himself.[9] Marianna Torgovnick comments on Maggie's avoiding positive knowledge, unlike Oedipus, and the way she buries her eyes instead of blinding them, making a human and unheroic compromise.[10]

In the scene—also commented on by Mattheissen—where Maggie and her father on one side and Charlotte on the other are framed in doorways at the opposite ends of the long picture gallery at Fawns, with the cluster of visitors in between, the "strained, obsessive regularity of its geometry" makes, says Holland, a prediction of the final sacrifice. James becomes the author "as watcher through the windows of his form . . . and the action it projects or the life it images" (EV, p. 334). In my reading, James will never leave off being the "watcher", not watching through the window only, but, and more importantly, watching its form as window, its effect as frame.

As for form, the "funny form" of Maggie's life as she refers to it is compared by Holland to the equally funny form of the novel itself, both ghastly and wonderful, as it makes a "perilous marriage"—always in crisis—with its materials, buying and owing and gilding and breaking and salvaging: "The fictive marriage subjects the actualities of the institution to an appallingly intense light while embodying also the promise or ideal communion of the form: yet the promise itself is flawed and must be recast in the crucible of experience" (EV, p. 363). As for casting out the flaw, the novel, like the principal figures, is "tense with terror while measuring the cost in beauty, integrity, and suffering which is exacted in the process of breaking with the past and redeeming it, while discovering that the bowl must not only be gilded to salvage the past but that it must be broken, it must be sacrificed in order to create even the promise that the reality it symbolizes may be transformed" (EV, p. 381). The whole symbol of the bowl is itself sacrificed for James, but "the lie which James' mannered style creates" is a proof that what does not show does not exist, and that the marriage can become genuine, unflawed, by pretending it is already just that. Thus, gilding the bowl is giving its form to the potential faith, and so the novel can make good on its promise.

Holland's final sentence finds a style quite as finely hammered as James's own, setting high and properly the insertions from James:

> Possessed and in possession, Maggie welcomes and returns the embrace, but "for pity and dread" of the devotion she has sought and he now tenders, she shields her eyes, from the impact of his faith and vision. The burden of confession which she has lifted from him is assumed by Henry James, acknowledging the responsibility risked and sanctioned in the "sacrament of execution" which in *The Golden Bowl* he made his own. (EV, p. 406)

I have chosen to mention the critical appraisal of James here, at the outset, as the frame for my own commentary on the Jamesian picture.

FIGURES AND FRAMES

I liked things that appeared, then one was sure. Whether they were or not was a subordinate and almost always a profitless question.
"The Real Thing"[11]

The painter in "The Real Thing" who finds the "real model" less convincing than the practiced professional model is opting, like James himself, for "art" against what purports to be "real" life. The fictive figure of "The Real Thing" is an artistic model appearing true, because since it is in fact "false," it can be variable, thus more convincing than the faithful and unchanging "real" figure, in its steady and thus unartistic single effect. James's high conception of his own art in his late period includes his passionate prejudice in favor of the visual and his defense of the deliberate crafting of vision within the art of the tale and the novel, implying all his ambivalent effects. "The Figure in the Carpet" (1896) questions the existence of a unifying figure invisible in every work, of which it could be said "When you do see it, you know." The possibility of there being only one real thing, present or absent, in every text's tissue, one figure or then one hole in the fabric, is put in serious doubt. "As a tissue tolerably intricate it was a carpet with a figure of its own; but the figure was not the figure I was looking for."[12]

Images of sight and nonseeing,[13] of insight and oversight, are strangely superposed and juxtaposed, themselves plainly of more interest than what is actually observed: "Nobody sees anything" (ET, p. 139). We are never certain whether or not we know the figure in the carpet or the text, but are only offered successive speculations; in the stories built around the central enigma, such as "In the Cage" (1898), the enigma as such is allowed no interest: "I have no idea," James responded to a question about the "real" plot therein, nor, he claimed, did he care. Thus the reader is meant to occupy just the position of the telegraph girl in her little enclosure in the grocery store, the limits to her understanding heightening her buildup of the story, whose lines are beyond her; this cage itself serves as the metaphoric frame for what ensues in our own reading of James, its optional inclusions and omissions.[14]

In her "framed and wired confinement," she is enclosed and distanced, for "this transparent screen fenced out or fenced in . . ." (ET, p. 174). Paradigmatic of James's approach, the framing metaphor illustrates in a self-reflexive pattern the peculiar ambiguities of the ground excluded and included, against which the figures move and are read.

Fenced in the frame as she is, the girl's interpretations have an intense plausibility, a "high reality," the "bristling truth," and no less extensive a self-deception. The height of reality as it is conceived in the cage encounters the other extreme which is the "deep down" of the "Figure in the Carpet," both vertical constructs depending on the observer within the tale, whose gaze is limited. From her confinement, the girl's view of the mysterious telegrams she sends is a second-order experience; what is coded and sent, or the texts within the text, has an occluded code of exchange, so that the girl's interpretation of that code and our interpretation of her interpretation are caged within the text.

> our interpretation of the text "In the Cage"
>> our interpretation of the girl's reading of it
>>> girl's interpretation of the code
>>>> code of text in telegram

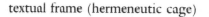

The tightly packed metaphor could be presented differently:

> textual frame (hermeneutic cage)
>> symbolic frame (telegraphic code)
>>> psychological frame (the girl's)
>>>> physical frame (her cage)

As for the "reality" of the picture outside the cage, at once symbolic, enigmatic, and fictive, it is "really" nonexistent, even within the conventions of literature. Of what the girl retains of it in the cage, she makes a tapestry, and her own woven text: "she nipped and caught it, turned it over and interwove it" (ET, p. 190); the very narrowness of the enclosure and its lack of margin heighten the mystery of her "high reading," her "prodigious view," her "immensity," these half-mocking terms to recur throughout James's later novels, particularly *The Golden Bowl*, where Maggie becomes little by little a skilled reader of a text as its own vessel, and hers.

Apart from the heavily outlined symbols of code and text-in-the-cage, other essential elements of psychological and architectural framing are put in play here: the captain around whom the girl's interest builds is glimpsed in the doorway of his apartment, before an open and lighted vestibule and a flight of quiet stairs. (What is lit up? What is led up to?) This is the prelude to a central scene of dialogue constructed around the two verbs of "seeing" and "knowing," dominant in the late novels at the moments of framed crisis and revelation, again, particularly in *The Golden Bowl.* "I know, I know, I know!" (ET, p. 227), the girl repeats to the captain about his affairs, about which, of course, she knows nothing. When she inserts herself into an imagined canvas to watch herself walk away from him (as the later heroines of James will often watch themselves in interior pictures they have constructed), his own invocation of sight "See here—see here!" suddenly resounds, together with her interior questions: What should she have been seeing, what has she seen awry? The brightly bordered scene endures, built up in her memory: "She had framed the whole picture with a squareness that included also the image of how again she would decline to 'see there,' decline, as she might say, to see anywhere, see anything. Yet it befell that just in the fury of this escape she saw more than ever" (ET, p. 245). The verb of *seeing* has absorbed that of *knowing,* and the self-aggrandizement has justified the construction of a more heroic canvas, which she strangely transfers into his own sight: "Deep down in his eyes was a picture, a scene—a great place like a chamber of justice, where, before a watching crowd, a poor girl, exposed but heroic, swore with a quavering voice to a document, proved an alibi, supplied a link. In this picture she bravely took her place" (ET, p. 250). So she plants a picture in the other, and paints herself into it, like the glorification of a further cage.

The dimensions of the heroic canvas finally suffer a deflation, in her final perception of what the buildup has been, if not of what it has been about; in an atmosphere entirely different from

the previous one marked by "knowing" and "seeing," the infla-
tion of hope undergoes "invidious shrinkings," like a return from
imagined canvas to mental cage. At the conclusion of buildup
and letdown, the girl is seen to make a few "sightless turns"
before she stands looking, sightlessly still, into a canal. She has a
course been looking sightlessly all the time, building a false canvas within the limits set by her frame. But that frame has also
framed that of the reader. The double seeing bestowed by an
acquired "high" textual consciousness only intensifies the irony
of the deceiving frame, exposed as such without any disclosure
of the engima: "She had framed the whole picture" (ET, p. 245).

PICTURES AND PORTRAITS

Not to walk straight up to the fact and put it into phrases, but to
surround the fact, and so to detach it inviolate . . .
    PERCY LUBBOCK, *The Craft of Fiction*

The kinds of borders set about the central figures are multiple:
they may be material, like the theater stalls in "Broken Wings"
of 1900, the opera stall of Flora Staunt in "Glasses," the fence
of "In the Cage," or symbolic, like the interior pictures built up
and dwelled on; or may make exterior reference to "actual" pictures, recognizable in the world of art. Similarly, the types of
constraint upon the reading of the text are multiple, as are our
responses to them.

"The Author of Beltraffio" (1884)[15] combines material and
"artistic" framing: the disciple sees the author's mysterious wife
repeatedly centered in the garden, or through some window, always holding her son as would a Madonna, or framed by the
loose folds of the thick curtain of trees, muffled in scarves like
the women of Gainsborough and Romney. The door frames in
which she successively appears, surrounded by silence, herald and
disguise her coming with exactly the ambivalence that each sight
of her arouses in the disciple and the reader. She is simply an
enigma seen as a picture, posing with her doomed son, "the

beautiful mother and beautiful child, interlaced there against their background of roses, a picture such as I doubtless shouldn't see soon again" (ET, p. 65). Since the doom may be her fault, the picture is both a tribute and, retrospectively perceived, a warning, doubly stressed by the highly visual aspect that effaces all the individual traces in its celebration of two classically lovely beings against the equally lovely, natural, and fragile backdrop, figures outlined on a ground. The topos of ephemeral beauty is suggested by the roses, as in traditional love poetry, and the child's imminent death is strangely heralded by the picturesque background for the one-time picture.

The central picture of "The Altar of the Dead" (1895)[16] has a hole within it, befitting the "hollow center" of the hero, who leaves a single empty place among the candles on the altar he constructs to celebrate the persons he has loved. This sets the entire story askew in its fiery frame, for the unspoken wrong committed by that erstwhile friend has an equally mysterious parallel in the wrong he has done the only other person in devotion before the altar with its "multiplied meanings," like a great text afire, whose significance can thus be adjusted to whatever psychological pattern the eyes and heart may select. The author of the altar discovers the lady's secret wrong, pardon, and devotion through a small portrait in her room, which typically acts as the scene's *revealer*. From that room his own future exclusion or framing-out is as clear as the portrait itself and her own setting in her votary museum: "He was now on the lower door-step, and his hostess held the door half-closed behind him. Through what remained of the opening he saw her framed face. . . . And she closed the door, shutting him out" (ET, p. 122). He cannot pardon, and she cannot forget, the unforgivable absence at the altar. So the candles must find a new arrangement that claims to be artistically motivated while in fact it is obsessive and compensatory:

> There came a day when, for simple exhaustion, if symmetry
> should demand just one he was ready so far to meet sym-

metry. Symmetry was harmony, and the idea of harmony began to haunt him; he said to himself that harmony was of course everything. He took, in fancy, his composition to pieces, redistributing it into other lines, making other juxtapositions and contrasts. He shifted this and that candle, he made the spaces different, he effaced the disfigurement of a possible gap. There were subtle and complex relations, a scheme of cross-reference, and moments in which he seemed to catch a glimpse of the void so sensible to the woman who wandered in exile. (ET, p. 130)

There is, he decides, room for just one more figure, as the structure or the formal *set* of the candles finally dominates the sentiment of hate: to rearrange the pattern is to pardon the offense.

In this story, which James ranged, understandably, with his "tales of the supernatural and the gruesome," the obsessed character arranges the blazing picture in his mind, while still troubled by that other portrait and by the lady's framed face in the door at the moment of his exclusion. At his death, another candle will be added to the altar, merging her devotion to both men with his symbolic resetting. The story has a peculiar unsavory and claustrophobic atmosphere, reminiscent of the cathedral scenes in Hawthorne's *The Marble Faun*, which James so admired. Hatred and fanatic devotion border the limited life devoted to worshiping death, as if the reader too were to be shut within the grill of the chapel and shut out from any understanding of the story's facts.

"The Way It Came" (1896), renamed "The Friends of the Friends,"[17] also turns about a portrait and a mystery, and is prefaced by a narration like an outside border that oddly frames the story. Its "inside" or first-person narrator herself tells a tale of uncertain truth and origin, concerning or not concerning herself, intended or not for possible publication or exposure, the result to be decided by the outside narrator, who tells it "the way it came." So the text in its sentimental and supernatural implications is put in doubt from the very outset.

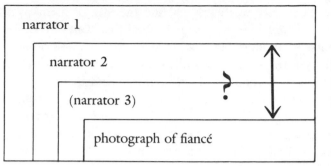

According to the inside narrator, her own projected marriage (or that of another friend, who would thus become a further inset) was undone by a photograph of her fiancé, shown to her closest friend, who then falls mysteriously dead upon arriving home. According to the fiancé, she had come to stand before him in silence, leaving an indelible memory, of which the narrator is increasingly jealous; the development hinges entirely on the exaggerated importance of one photograph and the fiancé's address on the reverse side, a sort of *backwards text*. Developed thus from front to back, this is one of the most aggressively haunted of all James's tales, obsessively "unreal"; the double relations between photograph or picture figure and the real figure, between exposure and cover-up, or front view and the reverse, mirror the complex irresolution of the Jamesian text in its own enigmatic and double appearance.

One of the most remarkable doublings, "The Jolly Corner" (1908) (ET), even later than the novels considered here, is entirely concerned to prepare the apparition of a double and the interpretation of these apparitions in a setting, like that of *The Sacred Fount*, deliberately evoking a nested structure. Rooms open upon rooms, thresholds upon thresholds, in an architectural frame within a frame quite as formally complex as the relations between the figures of the man and his double, awaited at length and finally bordered in a doorway, as he himself watches, bordered. The repeated openings and closures develop that suspense to which

James will eventually, as in *The Golden Bowl*, assign the term *delay*:

> He had come into sight of the door in which the brief chain of communication ended and which he now surveyed from the nearer threshold, the one not directly facing it. Placed at some distance to the left of this point, it would have admitted him to the last room of the four, the room without other approach or egress, had it not, to his intimate conviction, been closed *since* his former visitation, the matter probably of a quarter of an hour before. He stared with all his eyes at the wonder of the fact, arrested again where he stood and again holding his breath while he sounded its sense. Surely it had been *subsequently* closed—that is it had been on his previous passage indubitably open! (ET, p. 335)

Here the descriptions drastically retard the reading, preparing the halt at the most vivid turn of the scene; the sharp focus of the physical and topological descriptions so centered renders the scene uncomfortably present between its stark borders, stressed at length:

> How long did he pause and how long did he debate? There was presently nothing to measure it; for his vibration had already changed—as just by the effect of its intensity. Shut up there, at bay, defiant, and with the prodigy of the thing palpably proveably *done*, thus giving notice like some stark signboard—under that accession of accent the situation itself had turned . . . (ET, p. 337)

All the elements of a suspense story of vintage James are, as he would himself say, palpably proveably here: the heavy machines of thought and the frames of sight, an *arrest* of time and of motion, the soundings or vibrations of an interior conversation with the self, an outward sign of some hidden event determining the turn of the tale, however slight. The tale tells of the panic of a mind whose workings in slow motion are clearly glimpsed, against a vividly painted backdrop of theatrical arches and vistas, bright until they are clouded by this event. Only its nature can be suggested, the subject remaining unspecified, but there appears a nameless something to be confronted at the center of the shadow, as if in a place recessed to emphasize its outline: "The penumbra, dense and dark, was the virtual screen of a figure which stood in it as still as some image erect in a niche or as some black-vizored sentinel guarding treasure. ... It gloomed, it loomed, it was something, it was somebody, the prodigy of a personal presence. ... No portrait by a great modern master could have presented him with more art, as if there had been 'treatment,' of the consummate sort, in his every shade and salience" (ET, pp. 343-44).

This melodramatic insetting, darkly outlined after the highly theatrical buildup, enhances the ghostly figure, even by its strained rhymes, "gloomed, loomed," in a presentation quite unlike the undiscovered figure in the carpet or the undiscoverable engima in the cage. Whatever "truth" might be presumed in a text or an enigmatic tapestry intimated through the metaphoric setting, is irrelevant in regard to the intricate framing, whose primary and secondary construction, from several viewpoints, is itself the main subject and also object of our text.

SETTING THE SCENE: ARCHITECTURAL BORDERS

It was the light in which so much of the picture hung.
    The Portrait of a Lady

A picture is made, not just of, but within, the text, by the insetting of an interior frame to concentrate the reading attention, like the circle drawn around the relations to be focused. Outside and unseen fall the explanations of the engima at the very center of that circle: the method, used in an increasingly subtle and psychological fashion, requiring progressively more of the reader, will itself form the focus of my discussion of the works.

From the time of *The Turn of the Screw* (1896) to that of the *Sacred Fount* (1901) and the three great novels, *The Wings of the Dove* (1902), *The Ambassadors* (1903), and *The Golden Bowl* (1904),

James's fascination with exterior and interior framing reaches its height. Without wanting to make in any sense an exhaustive list of those techniques recognizable as such, I shall make a few suggestions only as to the recognition of a framed or "placed" scene, a bordered "arrangement" or "composition," terms heavy with implications as to the aesthetic, the economic, the thoughtfully managed, and the tastefully structural. The scene thus prominently outlined is noticeably associated with a rise either architectural or psychological, a figure with a clearly marked surround, and with a general metaphoric heightening, as well as formal devices of marking and setting off. The scene of interest is foregrounded, like some photograph whose setting and subsequent development may act as the central affair of the mind.

The architectural sense so vivid in the works after 1900 is visible before, but in the early novels serves a far more limited end.[18] The salient moments or the transitions between scenes are announced by figures standing in the doorway, for instance, whose entrances can scarcely be overlooked, and sometimes, as in *The Tragic Muse*, an actual picture is used to develop the plot or to reveal the character. These and other "artistic" objects, roles, and figures of the book concern representation itself, and could all be inscribed under Peter Sherringham's statement: "I'm fond of representation—the representation of life: I like it better, I think, than the real thing" (TM, p. 58). The latter concept, of course, puts itself into question in "The Real Thing."

Two scenes invite our close concentration on their borders, using inserted pictures and roles to deal with the motif of representation. Miriam's prolonged staring at Gerôme's portrait of the actress Rachel in the foyer of the Théâtre Français reemphasizes more visually still her own passionate vocation as an actress, sums up, as it were, the drama within its own pictured borders, in a genre mix. The art of dramatic representation is captured with the art of visual representation which, in a further complication, represents it and surrounds it, to preserve it against time. "She quitted her companion and stood looking at Gerôme's fine portrait of the pale Rachel, invested with the antique attributes of tragedy. The rise of the curtain had drawn away most of the company. Sherringham, from his bench, watched Miriam a little, turning his eye from her to the vivid image of the dead actress and thinking that his companion suffered little by the juxtaposition" (TM, p. 242).

Julia's intrusion upon the scene in the studio when Miriam is having her picture done by Nick makes an odd parallel to that pictured scene in the theater, but here she herself is the framed presentation, looking at the picture before her, itself the preparation for yet another picture in process:

> She had taken a step forward, but she had done no more, stopping short at the sight of the strange woman, so divested of visiting-gear that she looked half undressed, who lounged familiarly in the middle of the room and over whom Nick had been still more familiarly hanging. Julia's eyes rested on this embodied unexpectedness, and as they did so she grew pale—so pale that Nick, observing it, instinctively looked back to see what Miriam had done to produce such an effect. She had done nothing at all, which was precisely what was embarrassing; only staring at the intruder, motionless and superb. (TM, p. 285)

Here the motif of representation is once more center stage, as the portrait is again of an actress, thus a potential representation included in the canvas, doubly a representation. The interruption stresses all the more the undervaluing of the real—what is interrupting the representation—as compared to the represented canvas. The opening on to the outer world, represented by the carriage and the road, is closed up deliberately by the artist: "He closed the door of the studio behind her; his servant was still at the outer door, which was open and through which he saw Julia's carriage drawn up" (TM, p. 285).

The subtle framing is concentrated in these two major scenes and in the doorway presentation of persons: their first appearance being made generally upon the threshold, followed by a pause to call attention to the description; this architectural technique, stressed still more by the expected descriptive passage, is at times irritatingly typical of the early James.

A few more developed uses of both doorway and picture sequences are present in *The Awkward Age* of nine years later, where the first noteworthy scene is that of Mr. Longdon contemplating Van's photographs at length, with increasing excitement. His admiration and his "side-lights of shocks" are repeated throughout the introductory chapter, leading up to the crimson-furred frame around the photograph of "little Aggie," itself placed, in this peculiar presentation of innocence, within a deliberately erotic border, a come-on and a showoff of the second photograph, Nanda's, which Mr. Longdon will care about. The diminutives grate on the mind:

> She gave me the portrait—frame and all. "The frame is Neapolitan enough, and little Aggie is charming." Then Vanderbank subjoined: "But not so charming as little Nanda."
>
> "Little Nanda?—have you got *her*?" The old man was all eagerness.
>
> "She's over there beside the lamp—also a present from the original." (AA, p. 36)

Thus the first crimson-edged portrait prepares the second, in glazed white wood. Nanda's presentation is already markedly different from the showy red of the other borders, simpler and less ostentatious: but she is "gotten" too.

Later, this Aggie is outlined in the door at her entrance, "as slight and white, as delicately lovely, as a gathered garden lily" (AA, p. 87), with some emphasis on the gathering of the delicate riches, her very blandness emphasizing the innocence so strongly marked as to give hesitation. In contrast, Nanda's entrance is marked by a "stir of the door," and unanimous surprise of the observers, as she is greeted by a stillness and a silence within the room, which is concentrated in the person of her principal admirer: "All expression had, for the minute, been arrested in Mr. Longdon" (AA, p. 111). When, directly following this, Vanderbank's figure is framed in the same doorway, it only serves to emphasize the reading of the scene thus formed, so that all these three obvious presentations are composed into a picture of evident significance, focused on these latter three persons.

The photograph of Nanda continues to haunt the imagination in these pages, together with the portrait of her grandmother, so that her actual and present face is a recomposition of a picture already existing in Mr. Longdon's memory. Nanda, again like her grandmother, has a face that Sir Thomas Lawrence or Gainsborough or Raphael might have painted: thus the references in the world of art reinforce the art of the picture presently on the page to be read. Nanda's fate is in fact already framed within a future picture by the kind of verbal repetition so finely and clearly "worked" here, as if worked up to a summit of nervousness. Van, offered a sum by Mr. Longdon if he will marry her, is discouraged by the mother's harping on just this offer. Her repetitions jar the nerves and, more importantly for us and for him, act to border the picture of the hesitant bridegroom and the rich prize. From this moment, Nanda's fate is sealed, and these borders act out the sealing:

> '. . . so far as they count on you, they count, my dear
> Van, on a blank. . . . You won't do it.'
> 'Oh!' he almost too loudly protested.
> 'You won't do it,' she went on.
> 'I *say*!'—he made a joke of it.
> 'You won't do it,' she repeated. (AA, p. 218)

Nanda's subsequent entrance, as she is feathered and beribboned, in a light fresh fabric and pale colours, is prepared by a repetition of this bordering prediction: he won't go in, says the mother, for the plan. He won't, and again she repeats it, go in. The prediction is, of course, efficacious, by its very jarring nature and the implied shame in giving a positive answer.

As well as these verbal repetitions, the visual ones set the scene in much the same way. In Tishy Grendon's drawing room, the polish of the floor reflects the whole scene, making it all the more uncomfortable, and all the more to be reflected upon. Reflections in the glass precede natural sight, as if art were to take place before the ordinary vision; the action takes on an embarrassing tint, as if one were being spied upon. Van twists his moustaches, and then is aware of another pair of eyes: "While so engaged he became aware of something else and, quickly facing about, recognized in the doorway of the room the other figure the glass had just reflected" (AA, p. 276). The suggestion of surface contrasts with the suggestion of depth in such passages as the one directly preceding this one, as Mitchy, having chosen to be alone in the darkness, "face to face with the vague, quiet garden, still stood there" (AA, p. 274). The strong reflection upon the personality of the scene needs no further statement. Each of the characters and their relations does indeed have the outline James wanted for them here, as stated in the celebrated preface: "though the relations of a human figure or a social occurrence are what make such objects interesting, they also make them, to the same tune, difficult to isolate, to surround with the sharp black line, to frame in the square, the circle, the charming oval, that helps any arrangement of objects to become a picture" (AA, preface, p. 10).

Later, in the scene James presents as the height of his achievement, the sharp view of the Duchess is centered as she has composed the scene: "Look at her now . . . ," and this is the polish and the final picture we are left with, the real arrest of the figures within their own polish and their own frames, categorized ("poor Nanda's little case") and shrunk in the presentational manner; James refers to this scene as a masterly composition, "with all the pieces of the game on the table together and each unconfusedly and contributively placed, as triumphantly scientific" (AA, preface, p. 24). If, from the reader's viewpoint, the subtlety of the later volumes is missing here, this work, all the same, like the figures in the doorways, prepares the way for it.

We might read the framing scenes in *The Portrait of a Lady* also as preparations for *The Ambassadors* and *The Wings of the Dove*. The scene in which Isabel stops in front of a small picture at Gardencourt, with her eyes suddenly "suffused with tears" (PL,

p. 117), predicts the scene in which Milly stops before the Bronzino portrait, her eyes suddenly filling with tears, while the scene amid the "shining antique marbles" reflected in the polished marble floor below the dark red walls of the Capitoline (PL, p. 257) leads eventually to the picture in the National Gallery with Milly tired among the paintings, too weak to confront Tintoretto and Rubens.

The doorway framing—"Mrs. Osmond coming out of the deep doorway . . . dressed in black velvet," looking "high and splendid . . . framed in the gilded doorway," as the very "picture of a gracious lady"—not only frames the title, but helps to outline the later framing of Kate within the balcony window, and of Milly within the Venetian one (PL, p. 309). The recessing of room within room, the antechamber and the drawing room leading to another room, like so many nested boxes or delaying frames, is found again in Madame de Vionnet's pale chambers recessed into each other in *The Ambassadors*. The particular form of putting off sight and action that this recession represents is exemplified in the negation of the figures within the following scene, based on absence as much as on presence: "Pansy was not in the first of the rooms, a large apartment with a concave ceiling and walls covered with old red damask. It was here Mrs. Osmond usually sat—though she was not in her customary place tonight—and that a circle of special intimates gathered about the fire" (PL, p. 308). The intimates are framed in their absence, about the fire set far back, deeply recessed with the text as within the house, postponed until the second sentence, and the second room. It is the postponement itself that *gathers* the recessed inner scene, like a spatial parallel to the narrational framing insets of the story told about the fire and entitled "The Turn of the Screw."

Shams in The Sacred Fount

We were in a beautiful old picture,
we were in a beautiful old tale . . .
    The Sacred Fount[19]

This "small, mean story" that "worries one like the rat nibbling at the wainscot," as Rebecca West says of it, or this "nothing made out of nothing," is at the same time a capital text, framed or mock-framed about itself, full of self-consciousness and self-reference. From the beginning metaphor of the narrator as exhibitor and manager of the visual ("I turned the picture round," SF, p. 10), to its recapitulation near the end of his purposeful arrangement: ("It was as if I had hung the picture before her, so that she had fairly to look at it," SF, p. 285), the scope of the picture, however "enriched" and "revealing," is kept deliberately narrow. The terms are all diminutive: little gallery, small museum, small collection.

The observer's placement is made evident, the picture always less so. The scenes are set to be regarded, not clearly and straight on, but from their corners, at an angle, from out and in, in "clarity" and in dimness at once: "We were on one of the shaded terraces, to which, here and there, a tall window stood open. The picture without was all morning and August, and within all clear dimness and rich gleams. . . . We could just see, from where we stood, a corner of one of the rooms." (SF, p. 37). The "evidence" and the "relations" and their significance seem always to be presented in profile or from the back, so that nothing is simply observed. The borders, marked by windows, doors, or passages, or occasionally, by a long and spectacular row of trees surrounding the vista, enhance the center on which the whole picture is focused; all the more so, through the dramatic chiaroscuro lighting; the pictures succeeding each other, each held up rapidly in turn, prepare the picture gallery in the most famous and most heavily inset scene in the book, suddenly in close focus after a stated darkness: "I knew of some pictures in one of the rooms that had not been lighted the previous evening" (SF, p. 49). The gallery itself is given an inward-turned view: it is not just a "picture saloon" but a "pictured saloon," thus, at least potentially, already described at the moment when it is presented, as the polished and reflected setting for a discovery: " 'Why, here he is!' she exclaimed, as we paused, for admiration, in the doorway. The high frescoed ceiling arched over a floor so highly polished that it seemed to reflect the faded pastels set, in rococo borders, in the walls and constituting the distinction of the place. Our companions, examining together one of the portraits and turning their backs, were at the opposite end" (SF, p. 50).

The highly inset scene is dramatized by the observers' pause in the doorway and by the doubling of the painting in the floor's surface, as well as by the repeated back view of the observers absorbed in the pictures still further inset, until we are granted a view of the subject at the center of the picture on which all the attention centers, as if he were the fount of inspiration for the tale, and his inset contemplation, our own:

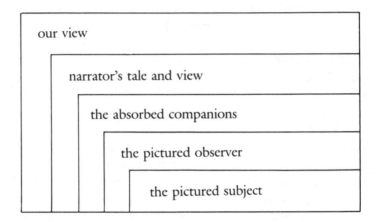

The pause prior to the picture's description, deliberately protracted within the room under the arched ceiling, pictures the central observer of the picture surrounded by the others, and therefore under the siege of gazes: "She was like an awestruck child; she might have been herself—all Greuze tints, all pale pinks and blues and pearly whites and candid eyes—an old dead pastel under glass" (SF, p. 51). A delay now ensues to stress the scene: against the slow-moving tide of arrest and suspicion with no resolution, the inset pictures will stand out, but the present one in particular by spatial insetting in the room with the rococo borders and by temporal insetting in a psychological delay, and the linguistic insetting in the present tense, set against the ordinary past narration: the young man in an old-fashioned black outfit, with a pale face and no eyebrows like a clown, holding a wax or enameled metal mask, while we stare at him. The frame is at least five-edged, with temporal, spatial, conceptual, and self-referring motifs, as well as verbal ones; the scene is spotlighted in the flow of the narration, which develops in the past but pauses to put all of this in the present ("the figure represented is").

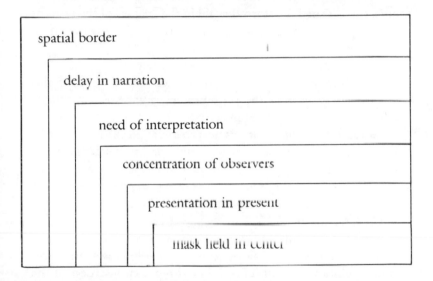

The mask as an object made present by and in the central picture is both a reduction and an enhancement, by compression and condensation, in the framed and concentrated space. As the developing object for the tale, it represents a perfect because enigmatic clue, at once superficial and central.

"The Turn of the Screw," with a Twist

How can you say I do anything so foul and abject as to state?
James letter to Hugh Walpole

The "Turn of the Screw" (1896) gets a tenacious grip on its included or enframed audience from the beginning ("The story had held us," TS, p. 7),[20] and holds that first included audience, and the second one we compose as readers, right to the conclusion in the literally end-stopped drama. The tale told by the governness, found and read by the finder to a circle of friends, shows an initial slippage in that the hold of the text depends largely on the recounted tension initially told by just the person who has not been able to take hold of or get a firm grip upon the events; the literal ardor of the fire around which the first audience is seated is gathered again in the "flame" of the governess's impulse at the end, so that the entire text is framed in an ardent round.

The real frame here is the receptive one, and in that the tale is distinct from the other framing and framed tales discussed in this volume. Here, each of the phantom appearances is surrounded either by a marked silence (an auditory frame), a sudden distance (a spatial frame), or an uncertain prolongation or delay (a temporal frame). Natural and architectural borders isolate the apparition situated atop a tower, on the other side of a window or of a lake, or upon the stairs, as well as metatextual references to the scene as scene or the page as page; the text is set for the mind as for the eye.

The Freudian senses of the turn, the set, and the screw at the center of sight are as intricate in their convolutions as the repetitions; Flora's insistent, effortful, and repeated insertion of the toy ship's mast into the hole gives a further turn to the fixation as it is "tightened in its place," preparing the turns of the rest of the tale. Many critics have commented upon the notion of turn and its own turns, and so I shall not stress them, except to say that upon these turns the focus of the reading is kept, and that they are what is framed.

Some of the framing mechanisms are expected, ranging from the visual surround and architectural silhouetting of Peter Quint at the window and later on the tower, to the other equally architectural and psychological framing of the apparitions; playing on the verbal as well as the visual and psychological, the bothersome "turn" of little Flora's back upon the vision of Miss Jessel on the opposite side of the lake, and the still more noticeable "turn" of her face to hardness at the second announcement of the apparition in the governess's eyes, give an odd twist to the otherwise banal exclamation of the banal Mrs. Grose, so rightly named: "What a dreadful turn, to be sure, Miss!" Even Miles, as he is "turned" out of school, counts in this verbal bordering and accentuation, until the repetitions and twists are tight: the double refusal of the vision by the little girl and the grown lady, the turning out of school and the turning of the back and the face, as of the mast in the hole, all cumulatively contribute, in their repeating parts, to the set-up for the governess's act, that fixation and that holding which bring about the terrible fall at the end into the mortal quiet of the day, into the stop of the heart, and the text with it.[21]

James's repetitions, in general, serve to isolate the stressed instant, and the revelations thereby exposed. Of Miles, the governess sees first his face surrounded by his sheets: like the transposition of the expression Mrs. Grose aptly applies to her after her second vision, "white as a sheet," the pair of imaged sheets supply a backdrop and border for his face then "framed in whiteness," in its bedclothes. Next, the borders are removed from his face for a less severe cropping, but are transferred to the object immediately beyond: "The frames and squares of the great window were a kind of image, for him, of a kind of failure. I felt that I saw him, at any rate, shut in or shut out" (TS, p. 113). The reader, too, sees the limits on sight, but is not allowed to make the image, for it comes prepackaged and preframed, obsessively: the rest and the "real" are cropped out.

The governess is always less visible than her obsession by which she mishandles the text, becoming herself its "horrible author." She glares in at us from the other side of the window, increasingly horrified by her own visions. But the culmination of her sight or her fantastic projection is exposed when the glare of Peter Quint beyond the pane is made an outward horror facing her inner one, preparing the final presentation and performance, melodramatic and appropriate, for her subsequent act: "The act would be, seeing and facing what I saw and faced, to keep the boy himself unaware." Each of the repeated terms, "act . . . act," "seeing . . . saw," "facing . . . faced," serves to stress the last and most awful repetition, on which the final fixation turns and by which it is betrayed, in the having, the catching, the holding of the boy in his fall, of the text in its conclusion, of the reader in the ardor of the fire, and in the overarching and underlying quiet of the day, for the end is bare to a fault.

Like the vision, the child, for whom the window is clear, is undone; the terrible end, commencing with the melodramatically rhymed verbal couple, "stare /glare," points at the "truth," fixing the final phrase and the ending border: the desperate attempt to catch, to hold, and to have, is only faced with "missing wholly," with a vicious "fall" and an eternal loss. The attempt at jealous contrastive possession, "*I* have you . . . but he has lost you for ever" (TS, p. 121), ends in dramatic and tragic arrest: "But he had already jerked straight round, stared, glared again, and seen but the quiet day . . . I caught him, yes, I held him . . . but at the end of a minute I began to feel what it truly was that I held. We were alone with the quiet day, and his little heart, dispossessed, had stopped" (TS, p. 121).

The whole tale, in its ironic catch and its fall, its tightly screwed support of the story, is really about the play of the held and the fixated against the free. The frame is one of reception and interpretation, unusually participatory in its requirements and in all its endless turns, befitting a story taut and twisted to its end.

The Ambassadors *and Some Arrangements*

... at last, in the high clear picture—he was moving these days, as in a
gallery, from clever canvas to clever canvas ...
    The Ambassadors[22]

IMPRESSIONS

By the time of *The Ambassadors*, the aesthetic sense of border is openly of greater interest for James than the rather dreary "plot."

What the reader sees, hazy or clear, is given its limits, as before, by the viewpoint of an observer interior to the scene, but here the viewer's highly developed sensitivity is strictly pictorial.[23] The plot is seen, like a moralizing conflict, with its clichés, stock figures and settings, and captions, not unexpected and not terribly interesting either. The interest is indeed developing in James for the frame itself as of greater import and complexity than the picture framed; but the impassioned reader of frames is likely to find this story, celebrated as an illustration of looking through a picture into a picture, unexciting: the excitement is, I think, to come.

An American friend is sent to recall the starving son of the States from the supposed guiles and wiles of Old Europe; but, having decided that the young man, greatly improved, should stay with the lady responsible for the improvement, and her daughter, deliberately made "as pretty as a picture," he will return empty-handed, wanting not to have profited by his ambassadorial mission.

The figures are placed by the naive gaze of Strether's artistic arrangements, of whose pictorial sense we have a clearer picture than of his character. Of the ways in which the elements are set, James says, in a letter to Hugh Walpole (August 14, 1912): "it is probably a very packed production, with a good deal of one thing within another."[24] This *production* and the very slight interest of the plot forces an equally detached "aesthetic" viewpoint on the reader, of what James calls, in the preface, "my demonstration of this process of vision."

Strether's sighting is already made, as if an impressionist open-air sketch, in the Luxembourg Gardens: "here, on a penny chair from which terraces, alleys, vistas, fountains, little trees in green tubs, little women in white caps, and shrill little girls at play all sunnily 'composed' together, he passed an hour in which the cup of his impressions seemed to overflow" (A, p. 53); and the Tuileries, where the picture plays surface precision against inset detail: "bareheaded girls with the buckled strap of oblong boxes . . . ancient thrifty persons basking betimes where terrace-walls

were warm, in the blue-frocked brass-labelled officialism of hum-
ber rakers and scrapers the deep references of a straight-pacing
priest or the sharp ones of a white-gaitered, red-legged soldier"
(A, p. 53).

In this composition, with its own "deep reference," the essen-
tials of Jamesian framing are already sketched: the scene held in
arrest within the flux is selected for its metonymic reference, according to the depth and prolongation outside its borders, in
allusion to the institutions of school, church, and army. The very
precision of the passage, with its hyphenated adjectives, specifies
the sharpness of Strether's sight, so strangely opposed to his slow
grasp of the outlines of human conduct and its implications. The
rest of the tale follows from the sureness of the visual composition whose limits he selects, and his far less sure understanding
of underlying meanings, suggested, on a second level, by the
expression "deep." That secondary picture is what James builds
for us, as a painter.

THE PAINTER'S EYE

Strether's sensitivity is a receiving one, as Chatman's studies of
the language of *The Ambassadors* have shown.[25] Like one of the
pictures in Chad's collection, what Strether sees is always heavily
bordered and deliberately set: "its frame was large out of proportion to the canvas" (A, p. 167). The conception and realization are tidy, and the limitations of the window are made visible
by the cropping of the picture, within the "oval" or rectangular
or square form of a window overlooking a body of water, of a
remembered picture superimposed upon a riverscape, of a door
or balcony or French window framing a presented figure. Strether
knows more than he shows, for example, about the article responsible for the wealth of the family whose friend he is; his
mention of it indicates one of the limits of the frame, which is
thus perceived by what it interrupts, by its cutoff points. Another
cropping is formed by the conclusion, since we never learn whether
or not the son returns to America, abandoning his mistress Madame de Vionnet: it is not that we care, but that the set-up, a

standard plot, makes one expect an ending statement which is, precisely, not forthcoming. The exterior frame is made visible to us just as the interior frame of the aesthetic composition around the French countryside or around a particular river scene is visible for Strether, and for us through his view.

Strether's sight is always and artistically connective, so that the series of small figures first glimpsed in the gardens prepares for the appearance of the figure upon the balcony, Little Bilham, who prefigures Chad himself as one picture prefigures and pre-frames another. The "meaningful perched privacy" that the balcony represents (A, p. 65) is concretized in a scene whose set-apart privilege will recur throughout the book as the parallel heightened luxury to the private insetting of Maria Gostrey's hearth, the spiritually comfortable refuge Strether is first seen longing for, but will finally refuse, in keeping with his neutral frame.

His initial presentation to Chad of the "desirable" future he should return to already appears as a "square bright picture" into which Chad should most perfectly fit: if that picture looks increasingly dull to Strether and to us, it is because of the vivid series of contrasting pictures. Pictures all along in the book are used as images and metaphors, rather than being seen in themselves or as their frames; this is why the story does not figure, on the reading list of the framing devotee, as having the same innate interest as those of the later James.

Framed pictures are used to contrast Europe and America the balconies looked up to and the hearths imagined, the gardens brightly and directly depicted or the countryside seen through a gilt frame, all represent Europe, whose doors and rooms give one onto the next, set into each other; in contrast, the doors of America are constantly open. The pictures are placed as in each other, thus the canvas of Lambinet is superimposeed upon a country scene, and the figures on the balcony are superimposed in their substitutions, or again, the faint pastel picture of a young European girl is superimposed upon the bright square picture of an American one; the superimposition is significant in its representation of the whole book and its amoral aesthetic message: two ways of seeing, according to national viewpoint.

What Chad has collected—Madame de Vionnet and Jeanne in their frames—develops in the reader's mind as a picture, with its focus progressively more centered and its figures sharper in retrospective contrast, whether superpositioned or juxtaposed. Strether has developed, like Chad, his collection of pictures, including the pastel oval portrait of Jeanne and those less appealing square bright pictures: the very softness of her faint outline prevents any direct desire and imposes rather a necessary aesthetic distance; "what was in the girl was indeed too soft, too unknown for direct dealing: so that one could only gaze at it as at a picture, quite staying one's own hand" (A, p. 143). Like a metaphor, the picture is exactly what cannot be handled or changed, while the faintness indicates its ephemeral character: "She was fairly beautiful to him—a faint pastel in an oval frame: he thought of her already as of some lurking image in a long gallery, the portrait of a small old-time princess of whom nothing was known but that she had died young" (A, p. 166). The faint portrait blurs, its outlines dim, unlike the durable brightness of the American one hung by its side in the gallery of the imagination. They are opposites in every way: moral, temporal, practical, and psychological, so that a choice is bound to be made sooner or later between the two kinds of picture and frame.

Its pastel medium challenging its duration, this portrait is also the opposite of the bright-colored lunch Strether shares with the girl's mother beside the open window at the waterside, with its clear order and its arrangement of the primary colors, red, yellow, and blue, as the perfect European replacement for the square bright American picture, substituting for possible moral judgment by the perfection of the picturing itself. The window frame neatly separates appearance and clarity from inner feeling: "How could he wish it to be lucid for others, for anyone, that he, for the hour, saw reasons enough in the mere way the bright clean ordered water-side life came in at the open window?—the mere way Madame de Vionnet, opposite him over their intensely white table-linen, their *omelette aux tomates*, their bottle of straw-coloured Chablis, thanked him for everything almost with the smile of a child, while her grey eyes moved in and out of their talk" (A, p. 192). Against the intense white of the picture surface, the grey eyes stand out as clearly as the red and straw and blue, for the picture is seen through the strength of her view, less pastel than that of her daughter. This portrait suffices.

Upon this bright picture, the far paler colors of her rooms, in their inward and nuanced recession one into the other, in their complication of faded tints and subtle insetting that imply old-world meaning, superimpose themselves in their high dimness. Behind the obviously framed scenes on balconies, in courtyards and at tables, in the gardens and at the hearths, this model of *mise-en-abyme* architecture forms an interior guide to the text, as, in *The Wings of the Dove*, the vistas leading to Lancaster Gate and to Matcham and to the inside of Dr. Strett's office deep within his home guide the reader's gaze further and further within, according to a series of recessions, toward a revealing episode deep inside the tale. In this case, Madame de Vionnet literally leads Strether along, intensifying his, and our, "sense of approach":

> But she went part of the way with him, accompanying him out of the room and into the next and the next. Her noble old apartment offered a succession of three, the first two of which indeed, on entering, smaller than the last, but each with its faded and formal air, enlarged the office of the antechamber and enriched the sense of approach. ... He stopped, he looked back; the whole thing made a vista, which he found high melancholy and sweet—full, once more, of dim historic shades, of the faint far-away cannon-roar of the great Empire. It was doubtless half the projection of his mind, but his mind was a thing that, among old waxed parquets, pale shades of pink and green, pseudo-classic candelabra, he had always needfully to reckon with. (A, p. 263)

The pale pink and green, these faint historical shades of the noble beauty of vanished Empire, dim in sound and outline like the portrait of Jeanne, subtle like the beauty of Madame de Vionnet, serve to superimpose in imagination the vision of the past upon the present experience in its own development by interior progressions and recesses. These framed and essential sights lead into, and open out upon, a civilization toward which Strether comes as an ambassador, significantly discovering this series of rooms recessed into each other, like further insettings in the discovery of the self. The room left in European architecture for hidden reflections contrasts with the enforcement of openness in American architecture, habits, and mind.

The scene at Mrs. Pocock's Paris hotel, demonstrating a convergence between American temperament and European architecture, includes high framing by balcony and French window. The concealed figure, with its "reflexion" in a leaf "folded back," as if it were a page, serves as the perfect model for a Jamesian text: "Both the windows of the room stood open to the balcony, but it was only now that, in the glass of the leaf of one of them, folded back, he caught a reflexion quickly recognized as the colour of a lady's dress. Somebody had been then all the while on the balcony, and the person, whoever it might be, was so placed between the windows as to be hidden from him" (A, p. 276). As with all the great novels of James, these ambivalent metatextual references are to be read within the most intricate framing structure. In this case, the *reading* values of the elements of hidden figure, the reflecting leaf and the backward fold, *concealment, reflection, reversal*, make a contrast with "the incessantly open doorways of home," honest and dull, that simple architectural statement marking the vast distance between concepts, between interior depth and exterior exposure.

Of all the framing convergences, revelations, and interior, aesthetic, and personal developments in sight, understanding, and presentation, the most elaborately worked-out is itself the most celebrated example of framing in James. Remembering a little picture found in Boston, a Lambinet[26] suggestive of the cool greenness of the French countryside, Strether makes an excursion the limits of which coincide exactly with the limits of that other picture's frame, the real and the aesthetic converging perfectly, as Boston remembered imposes its outlines on France experienced, imposing the past upon the present, art upon life:

> The oblong gilt frame disposed its enclosing lines; the poplars and willows, the reeds and river—a river of which he didn't know, and didn't want to know, the name—fell into a composition, full of felicity, within them; the sky was silver and turquoise and varnish; the village on the left was white and the church on the right was grey. It was all there, in short—it was what he wanted: it was Tremont Street, it was France, it was Lambinet. (A, p. 342)

After the initial *disposition* of the enclosure, its lines laid out, the willed suppression of detail (not to know the river's name) prepares the way for the direct felicity of experience; here a symphony of grey, silver, and white, accented with turquoise like some Corot, the opposite of the primary colors in the preceding restaurant scene à la Monet. More important still, the background is prepared for the dialectical crescendo: Boston–France–Art as the larger frame.

All day long, the superimposition of the frame upon the landscape continues with no effort, including all the temporal and personal elements, and no divergence from the dramatic lines, *scening* and *staging* the picture:

> He really continued in the picture—that being for himself his situation—all the rest of this rambling day . . . and had . . . not once overstepped the oblong gilt frame. The frame had drawn itself out for him, as much as you please; but that was just his luck. . . . For this had been all day at bottom the spell of the picture—that it was essentially more than anything else a scene and a stage . . . (A, p. 346)

The dramatic setting is perfect for observation; as if that were not sufficient, Strether observes from a raised platform what will be the specific stage, that is, the river. It is six o'clock, so that the early supper scene superimposes itself in a normal temporal progression for the reader upon the bright lunch scene by the Seine. The scene is further stressed by its presentational comparatives and implied superlatives: the Cheval Blanc seems "*the thing*" for a climax to the day, "even to a greater degree," he thinks, "than Madame de Vionnet's old high salon" (A, p. 347). Thus the entire scene is set in high and higher relief. Now within the general heightening, the specific focus on a detail makes a literal *arrest* of the picture in the flow of time: he "saw something that gave him a sharper arrest." The interruption heightens the suspense still further:

> What he saw was exactly the right thing—a boat advancing round the bend and containing a man who held the paddles and a lady, at the stern, with a pink parasol. It was suddenly as if these figures, or something like them, had been wanted in the picture, had been wanted more or less all day, and had now drifted into sight, with the slow current, on purpose to fill up the measure. (A, pp. 348-49)

As the focus becomes narrowed to the extreme, the verbal pattern and the psychological rhythm direct the gaze from the border to the central spot: the extraordinarily slow pace of the passage matches the slow-moving current, and the reader's expectation builds up accordingly, from the arrest to the suspicion to the confirmation of the detail. The picture is seen in slow motion or delay, as the eye takes in at a painfully slow pace, deliberately letting the mind of the reader outdistance it, the sharp detail of the bright spot made by the parasol, again pink against the green of the shimmering foliage, like an exact replica outside of the colors of Madame de Vionnet's rooms, preparing a repeat of her appearance. The aesthetic stress asserts, by implication, the "rightness" of the staging. And indeed the aesthetic border is "exactly the right thing"; the slow coming of Strether's consciousness develops now within a visible frame of verbally stated art, and not the moral one of life and judgment.

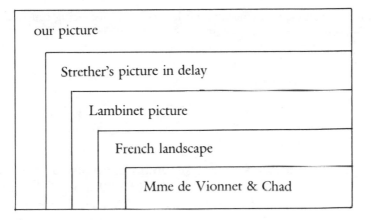

Here again and finally, *the frame is larger than the contained surprise*: since we have known all along that the couple are lovers, what could conceivably be, apart from the frame, the fascinated suspense created by the boat's arrival? Why should Madame de Vionnet shift her pink parasol so as to hide her face, and why should Chad stay slightly in retreat? Had the lovers not all along realized, as the reader must have, that the situation was *exposed*, staged in the open air? Seen "straight on," precisely by its cover-up—with the slow down, the arrest, and the focus of the gaze as it is directed—the arrival of the boat, as it is *wanted* and desired, in a transferral of the emotional to the aesthetic, can only be an anticlimax. These figures were to be expected, and so they came. The frame has been carefully placed and constructed, and the fill (as in Gombrich's expression of frame and fill) can only be aesthetic and not a moral or substantial surprise: the picture needed this spot of color, needed the arrival of a couple, any couple, in a boat, and there they are, the specific couple about whom the mind has been constructing its frames. Thus the possible letdown of the reader: all this frame to contain only what we already know?

Strether's discomfiture works almost as if it had been the discomfiture of some moralizing reader, transposed to his own personality whereas in fact his cool aesthetic sensibility is transferred to the reader, in a chiasmus no less effective for being only suggested:

In this exchange Strether takes up his ambassadorial role, for a diplomatic transfer of feelings, for the mediation of the attitudes and habits of two very different civilizations, the more subtle implications of the European ("leaf . . . folded back")—where leaf and fold and open door play upon each other in hiding and revealing each aperture or inset leading to the next—and the America, open and straight.

THE ARRANGING HAND

The irremediable distance between the two perspectives is made clear by example. Between the subtle colors and intricate reflections, the interior progressions, private high perches, and recessed hearths of France on one hand, and the openness and declared, if somewhat dull, "morality" of America, there is to be no absolute mediation. Mrs. Pocock terms Chad's development in Europe and his aesthetic arranging by the tasteful hand of Madame de Vionnet, not "fortunate," as Strether puts it, but rather "hideous." The very abruptness of her retort, "the manner of her break, the sharp shaft of her rejoinder," and her masculine march out of his hotel "straight across the court," make a telling contrast with the more subtle approach and slow revelations, the faded glories and rich presence, the inner recessions and settings of relations nesting within each other like so many rooms of an old apartment with all its memories in an old wise country.

In all three of these late novels, of course, the American and the European elements are thus balanced: in this one, the clear framing prepares the ambassadorial role of mediation. But

Strether's ambassadorial approach seems finally directed neither to the Americans nor to the Europeans, but rather to the reader as the supposed and predictable observer of the scene.

Acting as the hinge or mediating element in the center, Strether only observes, his empty hands witnessing to that. Between the two approaches, the direct and the reflected, the one instantly exposed or the one slowly unfolding from chamber into chamber, situated between the incessantly open doors and the private balconies set high with their folded shutters and their half-apertures of sight, their concealments and their parallel revelations, he takes an aesthetic stance and view. He looks before him at the arrangement and the composition, in just appreciation.

To reflect upon this, he takes his place upon the balcony, at the conclusion, as he had upon the platform above the river. Chad now replaces both Strether and his earlier representation in the person of Little Bilham, so that (as with the reversal of positions of Milly and Kate on one of the balconies of *The Wings of the Dove*) the high position finds its climax in its reversal. For Strether, now looking up from the sidewalk to the balcony, "it is as if his last day were oddly copying his first," so that the final frame fits just around to join the initial one. Thus the repeat of perception is rounded off, and the picture is completed.

It has become increasingly apparent to Strether that the whole experience has taken place within a work of art, surrounded by other works, not of life, but of art: "Between nine and ten, at last, in the high clear picture he was moving in these days, as in a gallery, from clever canvas to clever canvas—he drew a long breath" (A, p. 360). This "high clear picture" and this perception are prepared by the high perched privacy of the balcony, the restaurant lunch over the river, the view framed by the window, and by the observer's platform, from which he perceives the boat in its slow progress. All these perfect pictures are more subtle in their impressions and nuanced progressions than the square, bright one he might at first have regretted as an American temporarily expatriate.

Ironically, one requirement for the "spell of his luxury" as he pauses in this gallery of perfect pictures is that his hands will never be filled, his intervention will never be useful. The portrait cuts close to the finish, for as Maugham pointed out of James himself, "He did not live, he observed life from a window, and too often was inclined to content himself with no more than what his friends told him they saw when *they* looked out of a window" (in *A Writer's Notebook*, quoted in *The Dictionary of Biographical Quotation*, p. 415). Despite these high conditions of clarity, privilege, and luxury, Strether finally withdraws from the impressionistic pictures with their glorious colors, faded or primary, their memories and sounds, retreating from the frame of the rooms set into an interior progression and understanding, and even from the hearth offered as a haven. He withdraws with no collection except his memories of the scene, in which he served as the ambassador, as he did for our own. These pictures, we remember, were never to have been handled in terms of reality: "one could only gaze at it as at a picture, quite staying one's hand" (A, p. 143).

The Wings of the Dove *as Plotted Sight*

Yes, one has read; but this is beyond any book.
  The Wings of the Dove[27]

The presentation of *The Wings of the Dove* is nothing if not clear in its drastic outlines, as the heroines are placed in melodramatic opposition: Kate, splendid as a tiger in her vital beauty and her long black braid, poor and ambitious; against Milly, with her startling red hair and pale face, in her enigmatic malady, her riches, and her dovelike innocence; between them, dullish Densher as mediation, far less striking than either, loving Kate and acquiescing in her scheme to defraud Milly by pretending to love her in order to inherit her wealth, and then won over to "real" feeling by Milly's noble passive suffering, knowing, forgiving, and dying. The melodrama is both evident and engaging: Milly as a joyless Bronzino heroine in rich garment and rigid pose, or as a pale Maeterlinck princess in a Venetian palace, Densher and Kate posed in the vistas of the National Gallery for Milly to see them, and their relation. The manifold ironies of human cruelty and human anguish cram the stressed scenes, such as Kate and Densher taking tea while Milly is dying, as they supped when she was suffering. The horror of this novel comes unadulterated, heavily set in black borders.

SEEING AND SETTING APART

"She waited, Kate Croy . . ." (WD, p. 9). The opening scene prepares the entire novel as the text of Kate's anticipation, with the set already high in color: penniless girl, grasping father, scheming aunt. The stuff of terrible and traditional drama is exposed as the poor English girl with her beauty and brains is pitted against the rich American girl whom fate has doomed. The architectural setting already places Kate apart, looking down, like an eagle waiting to swoop in victory: first on a small balcony, then atop a long flight of stairs, two stressed positions whose dramatic verticals cross the horizontal "long straight vistas" leading to her aunt's house, where again she will live apart and upstairs. The interior violence of the story is prepared by just such outer images: the sentinel on watch, the animal of prey in hiding or about to pounce. The pulse of the plot line is quickened by the instinctive fear or delight of such preparation, as strong in its lines as some Napoleonic legend with the hero awaiting his moment.

Sitting far downstairs Aunt Maud was yet a presence from which a sensitive niece could feel herself extremely under pressure. She knew herself now, the sensitive niece, as having been marked from far back. She knew more than she could have told you, by the upstairs fire, in a whole dark December afternoon. She knew so much that her knowledge was what fairly kept her there, making her at times move endlessly between the small silk-covered sofa that stood for her in the firelight and the great grey map of Middlesex spread beneath her lookout. To go down, to forsake her refuge, was to meet some of her discoveries half-way, to have to face them or fly before them; whereas they were at such a height only like the rumble of a far-off siege heard in the provisioned citadel. (WD, p. 28)

The dark afternoon in the upstairs chamber of a citadel above the noise of the battle will be paralleled later with the enforced inaction of Milly upstairs in her Venetian palace, longing never to go down to life. Kate, "sensitive . . . sensitive," will go down now to do battle, "knowing," and again, "knowing," but Milly will remain up in that palace, to die; the adversary setup of eagle and dove is pictured here in preparation.

The settings are stately—great houses, gardens, palaces—and the borders picturesque. Kate is first sketched by Milly and her companion: "The handsome English girl from the heavy English house had been as a figure in a picture stepping by magic out of its frame" (WD, p. 125). The description of Kate as this "handsome girl" now joins "the sensitive niece" as a motif replacing what might have been specific description by the general. Her personality is perfectly adapted to her category, as the setting comes inescapably to dominate the individual: "The handsome girl was . . . the least bit brutal." If such brutality underlies Kate's sensitivity, Milly's eventual perception of Densher's gaze directed at Kate and the latter's silence itself form "a great darkness," as she says: this gloomy sight prepares the central tragedy of innocence betrayed and pardoning.

PORTRAIT PLACING AND REVERSAL

Set within a set, the central pictorially suggestive scene is laid at the extreme end of the long corridors in the majestic house at Matcham, centered as in a Watteau painting, in a tone as of "old gold" (WD, p. 150), kept down in accordance with the air, but indicating the symbolic value of the scene. Through the vast halls of armor and chests, lined with tapestries and pictures on the grand scale, Milly is led by Lord Mark toward the Bronzino painting, which will be the major developing or revealing object for her tragedy, embedded in the house and enframed deep within the memory of a tradition of poses. The sight of the painting, so profoundly inset,[28] is delayed until after the lengthy passage of the heroine along the great halls and among the groups of guests: "The Bronzino was . . . deep within, and the long afternoon light lingered for them on patches of old colour and waylaid them, as they went, in nooks and opening vistas" (WD, p. 158). All these openings, nooks, and niches stress the insetting of the picture, the discovering of which by Milly, and her simultaneous discovery of herself as she is perceived and as she is, are themselves inset and individually framed within the group set in visual, sociological, and emotional contrast to her.

This scene giving Milly away to herself and to the others is at the heart of the great novel as of the great house, set "deep within . . . the long afternoon light." Before seeing Bronzino's mannerist portrait of a young woman, the reader sees its effect upon Milly, which sets it already in a psychological surround: "She found herself, for the first moment, looking at the mysterious portrait through tears" (WD, p. 158). The self-recognition is as powerful as any mirror scene, adding an attendant figure to Milly's thin shape from now on, in the vistas of scene and self: "The lady in question, at all events, with her slightly Michaelangelesque squareness, her eyes of other days, her full lips, her long neck, her recorded jewels, her brocaded and wasted reds, was a very great personage—only unaccompanied by a joy. And she was dead, dead, dead. Milly recognised her exactly in words that had nothing to do with her. 'I shall never be better than this' " (WD, p. 159). The picture of wasting has already been announced as the object before which Milly will have "said all." The insetting of tragic portrait into tragic text is peculiarly visible here, exposing the joylessness as nothing else can. "She was before the picture, but she had turned to him, and she didn't care if, for the minute, he noticed her tears" (WD, p. 159). As if the narrator were inside the mind of Milly, this sudden intimacy intensifies her pain, as in a repeat, by her observing her own tears, within the line of another's gaze; even as she sheds them, she is made—or makes herself—into a picture.

The confrontation of pictured heroine and picture is inset within further borders; through the open door behind Milly's back appear three more figures including Kate, all held in a dramatic arrest by what they have "seen" and, by extension, found out. The halt of the spectators before Milly repeats the motif of self as picture, revealing, like the "kind" court they pay, with their "kind, kind eyes," the terrible surround of her fate: she too is read like a tragic figure against a rich ground of "recorded jewels" and wasted brocades, as an object of limitless aesthetic value. "Lady Aldershaw meanwhile looked at Milly quite as if Milly had been the Bronzino and the Bronzino only Milly. 'Superb, superb, of course I had noticed. It is wonderful'" (WD, p. 160). Of course, what is wonderful is in fact, although an object of wonder in its resemblance, quite terrible: but it is "only Milly."

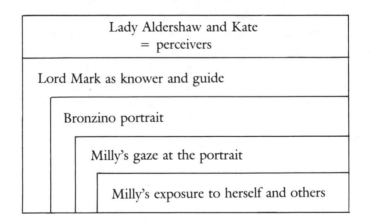

Milly is thus framed and hung in her true place, assigned to it by the appraising stares of others, both pictured and real.

Quite unlike the striking and somehow vulgar image of Kate and Densher perched, however gracefully, on their ladders, Milly's pose reflects the stiffness of the pictured heroine, placed and kept at a dignified, even solemn level and distance. The reader may recall the passage where Milly sits alone upon "the dizzy edge" of a high rock in the Alps, contemplating "a view of great extent" (WD, p. 93), for even there, the pose made it clear that she was reserved for "some more complicated passage," whose exact configuration was yet to be ascertained. It includes the future end, when the others will have left Venice, where she must die, forever set apart, lonely and distinct between her high and heroic borders. Over and over, before and behind her, psychologically and spatially, a chasm opens like a space set about her, boxing her off from the others. It is Milly who suddenly has to sit down while "the prospect, through opened doors, stretched before her into other rooms." This passage of seeing or "vista" works like a mental prospect, yielding the positive connotations of long stretches for the doom of an abyss.

The border is, as usual, marked by an absolute contrast, double in this case: gilt and pale, high and low, a sign as minimal as one word, here the adverb "aloft" (we remember the adverb as James's favorite part of speech) announces the analogy of the dove, both humble and soaring. "Thus it was that, aloft there in the great gilded historical chamber and the presence of the pale personage on the wall, whose eyes all the while seemed engaged with her own, she found herself suddenly sunk in something quite intimate and humble" (WD, p. 162). Aloft, she is also sunk; the passage contains in its depths and heights the abyss and the saintliness of her personal doom, parallel to the pose in the picture. Like a portrait of herself, she continues to smile fixedly, as the stale air of summer London replaces the Watteau-like vistas of Matcham and its dull gold, "the late hot London with its dance all danced and its story all told." Such exhaustion results in an automatic repetition of expressions: "dance . . . danced" and "all . . . all" represent a mechanical exhaustion; a seasonal emptiness reflects the terrible inner truth of Milly's self-consumption—like the season, she is all used up.

Milly's second meeting with Dr. Luke Strett, in his consulting room far back in a recess of his fine old house, relates, as the second panel of a diptych, to her Bronzino encounter, deep within the great house of Matcham. Both scenes are set deep into their physical surroundings and prepare a forced psychological revelation: "She had come forth to see the world, and this then was to be the world's light, the rich dusk of a London 'back,' these the world's walls, those the world's curtains and carpet" (WD, p. 170). As the world is suddenly put into narrow focus by the deictic pointers—"this . . . these . . . those,"—the office is made to absorb the Bronzino portrait's mortal lament ("Dead, dead, dead"), all its inanition and hints of doom: "she should be as one of the circle of eminent contemporaries, photographed, engraved, signatured, and in particular framed and glazed, who made up the rest of the decoration." For the third time Milly is tempted to tears, exposed as she is to pity and, worse, to self-pity. Made into a picture first by a resemblance pointed out from the world of history and of art, and next by the physical and psychological resemblance of her doom to that of other patients in the world of medicine, she is finally set into her pose as victim by her own imagination of a revolutionary heroine dragged silent to her fate, who serves as the developmental *model*. The portrait and the imagined role model work closely to give coherence to her own picture.

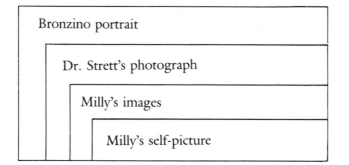

Then Milly's new knowledge, enclosed in the inner sanctum of Dr. Luke Strett's consulting room, with its framed pictures and their glazed truths, must be inscribed in the larger limits of human tragedy by Milly herself. Her realization of her "com-

mon" condition as she is alone makes a strong passage marked
by poetic rhythms and rich patterning, by a linguistic border
crossing verb with verb, and by the concrete image of a box as
if it were a coffin for the common perception of mortality, having become, finally, "the real thing." Repeating pointers direct
our attention toward the center of the scene: "this was . . . here
were . . . here were . . . here were . . ."

> . . . this was the real thing. . . . Here were benches and smutty
> sheep; here were idle lads at games of ball, with their cries
> mild in the thick air; here were wanderers, anxious and tired
> like herself; here doubtless were hundreds of others just in
> the same box. Their box, their great common anxiety, what
> was it, in this grim breathing-space, but the practical ques-
> tion of life? They could live if they would . . . they would
> live if they could. (WD, p. 179)

> . . . It was perhaps superficially more striking that one could
> live if one would; but it was more appealing, insinuating,
> irresistible, in short, that one would live if one could. (WD,
> p. 182)

The chiasmus reversing the final repetitive expression of the two
quotations makes a sharply patterned edge, a marked and sonorous border for Milly's moment of wider consciousness.

could live if they would	a	b
would live if they could	b	a
one could live if one would	a	b
one would live if one could	b	a

She has moved out in two stages beyond the individual and privileged revelation of an individual fate, doubled in the portrait, to
a doom shared by the several other patients in the framed and
"glazed" portraits, to a wider consciousness of suffering human-

ity, which *would* live if it *could*, prepared by her image of the revolutionary figure at the window. In a gesture of acceptance of the common lot, she "sinks" upon a bench, her physical attitude responding to the "intimate and humble" plight in which she sank just as she was "aloft" in the great picture gallery, after her lofty perch upon the rock. This humble pose predicts the end, when she will collapse against a window seat, in her Venetian palace.

VIEW AND FOCUS

While to Kate are given all the vitality, energy, and brutality in the book, painted as she is in large brush strokes, from Milly all is taken away; Kate was initially seen upon a balcony and at the top of a flight of stairs, positions indicative of domination, but when Milly is glimpsed on an overhanging balcony, supposed to respond to Kate's curiosity, she is ill at ease; later, Kate will take up her position upon the balcony, her figure seen framed by the window, clearly outlined and defined by her impatience and vigor, while Milly has only to smile "hard," to smile "cheerfully," to wind up "with a smile," this automatic grimace repeated over and over, covering up the fatality of the "real thing," once perceived in the park. After a long delay on the balcony, an arrest seen through the open window, Kate focuses the attention of the others on herself: "Kate had remained in the window, very handsome and upright, the outer dark framing in a highly favourable way her summery simplicities and lightness of dress" (WD, p. 195). The light/dark contrast picks up the motif of the contrast between the two girls, their poverty and riches, their black and red manes of hair, their vitality and sickliness. Kate, restless and charming as a cliché of herself ("the handsome girl was in extraordinary form"), paces like a panther, while Milly wears herself out in a catalogue of present participles, three of perception and one of defeat: "listening, watching, admiring, collapsing." It is the collapse that remains at the center of the picture, all lines leading from the side back into it.

Just as the Bronzino scene was set in a private gallery, its revelation of joylessness followed by Milly's two successive visits to the doctor and the revelation of his photographs, with their equally joyless glaze in the final lifelessness of his former patients, there follows now a modified replay in reverse, although more public than private, of those same pictures: Milly escapes the doctor's call on her by a visit to the National Gallery, where the pictures further reveal her exhaustion, for she will be "after all too weak for the Turners and the Titians. They joined hands about her in a circle too vast, though a circle that a year before she would only have desired to trace" (WD, p. 206).

The large room of the National Gallery now sets a major framed scene into a slow-motion exposure, initially opposing Milly to three American women who turn their backs upon her, offsetting her isolated figure with its Titian hair (James himself admitted in a letter to William, "I admire Raphael; I enjoy Rubens, but I passionately love Titian" [in Matthiessen, *The James Family*, p. 255]) before their eyes converge upon a gentleman visitor, by whom Milly suddenly feels her own held in an *arrest*. Their look has then worked as mediator for her own vision of him: this build-up takes its time, and the details of gradual recognition continue to work just as slowly: the gentleman removes his hat, taps his forehead with his handkerchief, as the camera appears to zoom in on an ever-narrowing close up. After an extreme *delay* and a deliberately retarding description, Milly eventually perceives that the head is familiar, that it is in fact Densher's. The framing effect here is worked from outside in, from exterior acts to interior realization, from single details to total effect, the accessory figures of the American tourists in the margin serving to concentrate the central picture. Importance is given to the dull Densher's figure by his being made the object of the others' gaze, as innocent guides to Milly's own interest in his nameless figure, her gaze increasingly narrowing its range, intensely trained on him until it is abruptly interrupted, even violated in its intimacy, for she observes herself to be suddenly observed observing Densher, by Kate Croy, who is plainly there to meet him. The scene has shifted from the Americans' admiration of an anonymous figure to Milly's excruciatingly slow realization of its identity, until the brusque, unpleasant interruption of her gaze, in a disturbing alteration of rhythm and direction, making its own exposure:

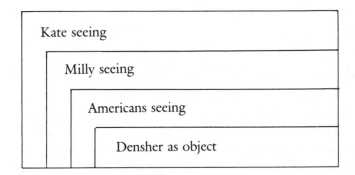

Several of the favorite Jamesian techniques for setting an episode apart are visible here: the stress on the pictorial setting in the National Gallery; on a single gesture, in Densher's tapping his forehead with his handkerchief; and on a single object, that handkerchief itself. Psychological pictures and revelations placed in a place of pictures make a metapictorial setting in which Milly's perception of Densher, converging with her sudden recognition that Densher and Kate are somehow linked after all, makes a turn in the text, now arrested for close observation. The textual self-consciousness is put in relation to Milly's own self-consciousness about her possible interest as a tourist in the National Gallery; to explain her presence, she refers to her own "unused margin as an American girl—closely indeed as, in English air, the text might appear to cover the page" (WD, p. 211).

The scene concludes by a series of striking verbal repetitions for a perfect formal closing edge, and it sets up a visible and audible distance between the reader and the figures in the story, as between the figures themselves, by the systematic use of the same categorizations already perceived, replacing individual thought, observation, and figures, by labels: Densher loses his

name for the category of "her young friend," Kate loses hers for
the threatening tag "the handsome girl," and Milly is patronized
as "our young woman," so that the reader is forced a step back
from the personal picture for a general one, neatly set in its repetitive borders. Milly's thoughts are laid open about what
Densher's sight of her must be: "feeling how much his view was
likely to have in common with—as she now sighed over it—*the*
view. She could have dreamed of his not having *the* view, of his
having something or other, if need be quite viewless, of his own;
but he might have what he could with least trouble, and *the* view
wouldn't be, after all, a positive bar to her seeing him" (WD, p.
215). Expressed in terms of sight and views, individual and public, emotional relations are seen depending as much on perspective, whether private or shared, as on knowledge; Milly's subsequent holding in of her private knowledge within its borders,
lest it explode into self-pity and confession, is admirably rendered
by the obsessive repetitions tightly controlling the "personal fact"
of Mr. Densher to which she has reacted too strongly. "She didn't
care now for Mr. Densher's personal fact . . . this personal fact
failed, as far as she was concerned, to be personal" (WD, p.
216): she consciously reins herself in to frame him out, to no
avail against the exterior frame-up of her emotions of which she
will be the victim.

PLOTTED SIGHT

In a horrible counterpoint to Milly's previous "view" of life from
the mountain peak when all seems stretched out at her feet, Kate's
own view, quietly implying Milly's imminent death, is revealed
to Densher at the top of the stairs, at the height where she has
been situated from the beginning. They are both thus perched
aloft, in a scene visually and conceptually equivalent to that of
their mutual ladder climb, during which they first glimpsed each
other as the unscrupulous, scheming, yet attractive beings they
are ("She had observed a ladder against a garden wall, and had
trusted herself so to climb it as to be able to see over into the
probable garden on the other side. On reaching the top she had

found herself face to face with a gentleman engaged in a like calculation at the same moment, and the two inquirers had remained confronted on their ladders" (WD, pp. 44-45).

What is at issue here is the imposition of one's own perspective and frame of reference upon another's: concern for Milly's own view is uppermost in Densher's consciousness, but Kate insists *in what light he must see*, that is, as she herself does: "The beauty of what I see! . . . He was really, notwithstanding, to hear more from her of what she saw" (WD, p. 238). The verb of seeing builds up in a menacing crescendo, assuming all action in itself; Milly remains the central spectacle, and Densher's discomfort is not only that of the observer of the scene, but the eventual actor. Kate's goal is to frame the scene properly for Densher's eyes, setting her sights on Milly, while separating with great care her seeing from her knowing, the other essential component of the Jamesian fiction of conscience; the supposed divorce of these two elements lends a terrible irony to the spectacle. The initial repetitions make a verbal border for the scene at the table focused about the absent Milly as the victimized object of pity, speculation, and finally verbal slaughter: "One *sees* her," says Kate, "more than one *sees* almost any one; but then one discovers that that isn't *knowing* her and that one may *know* better a person whom one doesn't *see*, I say, half so well" (WD, p. 247, my emphasis). From here on, Milly has no escape from the picture where she has been placed, seen, and carefully not known.

FIRST TURN: PICTURING

The heightened effect of James's masterly "confining" of the picture conserves energy within the extensive compression of his composition. When, in a scene he pictures, Densher drops Kate's hands to take Milly's—which in a sense he will never let go—the initial gesture remains fixed in our memory—"His corner was so turned . . ."—the rest, says Densher, will be left to Milly. She has now been worked into a picture imprisoned in her borders as she is doomed in her high and painterly palace setting, posed in the elaborate decor she has chosen. The scene is prepared and her fate covered over by the implicit consent of all, in care, silence, and watchfulness. No outward sign of tragedy is permitted to traverse this picture as long as the spectators are before it: the figures are framed as if forever, in a setting where time plays no apparent role, in a Venice the perfect place for a picture, and for its elegant decay.

One description, set in slow motion, isolated from the flow of the text by a tense change—it is written in a sort of dreaming present—makes a visible and temporal *delay*. The figures are observed as if from one step back and quietly, the active and the passive young women singled out as the two bearers of a massive symbolic drama. This inset piece, of a majestic, slow rhythm and heavily costumed, is markedly different from the rest of the text:

> Certain aspects of the connection these young women show for us, such is the twilight that gathers about them, in the likeness of some dim scene in a Maeterlinck play; we have positively the image, in the delicate dusk, of the figures so associated and yet so opposed, so mutually watchful: that of the angular, pale princess, ostrich-plumed, black-robed, hung about with amulets, reminders, relics, mainly seated, mainly still, and that of the upright, restless, slow-circling lady of her court, who exchanges with her, across the black water streaked with evening gleams, fitful questions and answers. The upright lady, with thick dark braids down her back, drawing over the grass a more embroidered train, makes the whole circuit, and makes it again, and the broken talk, brief and sparingly allusive, seems more to cover than to free their sense. (WD, pp. 314-15)

The visual borders are set, shaded twilight, around the nervous repetition of action. Extreme restlessness and deep motionless suffering are opposed in this splendidly mannered picture, both "confined" and of potential wide reach, yet the sense is so far covered over, as are the underlying questions. Milly now takes into her person all the drama that was only suggested in her encounter with the Bronzino heroine in her private borders, the doom weighing within her, about her, and over her, rendering the weighted silence of greater significance than the fitful talk ("brief, sparingly, allusive") as the scene incarnates the joylessness revealed by the other portrait, and increases a sense of dread. The style hangs heavy as the air.

Progressively and willingly, Milly is set apart in her high palatial framing: "Ah, not to go down!" she sighs. The major Venetian scene is set next to a window with the other faded palaces playing the same role of witness to a life gone by as did the Bronzino portrait ("dead, dead, dead") and the glazed photographs in the doctor's office, where death was indeed covered over, but no less terribly fixed. The signs of death come "slow," "lingering," "long": once again, Lord Mark is the witness to her weakness, as he presses her about her health:

> They were at the window, pausing, lingering, with the fine old faded palaces opposite and the slow Adriatic tide beneath; but after a minute, and before she answered, she had closed her eyes to what she saw and, unresistingly, dropped her face into her arms, which rested on the coping. She had fallen to her knees on the cushion of the window-place, and she leaned there, in a long silence, with her forehead down. She knew that her silence was itself too straight an answer, but it was beyond her now to say that she saw her way. (WD, p. 320).

Her pictured anguish, perceptible in the silence, the downward leaning attitude, and, once again, the seeing and knowing, is in exact correspondence with the former Bronzino revelation: the latter picture was spatially distinguished by its interior setting far within the depths of the house, and temporally by the traversal of long trophy-laden corridors. Here the scene is distinguished spatially by the border of the window frame, separating the exterior sights from the interior ones yet articulating them, as with the past, and distinguished formally by the extraordinarily slow rhythm, distinct from the pace of the surrounding passages. As in the Maeterlinck staging in the present that is descriptive of the two young women played against the surround of narrative past, the spatial and formal borders set off the scene, stressing its centrality.

Mark serves again as the personal developer of the situation within the highly impersonal decor, coolly observing Milly as she makes her confession of despair, sinking to her knees. Here her eyes shut upon the world she gives up, fading like the palaces, the whole passage situated as she and they are set in a marked *deceleration*: the delaying sense is intensified by the dragging of the tide in the canals and by the length of the silence, the temporal parallels to the human hesitation inside and the fading of palatial glory without. Milly's blocking gestures are those of defeat: closing her eyes, dropping her head, resting on her arms, falling to her knees, leaning against the coping for support, all made visible in the downward slant of her forehead. The spaces opening in her mind are beyond conjecture, as the exterior light is cut off, and beyond communication: "it was beyond her now to say."

The peculiar insetting of this scene recalls the great ambivalent end of *The Golden Bowl*, where Maggie will hide her eyes in her husband's breast, to conclude the text, but also in order not to read into his eyes or from them. Blockage of outer sight by the principal figure serves, whatever its other purposes, to curtain off the text from the reader, who may retain, particularly in James, the impression that something is to continue on the inside.

RECOMPOSURE AND DISCLOSURE

Densher has different sights to block out as he walks along what he envisages as "a high ridge." His advance from the metaphoric ladder on which Kate saw him to the actual stair of Milly's high palace has aroused his dread of the interior "decomposition" to which he refers, and of its recovering or "recomposition." Moral doubts assail him as to the "straightness" of his way, covered over by the aesthetic attitude, for he has only to cross the palace threshold to see the elements "compose, as painters called it, differently." The direction of his personal line, and what he will make of the composition and of himself within it, are determined still by his having made his turn. As Milly's companion points out, he is now necessarily *in the picture*. Kate's notion frames him in, pictorially and personally, and his own "personal fact," as Milly would say, has been responsible for a massive frame-up: aesthetics has covered over the moral disfiguration.

That frame-up has to be exposed; a dreadful scene of revelation shows the dark outline of the scheme in all its mercenary truth. Admiring Milly's long rope of pearls as it figures perfectly against her white lace dress, Kate confesses how deeply she desires the very symbol of the distinction between them, this self-picturing horrendously visible through her picture of Milly-as-other. The mixing of the aesthetic with the immoral is particularly vivid in the very first stroke she gives to her self-portrait, seeming to be only a generalising urbane judgment, which unfolds in a desire covered over and presumably excused by the clichés of fashion. Her seeing herself through her opposite, and confessing that sight, makes a picture sufficiently clear to reveal the whole plot to Densher for the first time, demonstrating that indeed pictures are more effective than words: now he sees, being quite "uncommonly" involved.

> "Pearls have such a magic that they suit everyone."
> "They would uncommonly suit you," he frankly returned.
> "Oh yes, I see myself!"
> As she saw herself, suddenly, he saw her—she would have been splendid; and with it he felt more what she was thinking of. (WD, p. 369)

In its extraordinary understatement, this scene reveals her person and her plan, both suddenly focused in a close-up, with Milly's pearls as the *disclosing object* for her, for him, and for us, doubly precious as they show up the envy they create by their very show, in the ghastly self-portrait blatantly mirrored: "Oh yes, I see myself." The reader who might wonder if indeed she does or can, or of what kind Densher's "feeling" might be, wonders still more at such a scene transpiring in Milly's own drawing room, concluding that Kate's predatory observations, together with the uncomfortable exaggerated repetitions of the dialogue—these automatic responses made in the guise of "normal" conversation—betray her operation as that of a mechanical figure, replacing not only human compassion but even natural parlance by obsessive patterning.

In some of the repetitious framing passages we have already seen in this novel, such automatic patterns serve already to mark the *differential borders*, where the recurring phrases, defining qualities, and fixed clichés of categories—"the handsome girl," "her friend," "the sensitive niece"—stress the neat ironies set within the borders. At the extremes, all trace of individual and mobile characterization is stripped away from the plot to form a text hardened into its successive frames, as visible and audible art objects devoid of human nuance and alteration, of the flexibility of a situation or a mind at ease. But nothing has yet equaled Densher's parroting responses, occasioned by his astonishment in this scene—paralleled only by our own—and fully matched, in their automatic drill and echo, by Kate's own repetitions and promises. The figures make a good match so far, each in the excessive mirroring of the other, as the tidy linguistic patterning of the dialogue reveals and betrays their underlying callousness:

> "Since she's to die I'm to marry her?" . . .
> "To marry her."
> "So that when her death has taken place I shall in the natural course have money?"
> . . . "You'll in the natural course have money. We shall in the natural course be free."
> "Oh, oh, oh! " Densher softly murmured.
> "Yes, yes, yes," (WD, p. 374)

As an unthinking ready-made device, impermeable to feeling, the final "Yes, yes, yes" sets a conclusively grating touch on the border of the scene, echoing rhythm of the "Oh, oh, oh! " like the reversed pattern on the outer edges of certain frames, described by Gombrich and others (see "Coming to Our Senses," above, in chapter 2, Perceiving Borders). Whatever trace of guilty conscience there might be is neatly put in wraps by the border in its repeats, like two pairs of three concluding notes in some piece of especially nerve-wracking music.

The dialogue, doubling the former neat repetitions, itself echoes, in Denser's equally callous suggestion, the preceding automatic volley:

> "If you decline to understand me I wholly decline to understand you. I'll do nothing."
>
> "Nothing?" It was as if she tried for the minute to plead.
>
> "I'll do nothing. I'll leave before you. I'll leave tomorrow."
>
> . . . "And if I do understand?"
>
> "I'll do everything."
>
> . . . "Well, I understand."
>
> "On your honour?"
>
> "On my honour."
>
> "You'll come?"
>
> "I'll come." (WD, p. 378)

The doubly terrible suggestion and corresponding response, as they match exactly to make a beautiful fit, are all keyed—to use Goffman's term—to the hard attitude initially taken within these borders; the perfect decorative device covers the inhuman action, perfectly.

SECOND TURN: EXPOSURE AND UNVEILING

Densher's previous deliberate "turn" toward Milly is given its reverie parallel to Milly's last turn in the opposite direction, from the will to live because of him to the abandon of that will because of his discovered deceit, "turning her face to the wall." As Dupee points out, her interior alteration is matched on the outside by a turn in the weather from clear to stormy, and by the "general arrest and interruption" of the Venetian figures serving as background for the scene; this delay, made so evident, silhouettes Densher's hesitation and his aimlessness, recalling our first vision of his vague wandering to and fro in Kensington Gardens. This later scene develops that primary one and keeps its pattern intact.

In a further repeat, Densher's own slow focusing on a figure

in Florian's café, detail to detail to find sight of the whole, re-
produces in kind and rhythm Milly's gaze in the National Gallery
as it first ranged over the general group, then over his own person as the object of the others' interest, before focusing on the
details: from his handkerchief, to his gesture of tapping on his
forehead, to his face, and finally, after the gradual buildup toward recognition, the sudden enlightenment as to the reason for
and the meaning of his presence. Here the narrowing range of
his gaze as it becomes focused serves to direct our attention slowly
and firmly to the center of the view, the suspense holding in an
outer delay the specific shock of perception and eventual central
revelation. Densher's individual arrest before the café, responding to the general slowdown in Venice that day, frames his own
process of recognition just as Milly's was framed by her arrest
before the American group's gaze at Densher. As she then first
saw his handkerchief, the object directing the inward focus, he
sees first two objects: a half-empty glass and then the newspaper
at which the nameless figure glances from time to time when he
is not staring at the wall. Since the recognition procedures work
in the same ways, when finally Lord Mark turns his head to
reveal himself exactly as Densher had last seen him at the palace,
the two revelatory encounters superimposed work like a double
exposure, like Milly's encounter with the Bronzino and the doctor's photographs. Densher is doubly exposed also, both in his
hidden scheme, and to the harshness of the outer elements.

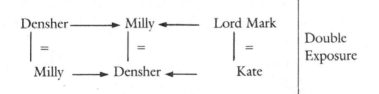

Close on the exposure of Densher by Lord Mark, both literal
and psychological, there follows a parallel unveiling, also literal
and psychological. When Milly's companion Susan arrives in his

room to explain Milly's feelings for him and to probe his, the metaphor used to expose her own sentiments subtly mingles outer with inner to disclose the latter, here literally unveiling it: "her face, under her veil, richly rosy with the driving wind, was—and the veil too—as splashed as if the rain were her tears" (WD, p. 403). The object of the gaze is of course already a symbol of a metaphor: the veil as the frame of visual reference has an unusual power of *fashioning*, for in this passage it both hides and reveals, both covers and uncovers face and feelings. The poetic cliché: rain/tears (as in "Il pleure dans mon coeur / comme il pleut sur la ville") is used to its full, but quietly. The memory of this tear-stained veil will remain in the reader's mind when Kate pushes up her own veil unevenly, in the final scene, superpositioning images triple in the reader's mind and perhaps within that of Densher, who is haunted at that point by the recollection of Kate's similar gesture when she previously came to his room, as predicted by the last automatic dialogue quoted above.

Finally, then, the three veiled and veiling incidents stand in relation to each other, as each concerns Densher, the two episodes with Kate framing the singular one with Susan Stringham as Milly's substitute, since Milly, who will herself never come to these rooms she so wanted to visit, is exposed vicariously in her:

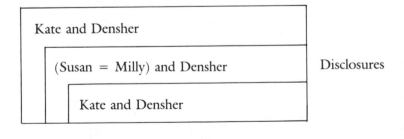

The relations of such encounters to each other act as the repeated encounters of Densher and Milly, each of which is prefaced, and followed, by an implicit or explicit encounter with Kate.

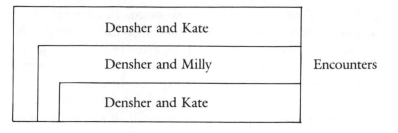

Densher's relations all along are neither free, nor completely disclosed: the interior sense continues to be veiled, at first from Milly, then from himself, and increasingly from Kate, once his disclosures of himself to himself have begun. Finally, he will step outside of the frame in which he has been implicated. Each of the three major disclosing situations mentioned above finds its climax when accompanied by an actual concrete gesture of greater or lesser unveiling before Densher's eyes. Kate's more drastic unveiling or unclothing depends on their agreed continuation of deception or veiling. But in the metaphoric turn from weather to tears, from Susan's exterior veil to her interior sadness seen, Kate's final self-revelation is gradually prepared, that is, the unveiling of her own grasping nature, paralleled by Densher's veiling over and refusal of what Milly has left to him, thus, his implicit redemption by the choice she gave him, and by his final protection of her privacy.

ARRANGEMENTS AND CLOSURE

Milly's condition itself remains closed until the end by an "impenetrable ring fence" made up of smiles and silence and fictions, of the priceless arrangements of appearance, which finally cannot prevent "the great smudge of mortality across the picture, the shadow of pain and horror, finding in no quarter a surface of spirit or of speech that consented to reflect it" (WD, pp. 432-34). As if to protect the smudged portrait of the doomed girl, a hard edge of verbal and conceptual distancing is developed around it by the repetitive technique previously described, where human discourse is systematically replaced by a reductive mechanical categorization. Densher, according to this system, becomes only "the specified . . . the specified," as if in some legal paper, having "his own view . . . his own view"; Dr. Luke Strett becomes "the great man . . . the great man . . . the great man," with stock gestures, closing his eyes or abstaining from speech. In their neutral or conventional labeling, these episodes make a convenient further frame for the distancing of what is too painful to contemplate, setting it apart in that other aesthetic space which leaves no room for moral surmise.

The English tea table, a polite and conventional picture, sets the dreadful scene of final unveiling, as Kate and Densher are confronted in a mutual uncomfortable scrutiny: she studies his face and he hers. Kate's customary "Won't you have any sugar?" is as normal in its setting and yet as inappropriate to the emotional charge of the conversation and the confrontation as was her former speech at Mrs. Lowder's dinner table about Milly as seen and not known: the two scenes may be superimposed in the reader's mind. To Kate's reassuring "But we've not failed," Densher's replying "Oh!" In its awful simplicity is the clue to his crisis of conscience, involving his picture of Kate as utterly changed, in "the light in which she struck the eyes he had brought back from Venice" (WD, P. 455). For his eyes, unclouded and unveiled by the successive scenes, the frame of reference has drastically altered.

Exactly responding to the three veiling and unveiling scenes discussed above, the three final scenes—the first at Lancaster Gate, the next at Kate's sister's house, the final one in Densher's rooms— merge for the reader into one continuous act, where Densher's horror of Kate's cruel lucidity and his own opposing deep reserve are increasingly portrayed. His rage slowly "turns" to "mere cold thought" during their mutual confrontations among the details and delays of these scenes, the most powerful of which is shaped by Densher's meditations before the window in Kate's room, where he gazes out into the lamplit fog, beyond her space within. Thus his final turn is away from Kate, physically and mentally, its force augmented by the slowness and the intensity of the buildup; when Kate throws Milly's last letter to Densher into the fire before he can read it, he reveals his turn away in the slightest of gestures and gestures withdrawn. His motion forward and then back, first to save the letter and then to let it and the corresponding knowledge be destroyed, acts as a double revealer for the situation and for both of them, as their lucidity and their obscurity are mutually framed before the fire in a last enduring picture, where their fear replaces their former love. The situation appears the same; all has altered.

On this scene at Kate's, already recalling another, the final scene at Densher's is superimposed, after a delay of several months. Or then, for the reader, it is inserted or inset into an architectural series, room set into room:

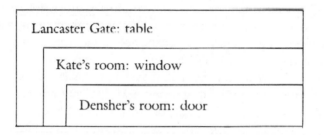

Kate now acts in keeping with the direction she has taken all along: "But she turned to the door, and her headshake was now the end. 'We shall never be again as we were'" (WD, p 497). This is the last set, through which she steps forever, to Densher's conclusive silence. So the book ends with her, as it began, and her final outgoing gesture coincides with the concrete frame of the door, as with the textual frame.

LOOKING BACK

Seen in retrospect, the novel seems a series of unambiguous and clearly bordered scenes, set in mutual response or even superimposed, but each with its moral import, quite unlike *The Golden Bowl*, where a certain ambivalence of style and sense will penetrate the settings, undermine the central scenes, and disquiet the memory. Settings of pictures and figures in *The Wings of the Dove* lead carefully into and toward each other: first, the home at Lancaster Gate, then the great house at Matcham, then the consulting room deep inside the doctor's house, and other pictures still:— the doors and vistas of the large hall in the National Gallery; the balconies and gondolas and cafés of Venice, its palace with the spacious and tapestried rooms and its watery landing; the parks and carriages, the private fireplaces and receiving rooms of London, with their windows looking out.

These settings and framings are indelibly impressed upon the reader's mind, as are the objects and figures they lead to, surround, and present, the language describing them, the metaphors they enclose and in whose light the figures are exposed, and the thoughts which they develop one within the other. Objects reveal and styles focus the figures as they make their turns, signal their delays, accelerate their gestures or retract them, all within the borders into which they are inset and composed.

" 'It was to *that* they reached,' " says Kate finally of the wings of the dove, and of their final forgiveness: " 'They cover us.' 'They cover us,' Densher said" (WD, p. 496). Given the several metatextual references to page and margin, to sign, prefiguration and end, we might take this repeated statement as a final curtain drawn down upon the textual scene, as an effective veil placed at last upon the sight and its object.

Collecting and Containing in The Golden Bowl

... to play the small handful of values really for all they were worth—
and to work my system.
Preface, *The Golden Bowl*[29]

At the summit of James's writing, *The Golden Bowl* is equally the summit of framing works. Introduced as a novel of seeing through one thing to another, illustrating the "indirect and oblique view" that the "writer's frame" can provide, its "shop of the mind, of the author's projected world," stands in exactly the same relation, I think, to James's work as does the artist's studio to the world of Picasso and other artists. It makes a summary of all the rest, collecting, then preserving and reexamining it. The extraordinary proliferation of terms in the preface having to do with the repetition of vision and action and dreaming shows how the reexamination frames the whole sight: re-perusal, re-appropriation, revision, re-writing, re-accepted, re-tasted, re-assimilated, re-enjoyed, renewal, re-representation, re-dreaming. The enjoyment of the bowl's contents is perceptibly increased by its being re-iterated, reframed by James's own visionary and conceptual efforts.

Works containing in themselves their own metaphors of value, price, and imperfection make the most perfect vessels to contain a multiplicity of readings. Since its publication, *The Golden Bowl* has aroused antipathy and passion, uncertainty and enthusiasm, and an attendant range of opposite reactions. The tense ambivalence in which the whole is held includes the moral issues, the evaluative terms, and the figures so melodramatically opposed: "Little" Maggie Verver, the American innocent, initially too attached to her collection-oriented father, Adam, is increasingly devoted to her "dazzling" Italian husband, Prince Amerigo, himself replaying a former mutual attraction with Maggie's friend Charlotte, who becomes, with Maggie's support, Adam's "great" and no less dazzling wife. The motifs of Eden and the New Country, of the great and the small opposed, are thus suggested from the beginning, and they contribute to that "small handful of values" James will play on here. Both dazzling figures have been chosen as prized collectors' items, beautiful and socially useful, from the beginning, when Charlotte's "value" is appraised as if she were a cabinet of treasures, until the end, when she and the Prince are seated at tea like two noble pieces of "human furniture" testifying to a great purchase price. The odd effect of people being evaluated like objects, with moral, mental, and material speculations subtly interwoven, furnishes the tense and glittering display of James's last great novel, where visual sensitivity is at its height.

His announced criteria of "large unity" and the "grace of intensity"[30] are fully met, while the unresolved ending, befitting the Mannerist art of his own "high" style, conveys both the "terror of life" and the splendor of conscious art. As James wanted the various windows that look in on and out from the text to show varying outlooks upon the object viewed, so the centrally focused bowl itself and the crack under the splendid surface are subject to drastic shifts in vision and understanding, which set them vibrating.

HIGH FRAMING

Virginia Woolf offers the best picture of James's art with its inimitable style, "which, as it imposes its stamp, sets apart the object thus consecrated and makes it no longer part of ourselves."[31] For the situation to be sufficiently "high" (a term that James repeatedly uses in the sense of great visibility, along the same lines as his recurring injunctions to "dramatise it, dramatise it!" NT, 17, p. xii), it must be removed from the ordinary world we inhibit by its singular form. Here the salient scenes are notable by their lofty and privileged settings (balconies, stairs, high rooms) or then by insetting and outlining (placing in a window or door, or raised upon a slight pedestal). These are the *rises* in the text, whose surface shimmers with "what is beneath it and what throbs and gleams through," for an effect of density (NT, 18, p. v). "We want it clear, goodness knows, but we also want it thick, and we get the thickness in the human consciousness that entertains and records, that amplifies and interprets it" (NT, 18, p. xix). As James chose his observing figures to be "registers or reflectors," sometimes intelligent, sometimes passionate, and sometimes just curious, working in alternation, so half of the novel is said to be composed of the Prince's view, the other, vibrant and not without lucidity. This double setting allows a multiplicity of viewpoints far beyond its supposed doubleness: but the duplicity pervades the text. What James said of *The Wings of the Dove* he could more surely still have said of *The Golden Bowl*: that between the face and the back of the medal he holds out, the observer may opt, for the medal simply hangs (NT, 19, p. viii). This image recurs in the latter novel, as if the prefatory metaphor had been absorbed, as Maggie imagines the portraits of the Prince and Charlotte facing each other, hung on a chain around her own neck; later, Charlotte will be pictured with a silk cord around her neck, held by Adam. The images themselves dangle, mutually determined in their double suspense.

The "highest" scenes, variously set apart by repetition, cropping, retarding, insetting, and outlining, can refer to the overpowering central metaphor of the golden bowl itself, the deceptive, splendid, and faulty vessel of the novel taking its name and form, even down to the crack in the center of its consciousness, divided between Prince and Princess. However the title is interpreted—as the golden pitcher "broken at the fountain," or as in Blake's question: "Can wisdom be kept in a silver rod / Or live in a golden bowl?"[32] the secret of the novel flawed in its center is both gilded and guilty, for the "fault" is contained in the text like a deep ambivalence corrupting all the relations between figures and actors, readers and inside observers. In his preface to the novel, James speaks of the re-vision, the rereading, and the redreaming of his own text, displayed in a "shop of the mind . . . in which objects are primarily related to each other" (GB, p. 13). The object is not simply found but rather *encountered* as if it were on the same level as the encountering mind, the accurate projection of the creator's mind, and of equal measure.

FLOWER AND VESSEL

The first scene noticeably exhibited shows two characters face to face at tea, the Prince and Fanny Assingham,[33] who has arranged his marriage to Maggie. The first metaphors of ship and direction, together with the verbs of seeing and knowing, prepare for the text as *vessel*:

> "I must keep your sail in sight for orientation. . . . You *must* be my lead." . . .

"What vessel, in the world, have I?" . . .
"I shall keep this spot in sight . . . I can do pretty well in
anything I *see*. But I've got to see it first. . . . Therefore it is
that I want, that I shall always want, your eyes. Through
them I wish to look—even at the risk of their showing me
what I mayn't like. For then," he wound up, "I shall know."
(GB, pp. 45-48)

This typically oblique dialogue prepares the scene of Mrs. Assingham's breaking the vessel, at which point she will indeed
show him what he will not like to see, but will then know. It is
the first of many passages heavily bordered by its motif of perception, picturing two people staring, as it were, at their own
pose and at their joint silence, in mutual and knowledgeable contemplation:

> The unspoken had come up, and there was a crisis—neither
> could have said how long it lasted—during which they were
> reduced, for all interchange, to looking at each other on
> quite an inordinate scale. They might at this moment, in
> this positively portentous stillness, have been keeping it up
> for a wager, sitting for their photograph or even enacting a
> *tableau vivant*.
>
> The spectator of whom they would thus well have been
> worthy might have read meanings of his own into the in-
> tensity of their communion. (GB, pp. 49-50)

This picture serves at once as a *delay* around the dialogue, a temporal marking, and as an interior photograph, a developing and
revealing picture consciously set, and set about, with multiple
implications: "The spectator of whom they would thus have been
worthy might have read meanings of his own into the intensity
of their communion." Before this observing audience, appraising
the "just value" of relations and potentialities, Charlotte displays
her will-to-the-top in the metaphoric staging of her past and
future relations with the Prince, setting the picture before his
eyes for him to fit it into her own framing: "She would take it

high—up, up, up, ever so high. Well then, he would do the same; no height would be too great for them" (GB, p. 62). Indeed, the arrangement will be constantly vertical, with Charlotte's majestic beauty poised on stairs and balconies; in the first of these public presentations, her slow rise up the monumental staircase to await the Prince, wearing her "high" tiara, shows off her "high" delight in the highest society and her "high" self-conscious stance. The jarring repetition of this word as her leit-motif keeps her always visible and always on the rise, until she and the Prince make "their conspicuous return together to the upper rooms," at the summit of all the converging gazes: their shining appearance is, thanks to her, carefully framed, placed, arranged, and privileged, to be speculated upon. The picture is extreme beyond measure, their aspect at once "outshining, over-looking, overtopping"; it would take a golden frame to set it off, or a golden bowl to contain it.

A series of liquid metaphors links the container and its content to the vessel where ideas are floating about, plunging, or sub-merged, and from which they are served. Thus the recalled scene of Charlotte's finding and offering and the Prince's rejection of the gilt-covered crystal bowl in the past is ironically replaced in the present by a mere teacup; on a rainy day, these two drink a toast, but only in tea, to their "sacred" duty toward their spouses, before celebrating on the contrary their own renewed passion, high through its own textual "rises" and its innumerable meta phoric elevations. They have "led up" to this sublimity, thinks the Prince. This high crisis within a tea cup as a "safe" and social receptacle for communion ("a kind of unexampled receptacle, letting it spread and spread, but at the same time elastically en-closing it, banking it in, for softness, as with billows of eider-down," GB, p. 227) is placed in an implicit relation to the fragile bowl, the finality sensible in the words "break," "shatter," and "crack," all suddenly appearing in this densely erotic passage in its own "spread" and violent shattering: "Then of a sudden, through this tightened circle, as at the issue of a narrow strait into the sea beyond, everything broke up, broke down, gave way, melted and mingled" (GB, p. 237). The text itself has tightened like the circle in the hold of tension and release. The action here, as elsewhere in the book, is interior and sensible in vibration rather than linear and active: this communion in a chalice, as a desire fulfilled, quivers before the reader's eyes throughout the novel.

Superimposed upon that tense scene of desire and communion is the "great painting" of the Prince's collection, holding the same two figures up to view, a "bright" picture perfectly varnished and framed for him to "hang." The day breaks at Matcham, blooming like a gigantic, desirable flower, which he has "only to gather." The aural increases the visual brightness; the suggestive "chink of gold" flashes like a mirror in the sun, reflecting the picture in a sudden hardening of the flower from its natural beauty into gold and, as crystal, sparkling outward with its bloom. The vaguely unpleasant offer of her beauty, built up in value, makes a material hardening of the natural, as, silhouetted on the balcony "like a blossom," she tosses him a "rich" white rosebud, a metaphor repeated five times. It continues to grow "richer" and larger and lovelier, in the image fusing gold and flower, day and pearl. The hard worth of the whole gift is ironised by his having "sold himself" for this situation whose images now flicker upon each other in a silent filmic sequence focusing on his freedom, seen "as some huge precious pearl. . . ." Here, precisely, it was, incarnate; its size and its value grew as Mrs. Verver appeared, afar off, in one of the smaller doorways. She came toward him in silence, while he moved to meet her; the great scale of this particular front, at Matcham, multiplied thus, in the golden morning, the stages of their meeting and the successions of their consciousness" (GB, pp. 268-69). As the balcony recalls the other balconies where we have seen Charlotte, and the framing door, other doors, the approaching figures enlarge steplike "in stages." The flower, changed to pearl, increases in the mind and before the eyes, not in a continuous flow, but in nervously lit bursts of consciousness. Now the teacup and the chalice of the former buildup lead to the central image of communion: "I feel the day like a great gold cup that we must somehow drain together" (GB, p. 269), he says, and the sacralized and present cup, now as great as the bowl and as rich in its gold, is to be drained and "sounded." In that verb the tone of the crystal sounds through the gift itself, and the phrase "gilded crystal bowl" appears as the verbal and visual summit of the day's rise.

As indeed this scene is plumbed and "sounded," a further irony is heard in the conversation beneath "tiers of windows," where the potential implications of pain and tears underlie a dialogue already vibrant in its understatement: "Don't you think too much of 'cracks,' and aren't you too afraid of them?" asks Charlotte. Risk for yourself whatever you like, he responds, stressing how sure his own investments must be, and her own solitude. They may drain the golden cup of a single day, but, as he need not point out, he has already refused the "whole" golden bowl, refused it wholly, in act as in metaphor.

IRONIES OF SEEING

In the second book, the mental vibrations are attributed to the Princess, as she gazes at the suggestive metaphor of an ivory tower, itself transformed into a marvelously "outlandish" pagoda, as excessive as the former construction of the scene of Charlotte and the Prince "outshining, overlooking, overtopping" on the staircase. The Princess "vibrates" with desire before the porcelain-covered pagoda as the princely continuation of her coveted tower, tinkling with tiny silver bells like quite a good investment, shimmering in the light but impenetrable from "little" Maggie's height; the windows are placed very high, she says, recalling Charlotte's "high, high, high" and her "up, up, up." Her realization, if "rightly looked at," of the intensity of her own passion before the princely tower coincides with the pretense by Charlotte and the Prince of seeing Gloucester Cathedral, their excuse serving as the ironic equivalent of that tower imagined, so that the real church tower as the falsely stated object of desire covers over both the suggestive metaphor and the erotic reality.

Maggie's vibrating desire and its imagination prepare the great scene of homecoming for which she bedecks herself in jewels to sit as for a picture, waiting, marking a temporal delay, a spatial void of action, and a great silence at the novel's center; the Prince appears silhouetted in the door, contemplating with surprise the unaccustomed: Maggie's presence and her ornaments, which the reader is given to see again in his surprised pause before the static silent scene. He registers only blankness as the scene focuses on his sight and on the repeating words of the verbal border: "She had naturally had on the spot no ready notion of what he might want to see; it was enough for a ready notion, not to speak of a beating heart, that he *did* see, that he saw his wife in her own drawing-room at the hour when she would most properly be there" (GB, p. 310). The repetitions overstating the understatement have the pulsations of that heart beat. Over the "immense little scene" is superimposed a cliché-type scene of the waiting wife and the errant husband returning. On the golden cup of the day for the other couple, she superimposes, in her thought only, the unspoken and suggestive biblical image of her anguished desire and pain: "my cup runneth over": "It's all very well, and I perfectly see how beautiful it is, all round; but there comes a day when something snaps, when the full cup, filled to the very brim, begins to flow over. That's what has happened to my need of you—the cup, all day, has been too full to carry. So here I am with it, spilling it over you—and just for the reason that is the reason of my life" (GB, p. 311). But the Prince goes upstairs for a bath, alone, as if to wash off what she spills, balancing Maggie's imagined "bath" of sweetness wherein he and Charlotte have attempted to drown her sight. Maggie's mental images follow in rapid succession, governed by the "fortune" of "having such a dazzling husband," as a possession of great worth.

In a contrasting imagined scene, she and her father are driven in a carriage by the other two: will she leap down from the carriage to make her own destiny? Whereas Charlotte's seem given effortlessly to her, all Maggie's pictures are of her making, and are hung in memory around her neck like a string of pearls, arranged as if to choke her—haunting, like the two-faced locket she imagines about her neck, with pictures of Charlotte and the Prince closed up together, the exact opposite of the Prince's pearl of freedom as it grows, to his advantage always.

Her perception clarifies: as Charlotte watches and waits, with her beauty framed by a window, Maggie sees the situation in high color: "And in the light, strange and coloured, like that of a painted picture, which fixed the impression for her, objects took on values not hitherto so far shown" (GB, p. 320). This explicitly pictorial framing, like that of the Prince in the doorway, like that of the three figures around the bridge table outlined in the light, reveals what is within, as well as outside, the text.

Against the Prince's natural superpositioning, like that of Charlotte, Maggie has to struggle; he stands on a step raised slightly above hers, as they return home, and the straight line of the servants attending them prevents any swerve in custom. This revealing straightedged picture too is, like any of the other framing fictions, "tremendously ordered and fixed." The Prince's dread of disorder, of cracks in the setup, glazes over the picture surface. Of course, the whole picture has been arranged for Maggie so that its domestic order is a cover-up, cropping off the natural suspicions at the edge. There are repeated gestures and visiting habits, arranged to such a point that the normal situation—Maggie's being at home when the Prince returns—appears abnormal. But the arrangement takes over, and the repetition becomes nervous as Maggie observes it: Charlotte standing at the window, Charlotte pacing up and down. Charlotte's movements are no longer ascending; they must all occur in a limited space. Repeatedly, she resembles the lady of a Whistler painting, for example, a symphony in yellow: will the Prince not tire, wonders Maggie, of seeing Charlotte displayed, "always up on the rampart, erect and elegant, with her laceflounced parasol now folded and now shouldered, march to and fro against a gold-coloured east or west?" (GB, p. 39). The superb harmony of tones and of ordered pacing takes at least visible precedence over natural emotion, this painterly touch especially on view in the central picture of the novel, where that gold-colored horizon is replaced by the gold of the bowl itself, which Maggie has purchased, now posed on the edge of a mantel, and in front of which she stands as an elegantly dressed young woman in an oriental Whistlerian mode.[34]

BREAKAGE AND ARREST

Like the first scene commented on here, the central scene is introduced for our perception and for that of the included figures by the key perceptual notions of seeing and knowing. The story of the bowl as a cracked gilt cup is told as an *inset* into the text, as the merchant exposes the previous intimacy of the Prince and Charlotte neatly displayed in his memory, the latter triggered by their photographs, side by side, those revealing objects so preciously standing for show, pictures at an exhibition of betrayal in Maggie's own home: having thus so unwittingly arranged the exhibition and then purchased the bowl, she has provided the setting for the pictures and later for the revelation. At Mrs. Assingham's counsel to make light of it all, "I see," says Maggie, but she turns away toward the outside to look, not out at its light, but in, while hiding from view. This reverses the previous pictures of Charlotte's high framing on balconies, at windows, at doors, for she conceals herself: "moving to the window as if still to keep something in her face from sight" (GB, p. 419). The background is set in red, in preparation for the ensuing action, which takes place silhouetted against this light: "She had come away from her window, one of the three by which the wide room, enjoying an advantageous 'back', commanded the western sky and caught a glimpse of the evening flush; while Mrs. Assingham, possessed of the bowl, and possessed too of this indication of a flaw, approached another for the benefit of the slowly-fading light" (GB, p. 420). The high stress falls, against this dying light, on the indications of seeing ("caught a glimpse"), possessing (at once the knowledge, the proof, and the flaw), and imperfection (the flaw itself): the evening's flush suggests a strong human emotion, transposed even upon the background of a natural setting. The scene is placed in high lighting, verbal and visual.

A temporal *delay* ensues, before the bowl's breaking, over which the one who arranged both marriages officiates: in the redness, after the revelation and this silent prelude, the central ceremony is sensed as inevitable and fitting. As Mrs. Assingham raises the bowl over her head, she smiles solemnly at Maggie to signal the start of the culminating act, in a perfectly framed moment where the evening glow will be reflected in a double flush upon the figures themselves:

> So for an instant, full of her thought and of her act, she held the precious vessel, and then, with due note taken of the margin of the polished floor, bare, fine and hard in the embrasure of her window, she dashed it boldly to the ground, where she had the thrill of seeing it, with the violence of the crash, lie shattered. She had flushed with the force of her effort, as Maggie had flushed with wonder at the sight, and this high reflection in their faces was all that passed between them for a minute more. (GB, p. 421)

Around the shattering, a silence and a pause. Suddenly, the Prince, framed in the doorway, is watching Maggie, as upon his previous return. She will try to repair the bowl, but in her own fidelity and passion can significantly carry at the same time only two of the three fragments to pose them on the mantel, as if it were a ritual altar for remarriage, for communion, and for reconciliation. The foot of the bowl, solid and detached, must be placed between the others to save the whole, and if the three parts will not stay joined, the image just repeats the problem of a man between two women, a situation that can be handled only by covering over the fault, as before, or its exposure, as at the present: "She could only lay the almost equal parts of the vessel carefully beside their pedestal and leave them thus before her husband's eyes" (GB, p. 424).

In the total silence still surrounding the scene and focusing its central act, at the side of which picture stands the Prince in his own door frame, the ritual manner and dramatically slow gestures of the Princess, all as unaccustomed as her elaborate costume, make symbolic reparation for both the crack and the breakage, neither of which are due to her; only the innocent victim, having suffered, can repair. The oppositions between dark inner state and outer light, and between inner impatience and actual act place a contrasting paradoxical and psychological border around Maggie's act: "it had all seemed to her to take a longer time than anything she had ever so quickly accomplished." Her perception forces his, for she has made him see her knowledge, and that changes all. The high scene is worked up to painful pitch by the repetitions of the words, nerve-wracking in their obsessiveness, and necessary: "though the bowl had been broken, her reason hadn't; the reason for which she had made up her mind, the reason for which she had summoned her friend, the reason for which she had prepared the place for her husband's eyes; it was all one reason. . . . Only *see*, see that *I* see" (GB, pp. 424-25).

Even Maggie's interior meditation has its own repetitive verbal borders that call attention to her smashing the object, as if it were some fetish with magic power, bestowed now on the one who most needs it: "her husband would have, on the whole question, a new need of her, a need which was in fact being born between them . . . would indeed . . . be *really* needing her . . . a proved necessity to him" (GB, p. 426). Once again, the language stresses vision itself, the real central act to be contemplated and valued, more than the pictures that have brought it about: " 'Yes, look, look' . . . 'look, look . . . Look at the possibility' " (GB, p. 427).

In the strong scansion of the dialogue, the repeating key words alternate with marked pauses for the interior development of the knowledge referred to:

"Oh, the thing I've known best of all. . . . That, I think," she added, "is the way I've best known."
"Known?" he repeated after a moment.
"Known. Known that. . . . Known there were things . . ."

"Would they have made a difference if you *had* known them?" (GB, p. 435)[35]

"What I know," she repeats, and this incessant and deliberately inhuman or unnatural iteration of her knowledge, "her repeated distinct 'know, know,' " strongly affects the Prince's nerves, as well as the reader's own. This artificiality or mechanical repetition draws a heavy border around the scene, set apart obviously as the verbal automatism of the hurt mind isolates it and its interlocutor, an obsessive framing, spectacular in its degree. Maggie's need for the Prince to recognize her knowledge composes this symphony in one color, this scene keyed by one tone, this vision prepared at length by all the preceding pictures of the novel:

> "Your knowing was—from the moment you did come in—all I had in view." And she sounded it again. He should have it once more. "Your knowing that I've ceased—"
> "That you've ceased—?". . .
> "Why, to be as I was. *Not* to know."
> . . . "Then does anyone else know?" (GB, p. 437)

In front of Maggie rises a clear mental picture of her father and Charlotte "having gropingly to go on, always not knowing and not knowing. The picture flushed at the same time with all its essential colour" (GB, p. 437). Just as she will demand that the Prince *see*, she will not enlighten Charlotte, seeing that he does not either; the latter will finally be cut from the picture, framed out into the darkness of the new world, leaving Maggie with the wisdom and the melancholy of the old. The knowledge of her father is perhaps identical to hers, yet neither she nor we will ever know, for this is one of the brilliant borders of the painting as it is psychologically cropped.

In its conclusion, the scene is set aside by yet another arrest: " 'Find out the rest—.' 'Find it out?' He waited. She stood before him a moment—it took that time to go on" (GB, p. 438). And then, with the most minimal of gestures, she rings a bell to stop the action short, summoning a servant to clear up, but more meaningfully, putting the final touch upon the scene: "Find out for yourself." She has given, for the first time, and for all time, *the order* that will prevail.

This great passage, discussed at length in its centrality to the novel, betrays an enormous tension in the slowness of its gestures and pauses, its arrests and hesitations, its silence and its high stress. The borders of verbal reinforcement are themselves clearly set into the opening and closing, or the top and bottom edges of Maggie's initial exposition: first, of her private knowledge and her final injunction to the Prince to search for his own knowledge, relating to the knowledge of others, where the jangling repeats set the scene apart. Second, by the opening of the door for the Prince, which initiates the passage, terminated by the closing of the door upon him. In sum, the extraordinary scene of the breaking of the vessel, after the slow and costumed ritual of sacrifice, prepares the two partners' perception of a new mutual understanding, repairing at last the *fault* between the two parts of a text, the flaw in perception which neither alone could fix, now made positive as a formal and psychological *brisure* or articulation between the two viewpoints.

PLAYING AND PERSPECTIVES: DIPTYCH

One of the last splendidly framed scenes already referred to hides within itself multiple perspectives on dignity and ugliness. Maggie stops on a dark balcony, *arrested* before a brightly lit window, where the others are tranquilly playing bridge, psychologically paralyzed before the spectacle of the others revealed in their true situation: her "husband's mistress" and her "father's wife" exposed as the same person. The recognition is heavily set in a visual border like that of the Prince on the two occasions he hesitated in the doorway, before the spectacle of Maggie waiting, that is, of Maggie having understood. As she glimpses now the back of the stage props, the evil "behind so much trusted, so much pretended, nobleness, cleverness, tenderness" (GB, p. 459), the echo of the final syllable triply stresses the irony of the scene where feelings are exposed as what they are, against what they seemed. This was a good game.[36]

Faced with the opposing group from which she is isolated, she walks by on the balcony, stops, looks again, and suddenly rises to the height required of her. For the second time we see her so raised, visually and morally, and she will not fall. The Judas kiss imposed on Maggie by the tigress Charlotte—so that Maggie will accord Charlotte an implicit pardon, taken by force, for what is never confessed—sets this highly visual encounter in a sacrificial light. We are reminded, here again, of the sweetness of Milly wronged, played against Kate's vital brutality. Charlotte's high positioning on the stairs, the balcony, the tower, and at the window, have been gradually replaced by Maggie's own window framing against the red background for the breaking of the bowl, and now this exposed height. Later she is at a higher-perched window, in her "high room," whose shutters frame her like those of a camera that has finally found its object. Her intense and self-made passion is focused at the center of the picture now, replacing the glorious beings so naturally endowed for "outstripping" and "outshining."

As a parallel, Charlotte replaces Maggie in the images of claustration; where Maggie formerly sensed herself forced into a series of imprisoning metaphors—a tepid bath whose walls block her sight, a pool of despair, a garden too small—so Charlotte, who has been, in the Judas scene, compared to a tiger just escaped from his cage, is now compared to an anguished creature whose cries Maggie hears with sympathy, hiding her head from them in the cushions of her window seat. This image superimposes itself upon that of Milly with her head down, leaning in despair against her palace window, picture fitting upon picture.

In a like superposition and an implicit response to this high scene is set a second, where these figures are again the principals: in the outside rotunda where Maggie comes to find and release Charlotte from her suffering. At this point, we see through Maggie's eyes, which are like frames for our own vision, and Maggie has seen Charlotte from the window; as we focus on Charlotte, descending the stairs, at first only the pale green of her parasol is visible—again, like a colorful spot on some canvas of Whistler—so that the majestic figure meant for, and now accustomed to, monumental stairways and balcony parade is reduced to this mere impression of an accessory object, only a colored spot, going downward instead of up the "rise." Her green parasol makes a spot of color in the canvas, as does Madame de Vionnet's pink parasol coming down the river in *The Ambassadors*.

The former high and dramatic lighting of the bridge-playing scene whose bright window frames the players, the rectangle of their lighted window against the dark of the balcony, is now echoed by the full tones of light and dark in the vine-covered retreat, deeply shaded after the sun-struck paths of noon.[37] En-fevered, Charlotte is caught again like a caged animal, trapped in a frantic pose: "Charlotte had paused there, in her frenzy, or whatever it was to be called; the place was a conceivable retreat, and she was staring before her, from the seat to which she ap-peared to have sunk, all unwittingly, as Maggie stopped at the beginning of one of the perspectives" (GB, p. 508). The verbs replace Charlotte's former lofty actions by signs of defeat: "paused," "staring," "sunk" into a seated position, she looks at nothing, while Maggie stops short in a voluntary arrest, placed "at the beginning of one of the perspectives," to look at this figure who has betrayed her but for whom she will provide the excuses and the departure.

Then the positions of imprisonment and liberty, of sunkenness and rise, will be reversed by Maggie's repeated generosity, and Charlotte, presumably unaware of her knowledge, will be able to make one more elegant traverse over the threshold of the ro-tunda outward, toward an apparent freedom. As Maggie replaces her within the drama of the cagelike rotunda, the latter subsumes in its borders the motif of the pagoda from Maggie's imaginary garden earlier, where Charlotte seemed to be enclosed with the Prince: the setting of this scene is superimposed upon that other. Maggie sinks down, *repeating* Charlotte's exact attitude, when she "appeared to have sunk." Ironically, by becoming her re-placement, by her humility, and her generous silence, Maggie has risen to the high position Charlotte has once occupied: "She watched her, splendid and erect, float down the long vista; then she sank upon a seat. Yes, she had done all" (GB, p. 514).

But in spite of this vaguely Christlike reverberation of Maggie's words—"she had done all"—and her sacrificial and vicarious positioning in Charlotte's cage—the latter's elegant figure never stops crossing the "further end of any perspective" (GB, p. 521), that is, any perspective Maggie might have, as Charlotte obsesses all the alleys of Maggie's perplexed mind. The irony of the vessel broken is that it remains to haunt the spirit: Maggie's vivid picturing of Charlotte's imagined discourse that might be addressed to Maggie herself, is keyed by the metaphor of the golden vessel with its conscious and heady, if interrupted, nourishment. Charlotte might well say, "You haven't been broken with, because in *your* relation what can there have been, worth speaking of, to break? Ours was everything a relation could be, filled to the brim with the wine of consciousness. . . . Why condemned after a couple of short years to find the golden flame oh, the golden flame!—a mere handful of black ashes?" (GB, p. 521). Maggie's self-torture in those words, projected into the other's mind, finds the images of cup and contained ardor to refer to her own cup of desire, with the gold as enhancement of the sparkling and ardent beverage, and the black as the bitter dregs remaining when ardor has burned itself out. In the reader's own framing of the implied and inset discourse, the first ritual of the polite teacup, leading to the cup and bowl of the glorious and illicit day, as to the golden bowl itself, creates in this projected and imagined picture the intense vibration characteristic of a Jamesian text at its height of arrangement. This is a perfectly "composed" picture.

FINAL PICTURE

On the eve of the Ververs' departure for America, a scene thus bordered with a sharp temporal and spatial edge makes a diptych. In one half of it, Maggie contemplates her father contemplating the Florentine painting he had given her and her husband for their wedding gift, a past which now serves in the present as the interior or framed frame, as the developing object. Resembling Adam's conscience as his daughter sees it, the pictured present, unlike the bowl almost given to the Prince by Charlotte for the same occasion, has neither fault nor crack: "the beauty of his sentiment looked out at her, always, from the beauty of the rest, as if the frame made positively a window for his spiritual face" (GB, p. 541). This is, of course, her picturing of the picture, where she insets his face in a transfer of value preparatory for the scene.

The other half of the diptych, formed by the Prince and Charlotte seated in conversation nearby, taking tea, refers back to the initial tableau of my discussion, to the Prince seated in conversation at tea with Mrs. Assingham. It also refers back to or contains the tea-taking scene between the same splendid couple when the entire text, and their lives with it, temporarily "broke up, broke down," under the force of their passion concentrated in a cup, a reduced model of the bowl:

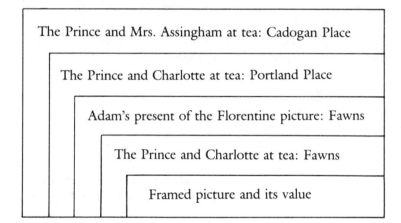

The present scene has the same kind of aesthetic value as does the Florentine painting, giving it price and frame, just as the "real" Lambinet painting in *The Ambassadors* frames the fictive scene on the river, but the pictures are real at one remove: this "real" and this "artistic" applied to pictures and to scenes are constantly set in a mutual vibration, within the fictive frame. What, after all, is "real" in a painting? In James, the "natural," apart from the pictured and the social, has a peculiar status. "The two noble persons seated, in conversation, at tea, fell thus into the splendid effect and the general harmony: Mrs. Verver and the Prince fairly 'placed' themselves, however unwittingly, as high expressions of the kind of furniture required, aesthetically, by such a scene" (GB, p. 541). The juxtaposed use of the terms "placed" and "high" gives the same effect as Charlotte's first being presented as a cabinet of elegant treasures. These two figures, visually suited to each other, bear witness to a high power of selection: "*Le compte y est.* You've got some good things" (GB, p. 541), says Adam to Maggie. The suggested awfulness of collecting people as if they were fine paintings and furniture is matched by the irony of the split between value that is real and value that is only apparent: "They were parting, in the light of it, absolutely on Charlotte's *value*" (GB, p. 545). As to whom the value *is* valuable, and of what sort it is, as to its fluctuations in worth, the question is left open.

After seeing the carriage off, Maggie makes her final rise, back up the stairs, alone, replacing Charlotte who once mounted in pride, and then descended to find refuge. Just as before in the pagoda she had replaced her in humility ("sank"), Maggie ends by replacing Charlotte at the height. When, after a *delay*, she goes out upon the balcony, she takes up her official position there, not of show, but of situation.

Charlotte on "diplomatic stairs"

Charlotte on Portland Place stairs

Charlotte on Matcham balcony

Charlotte on Eaton Square balcony

Charlotte at Eaton Square window

=	Charlotte joins		Maggie on Fawns balcony	=
			Maggie at Fawns window	
	Charlotte down	&	Maggie up Fawns stairs	
			Maggie on Fawns balcony	

The emptiness around the scene is spatial also, and silent, suddenly fraught with emotional weight, that of a loneliness corresponding to the emptiness around: Maggie on the balcony watching the departing carriage sees only a "great grey space, on which, as on the room still more, the shadow of dusk had fallen. Here, at first, her husband had not joined her" (GB, p. 546). To the end, fast approaching now, he will keep, at least in appearance, that role of husband, rather than the coldly formal title of "The Prince." But the loneliness is no less sensed.

The shadow, in falling, prepares a bare stage for the ripened fruit, which has taken the place and the color of the golden bowl, here in this room they now have the "freedom" to dwell in together. A remarkable stillness surrounds the final vigil or watch, in the emptiness of the room, creating in the text a marking pause for stress: "so that whatever next took place in it was foredoomed to remarkable salience" (GB, p. 546). And directly set into that border of silence, the question is uttered toward which the rest of the volume has slowly led: "She knew at last really why—and how she had been inspired and guided, how she had been persistently able, how, to her soul, all the while, it had been for the sake of this end. Here it was, then, the moment, the golden fruit that had shone from afar; only, what *were* these things, in the fact, for the hand and for the lips, when tested, when tasted—what were they as a reward?" (GB, p. 546). As with many of the other moments held in tight borders, verbal and perceptual, knowledge is the guiding and initiatory concept. The golden bowl stands here as the unique referent for this golden fruit in full focus, centralized as an apple without Adam, and held up finally so that its contents may be tasted as the bowl was held up to view.

Her husband opens the door, and as he is outlined there, Maggie's view of him is "renewed in intensity," while accompanied by an awful suspicion of the high price he must pay her for her past pain. Her generous and real terror at the confession which he owes and will have to pay makes her refuse speculation, interest, and self-interest. From that moment on, the vocabulary of

value received and appreciated, of debts and accounts to be settled, can be thrust aside with all the trappings of gold, paying,
amount, number, moneybags, and even all reward. Like Densher's not wanting to know even the sum of Milly's gift, involved
as he finally is in no terms but the moral, Maggie here "finishes"
off—for it is indeed the "end," the subject in a manner whose
expression assumes a majestic resonance, a verbal rise to correspond with her moral and physical rise already documented and
pictured. Her terms, for she has completed her final rise in stature, are those of an absolute pardon and an inescapable love,
"for everything that was deep in his being and everything that
was fair in his face" (GB, p. 547). Instead of awaiting her husband's confession, she offers, in conclusion, a eulogy of her rival,
inspiring not only his admiration, but also his last *delay*: "It kept
him before her therefore, taking in—or trying to—what she so
wonderfully gave" (GB, p. 547).

That his statement, on which this novel of seeing and picturing and consciousness concludes, can be so diversely interpreted
indicates that the last essential work of framing is to be left to
each reader: "close to her, her face kept before him, his hands
holding her shoulders, his whole act enclosing her, he presently
echoed: "See? I see nothing but *you*.' And the truth of it had,
with this force, after a moment, so strangely lighted his eyes that,
as if for pity and dread of them, she buried her own in his breast"
(GB, p. 547). For "pity and dread": Maggie's long ordeal has
here its Aristotelian catharsis, in the drama finally enclosed in her
husband's eyes for its only frame, now that the others have departed—characters and props alike. There are no more objects in
this final scene, neither paintings nor bowls, nothing to collect
or to recollect, in the bare light.

The steep price of lucidity arouses pity and dread, even after
the subsidence of the former terror; Maggie and Amerigo pay
equally for the knowledge and the pain, in their mutual loss of
Charlotte's high brilliance on one hand, and of Adam's quiet
affection on the other. The question of values must be left open
on the psychological as well as the moral side. It is deliberately

"kept" at a problematic peak: Just how high has Maggie risen in her husband's eyes by the truly terrible intensity of her passion? Is that increase in stature and situation sufficient to compensate for the other losses? Is the apparent fate of these unlike beings fearful after all this pain, most of it unspoken? And, gathering into itself all the other questions: Is the golden fruit to be a bitter one, or another and better "great gold cup" of day, freely enjoyed?

Presumably, *The Golden Bowl* represents, also, the Prince and not what he might have seemed to be; he is repaired, to some extent, by Maggie's knowledge, as she restores to moral order what was originally presented as "disordered." Maggie, formerly seen as "little," like "little Aggie" and even "little Nanda," grows by accepting, with a great deal of dignity, a certain and terrible ambiguity. As Adam says to the Prince, "For living with, you're a pure and perfect crystal." The value of such crystal and its durability, the worth of the "golden fruit" and its perishability, are put in question by her newly exploring sensitivity. The paradise she expels from Fawns, and from which she is thereby expelled in her turn, will retain at least the shadow of a crack, its ineffaceable memory in her mind, as in ours.[38]

No less crucial a question remains: What does the frame hold when there is only half a picture? "I see nothing but *you*": Is the ambiguity visible to Maggie also, and is it intended in the text? Does the reader's individual frame here occasion a "misreading" or a warp in the structure perceived? The uncertain note *sounded*, deep and probing, is potentially far more destructive than the fiction the cup seemed to contain. This lack of final knowledge might prove more awful even than the double betrayal in the tale; knowledge not given cannot, even by passion, be redeemed.

Such enclosure of knowledge and enigmatic sight together in a vessel whose very crack guarantees its interest, its modicum of substance, and its maximum of tension, composes the high style of the whole. The glittering language of evaluation, price, and gift turns finally about itself, framing a work essentially unframable and uncollectable and so, by a final paradox, fully repaying the reader's principal investment.

RECALLING AND RESTORING IN PROUST'S TIME

J'avais vécu comme un peintre. . .
  Le temps retrouvé

Lasting and Overlaying

Throughout *Combray*, a few things endure: Marcel's sobs, quieted once, but like the convent bells covered over in the day, heard again in the still evening; or the smell of "invisible and persistent lilacs" through the rain; or a moonlit night "ruining," by dissolving, the profile of whatever it touches. The reader is brought to the keenest awareness of such sensations, to the sound, scent, and sight of the three parallel and persistent experiences, often by a comparison with something else and some other moment, that is, by a transposition of the remembered element into the world of the presently perceived. In these repositionings or overlays, the original sensation is displaced and replaced both beneath and above the sensations of the moment, transforming the thinness of any individual experience into the densely poetic stuff of memory.

Now in both temporal and spatial superpositioning, the reader must be dependent. Given a necessarily linear script, the reader depends upon the narrator's backward reference for the alignment of one episode under another's time and place, the remembered sight or sound apprehended once more, literally, brought back to the senses by the triggering moment, through which the past can be seen, as through a transparency. That the two episodes of past and present are not exactly coincident allows the moment seen through the more recent overlay to be set in temporal and spatial borders made by the framing present. But frequently Proust's patterning of the original episode, influenced or not by what it is seen through, is noticeable; it is that visual and sensual patterning which occupies me here.

A good place to study the patterning of elements is the remarkable portrait gallery constructed over time; Swann's portrait, that of the "first Swann," prior to his obsession with Odette, is announced as if by a surrounding border, by the threefold difference between the two bells, the one he might have sounded, and the one he did in fact sound: the former harsh, rasping like iron, incessant, and icy; the latter, with a double ring of "two shy peals . . . timid, oval, and gilded." The contrast between the rasping and the timid, between the jangling and the oval sounds, as it increases and dies out delicately, with its greatest volume in the middle, places Swann exactly in his own "tonality," among the other portraits of family and friends, and brings back, with his portrait and into it, all the leisure, warmth, and fragrance of Sunday dinners. His personality and corporeal self are as if emptied out to receive these qualities, which are ranged in what is apparently a descrescendo in size and importance, and is in reality a crescendo in its power of prolongation in the text: "fragrant with the scent of the great chestnut tree, of baskets of raspberries and of a sprig of tarragon" (I, p. 21).[39] Shade and massive unity (the chestnut tree) give way to the many smaller objects (the raspberries in the basket) and finally to the smallest (the sprig of tarragon), until they fill out the person Swann is, remembered by Marcel, whose memory is thus the entire screen for this Swann as we see him. He is, of course, other; but in this moment, his outline permits the sprig of tarragon to endure, put in the stressed position at the end of the sentence and the memory, extending itself in the imagination through the succeeding pages, to be then joined by the lilacs, themselves still persisting. The bell too will sound again, at the conclusion of the novel.

Translating

What I have called superpositioning is further explained by the persistence of all the unspecified, unmemorable, and unfruitful hours of twilight and of dawn, sensible as a continuum, under the linear process of the everyday, recalling this memory fixed in the chill of an evening or the heat of noon. A present experience imposes itself, the two moments interpenetrating in their oppositions, and exchanging their substance. An abrupt difference makes itself felt in attitude, atmosphere, and color, perceived through the translucent quality of these sensations: "But between the memories that had now come to mind of Combray, of Doncières, and of Rivebelle, I was conscious at that moment of much more than a distance in time, of the distance that there would be between two separate universes whose matter and substance were not the same. Had I sought to reproduce in writing the element in which my most insignificant memories of Rivebelle appeared to me to be carved, I should have had to vein it with pink, to render it at once translucent, compact, cool and resonant, a substance hitherto analogous to the sombre, rugged sandstone of Combray" (II, p. 413). The operation of translating one memory like one material into another, of displacing the primary qualities of the substance first perceived into those of the second, is both mobile and static. In one moment, another infuses itself, so that both finally remain conjoined.

It has been abundantly shown how descriptions in a literary text do not depend upon "real" appearances, but may in fact be at their most vivid when they contrast with that "reality" [40] The shifting of a perception often occasions an intense rereading, an arrest of the gaze refreshed with memory of past arrests. Thus two of the most celebrated descriptive passages in Combray can be seen as logically impossible superpositions, and all the more poetically viable. First, a tapestry is placed vertically in the text, upon the upward slope of a hill; here a single poppy on the border announces the entire stretch of poppies in the center, where inch by inch the red switches to blue until there is a sudden and unforgettable sighting, in the imagination and its vivid picturing, of the sea, motivated through the pennant of a ship, itself imagined as passing. The tapestry motif permits the overlay and the transformation, holding the double experience as it is surely held, and by the same means, in Rimbaud's poem "Marine." It is essential to notice that the observation makes the composition by interpreting it from the start.

> My eyes travelled up the bank which rose steeply to the fields beyond the hedge, alighting on a stray poppy or a few laggard cornflowers which decorated the slope here and there like the border of a tapestry whereon may be glimpsed sporadically the rustic theme which will emerge triumphant in the panel itself; infrequent still, spaced out like scattered houses which herald the approach of a village, they betokened to me the vast expanse of waving corn beneath the fleecy clouds, and the sight of a single poppy hoisting upon its slender rigging and holding against the breeze its scarlet ensign, over the body of rich black earth from which it sprang, made my heart beat as does a wayfarer's when he perceives upon some low-lying ground a stranded boat which is being caulked and made sea-worthy, and cries out (although he has not yet caught sight of it), "The Sea!" (I, p. 151)

That tapestried passage, the culminating moment of perception, is itself spatially bordered by two views of the hawthorns, one directly after it and concerning a further attempt at perception and absorption: "And then I returned to the hawthorns, and stood before them as one stands before those masterpieces which, one imagines, one will be better able to 'take in' when one has looked away for a moment at something else; but in vain did I make a screen with my hands, the better to concentrate upon the flowers" (I, p. 151), for he is not able to become one with them and their feeling. It is rather the imagined that he grasps, the sea from a boat, the field of corn, and the scarlet rigging from a poppy, than the sight directly before him. The superpositions of two differing sights as they determine the richness and density of the sensations and of the memory are crucial to the feeling, and the hold of him upon them, and them upon him in turn.

This passage leads to another, where jasmines on either side of Gilberte border the sight of her, which is thus forever set apart. Her black eyes sparkle, and in the subsequent memories superimposed upon this one—with a spatial and temporal illogic that reinforces the poetic logic—the recall of their brilliance represents itself wrongly; in the final paradox that outlines the perception, had her eyes been even slightly less black, "I should not have been, as I was, especially enamoured of their imagined blue" (I, p. 153). The original French version says nothing here about imagination, only about color, as if the translation itself were grappling with the illogic of love, and spelling it out. The mistake, correct for the eyes of love, permits the positive double vision of one element through the other, intensifying both possibilities.

As the sea is transposed upon the ground of the tapestry bordered in a mille-fleur design, so are blue eyes superimposed upon black ones, for these pictures hedged in jasmine, in hawthorn, in poppies, and in a thousand flowers. These are contradictory and evocative superpositions, and the visual and conceptual difficulty they make claims our full attention, deepening our sight.

Displacement, Reinsertion, and Reframing

One of the most consciously metatextual passages describes the bell-towers of the three churches, two of Martinville and one of Vieuxvicq, being displaced by an optical illusion that is in fact the narrator's own, as he moves in the carriage at the moment he observes them.

> At a bend in the road I experienced, suddenly, that special pleasure which was unlike any other, on catching sight of the twin steeples of Martinville, bathed in the setting sun and constantly changing their position with the movement of the carriage and the windings of the road, and then of a third steeple, that of Vieuxvicq, which, although separated from them then by a hill and a valley, and rising from rather higher ground in the distance, appeared none the less to be standing by their side. (I, p. 196)

Long after they are outlined for his sight and ours, they are reframed as a picture in the second moment of their perception, within the restaurant scene with Robert de Saint-Loup, and then in a final scene in the borders of Marcel's window as he lies in bed. Displaced, reinserted, and reframed in the text at these points, the memory of the first bell-tower passage and of its former rein-scription in writing is developed to its fullest over the time of the novel. This textual memory also directly motivates the meditation on altered substances just quoted, as they are uprooted and then transposed into one another. Just so, this former and highly self-conscious passage is transposed here, textual matter into textual matter.

Originally concerned with a scene in apparent motion, this description-in-passage exemplifies many of the perceptual oddities characteristic of framing passages in general, doubly privileged as the bearers of a "special pleasure." Contrasts stake out its borders: the two towers contain and cover a secret meaning, clearly there but nonetheless mysterious; they at once show and hide, being near and far. They show displacement, as the two bell-towers of Martinville seem to change location, and the tower of Vieuxvicq moves to join them, and yet their surface is sunny; shifting in the sunlight, the lines are held, their verbal recall repeating at short intervals, as if to stress their retention in the memory and, as in writing, in the heart:

> noticing and registering the shape of their spires, their shift-ing lines, the sunny warmth of their surfaces . . . (I, p. 196)

> those shifting, sunlit planes . . . (I, p. 197)

> their outlines and their sunlit surfaces . . . (I, p. 197)

Reframed in the inserted text of Marcel's page of writing, the outlines yield up once more their secret:

> . . . the three steeples were always a long way ahead of us . . . motionless and conspicuous in the sunlight. Then the steeple of Vieuxvicq drew aside, took its proper distance and the steeples of Martinville remained alone, gilded by the light of the setting sun which, even at that distance, I could see playing and smiling upon their sloping sides . . . (I, p. 198)

its steeples and that of Vieuxvicq waved once again their sun-bathed pinnacles in token of farewell . . . (I, p. 198)

then the road changed direction, they veered in the evening light like three golden pivots, and vanished from my sight. (I, p. 198)

forming now against the still rosy sky no more than a single dusky shape, charming and resigned, and so vanishing in the night. (I, p. 198)

Here the sunny shell of the surface has been ripped open for the hidden secret to appear, just before these lines go black in the setting sun, marking the bottom edge of the picture by the cessation of light of sight, as by the unity of the shape turned dark. When at the conclusion of Combray this passage is transposed in the reader's mind, reframed within the concluding pages of the entire novel, the perception of a whole life is revealed, through a breach in the line of trees and rock blocking the sea from view, directly preceding the passage when the sun goes down upon life and text.

In the windings of life-and-text, these views and these revelations contained by the towers will be covered over: "From time to time a turn in the road would sweep them out of sight; then they came into view for the last time and finally I could see them no more" (I, p. 198). Transcribing that vision upon this page, Proust as Marcel rids himself of it in part, and at the same time retains those lines, that clarity, and that secret. Of the latter, displacement is an essential part, and the hiding of sight by the traveling glance.

Returning, Repetition, and Recall

The repetition of a view may serve to intensify the passage inserted within it, all the more when its development works in a crescendo toward a tragic end, as in the case of the grandmother's stroke.

After the shock of her first attack, the subsequent chapter opens with a repetition marking its upper edge; this is the start of a new section, and a suggestion of some message to be brought, here an unwelcome annunciation hinted at with an odd and revelatory street name: "We made our way back along the Avenue Gabriel, through the strolling crowds. I left my grandmother to rest on a bench and went to get a carriage. (II, p. 323). The isolation of the central characters from the crowd is seconded by their recrossing the avenue, like a trumpet of doom instead of birth, announcing the Grandmother's death. It will be brought into narrow focus by a series of nesting frames repeatedly bringing the convergence of image and emotion ever closer into the center. The sevenfold repetition of the horse-carriage in which the old lady is seated is made to enclose, more and more evidently, the presence of death itself, which will ride along, inevitably taking possession of her as Marcel watches, helpless, and the reader with him.

The initial presentation is announced with no sense of menace, the very routine nature of the gestures seeming to prevent any recognition of the mortal "assault and possession" gradually penetrating the consciousness as it penetrates the body. Death's intrusion into the living presence is heightened by this carriage's first image of innocence: "You insist on your daily outing . . . you have hesitated over which coat to take, which carriage to call; you are in a carriage, the whole day lies before you, brief . . ." (II, p. 325)

Only the day's brevity gives any clue in the text that the announced theme, "the time of death," which initiated the paragraph is about to enter in increasingly full force. The generalization about the outing is followed by a luncheon ritual whose very normality is stressed by an apparent statement of similarity which is really that of difference: "the same outing as that of healthy people . . . ill as my grandmother was, there were, after all, several people who could testify that at six o'clock, as we came home from the Champs-Elysées, they had greeted her as she drove past in an open carriage, in perfect weather" (II, p. 325).

For the first time, by being superimposed on the acknowledgment of death, the pictured return cloaks death's reality with routine gestures of returning, greeting, passing by. The Elysian Fields referred to in the Champs-Elysées put their own ironic touch on the scene, in which the outside observer (like Françoise for the later scene on the stairs) provides a halt in perception, an arrest in the passing flow for a picture which must be reexamined: "Legrandin, making his way toward the Place de la Concorde, raised his hat to us, stopping to look after us with an air of surprise" (II, p. 325). This arrest and his surprised look force us to look again at the moment when the picture is taken, to reconsider the scene in its insistent framing. This first repeat strengthens the initial impression of the mortality signaled by what is to be a deathride: "Yes, it might have been said that a few minutes earlier, while I was looking for a carriage, my grandmother was resting on a bench in the Avenue Gabriel, and that a little later she had driven past in an open carriage. But would it have been really true?" (II, p. 325).

After an intervening passage, the text makes a second repeat of the scene and its appearance for the same onlooker, Legrandin: this is a rerepresentation of grave consequence, since doubt now enters by a fatal crack in the observing habit: "And if Legrandin had looked back at us with that air of astonishment, it was because to him, as to the other people who passed us then, in the carriage in which my grandmother was apparently sitting on the back seat, she had seemed to be foundering, slithering in the abyss, clinging desperately to the cushions . . ." (II, p. 326). The reality is perceived only by the observer outside the scene, who thus projects the truth underlying the text, forcing a rereading of the picture. The scene is made more poignant by the narrator's seeing the grandmother as an object for the first time: "She was not yet dead. But I was already alone . . . this nonbeing . . . that my grandmother would shortly be" (II, p. 313).

These initial presentations, then, prepare the extraordinary picture of the funeral carriage as the focus centers more and more closely upon the entrance of death into the mind and body, parallel to the entrance of that carriage into its final resting place. The funereal picture projected against the red wall with its heavy outlining takes on a solemn significance; this scene is set in astonishing relief by techniques of contrast and repetition, where even the final verb of the black-bordered passage, "nous repartîmes," picks up on the verb opening the initial section: "nous retraversâmes l'avenue Gabriel."

Here the complete picture is bounded by the terms: "nous repartîmes" (we set out again), "nous retraversâmes" (we made our way back), "nous arrivâmes" (we arrived). Between them is the space of an epic picture:

> The Professor continued to storm while I stood on the landing gazing at my grandmother, who was doomed. Each of us is indeed alone. We set off homewards.
>
> The sun was sinking; it burnished an interminable wall along which our carriage had to pass before reaching the street in which we lived, a wall against which the shadow of horse and carriage, cast by the setting sun, stood out in black on a reddish background, like a hearse on some Pompeian terra cotta. At length we arrived at the house. (II, pp. 328-29)

The passage is outlined in black against the red backdrop, where death enframes the lonely figures forever. The downward path from the return along the Avenue Gabriel to the return of the funeral chariot like a pyre in the blaze of the setting sun and the sad arrival, explains the gesture of the grandmother in the carriage, lifting one hand ("what does it matter?"), as if the trumpets were to sound now, in the gathering silence.

Upon the return of the carriage, a silent drama is enacted with an observer to intensify its tragic impact. In the slow ascension of the stairs by the grandmother and the mother, one turns her head away, the other veils hers, each covering over her suffering at the other's suffering:

So they went up side by side, my grandmother half-hid-
den in her shawl, my mother averting her eyes.

Meanwhile there was one person who never took hers
from what could be discerned of my grandmother's altered
features . . . (II, p. 330)

Françoise watches the scene indiscreetly and sympathetically,
perspicaciously and offensively at once, seeing everything and
judging nothing, in the pose of the observing bystanders in the
most famous Crucifixion scenes. To this highly visual moment,
reminiscent of Mannerist art, in which one veiled figure turns
aside from another, and to the intrusion of the observing eye,
the reader might apply one of Erving Goffman's frames: into the
front region of the performance as it is acted out, the reader
projects the tragic "back-knowledge" both figures hide from each
other. This reading of the scene is included, if not understood,
by Françoise, as her seeing is caught in the narrative mode, which
in turn is part of our reading. As the carriage scene projects what
it frames, showing to Marcel the private tragedy in a public space,
so the stairs scene elevates as performance what is played out in
a middle space by the performers for themselves. Françoise's other
reading, however ignorant, is included in the script.

At the end of the chapter, on "this funeral bed", thus marked,
like the carriage, by the solemnity of this specifically mortal cap-
tion, death enters once more into the body, but positively now.
For finally the face of life is superimposed upon the other, youth's
traits placed upon the mask of death itself, and at the very end
of the passage, the essential characteristics that had been temporarily covered over, are restored to the being whose memory
provides a central touchstone to Marcel's consciousness and connection with himself. By the third and final crossing of that avenue announced by the name of Gabriel, a retraversal backward
in time is made on the very deathbed: "Life in withdrawing from
her had taken with it the disillusionments of life. A smile seemed
to be hovering on my grandmother's lips. On that funeral couch,
death, like a sculptor of the Middle Ages, had laid her down in

the form of a young girl" (II, p. 357). This transfiguration of the border experience, with the most absolute contrast available— death with life—permits the latter to win out, precisely through the creative hand of death itself, expert at superimpositions.

Door and Window Frames

Through a door or reflected in a mirror, in a box set apart, the figures glimpsed in a constricted view or blocked off are all the more visible, their actions stressed all the more vividly in their nature, often startling to the extreme. Charlus—Proust's most deliberately shocking creation—is over and over displayed to the reader, exposed through a half-cracked door, his naked neck contrasting with his top hat laid to the side, or then reflected in a glass, forced upon the observation of Marcel and the reader.[41] Above all, the mating scene is startling: Marcel watches Charlus through a ground-level window, seeing him outlined against the strong light, while waiting for the bee to visit the orchid, whose petals stand ready. Now the play of male and female, of stamens and styles, is emphasized, highlighting this extraordinary scene:

> My curiosity emboldening me by degrees, I went down to the ground-floor window, which also stood open with its shutters ajar. I could distinctly hear Jupien getting ready to go out, but he could not detect me behind my blind, where I stood perfectly still until the moment when I drew quickly aside in order not to be seen by M. de Charlus, who, on his way to call upon Mme de Villeparisis, was slowly crossing the courtyard, corpulent, greying, aged by the strong light. (II, pp. 623-24)

A sort of mating dance takes place, where the insect comes to the flower, and male to female:

> But more astounding still, M. de Charlus's pose having altered, Jupien's, as though in obedience to the laws of an occult art, at once brought itself into harmony with it. . . .

Meanwhile Jupien . . . had—in perfect symmetry with the Baron—thrown back his head, given a becoming tilt to his body, placed his hand with grotesque effrontery on his hip, stuck out his behind, struck poses with the coquetry that the orchid might have adopted on the providential arrival of the bee. (II, pp. 626-27)

This scene, already strong, is still intensified by the superposition upon it of another, Marcel's remembering the time he watched at her window Mlle Vinteuil and her lesbian friend, posed against the strong light, with her father's picture in prominence: then too the window framed the perfect picture, and even the picture within the picture. Still later, with Albertine, this latter scene returns as background and controlling force: "Behind Albertine I no longer saw the blue mountains of the sea, but the room at Montjouvain where she was falling into the arms of Mlle Vinteuil with that laugh in which she gave utterance as it were to the strange sound of her pleasure" (II, p. 1154). Thus the same scene—that of the window at Montjouvain with its mixture of sound and sight, framed simultaneously—serves as the intensifying agent for two later scenes. As if the first occurrence of the sight did not suffice, it is then transposed upon or behind another sight, and still another, memory deepening experience by suggestion beyond the present vision.

One of the most revealing pictures of the heavily bordered sort opens the doors on a restaurant shrouded in outer fog, into whose warm and bright interior the gaze is led by a beam of light as dramatic as in some Rembrandt picture set in a strong opposition of bright and dark. Marcel, stuck in the revolving door for a long and ludicrous instant, is then shuffled off to a badly placed table until Saint-Loup, like some avenging hero, rights matters in one of the most dramatic scenes of the novel: running along the tops of the red velvet dining benches, trampling down the symbols of luxury, toward the table where Marcel sits in a draft, he brings—while the others stand watching in frozen and paralyzed attitudes—the Marquis's vicuna coat to cover Marcel's shoulders. The scene is spelled out in three installments, each adding to the effect of the whole, as the successive renderings are positioned one above the other:

> Saint-Loup reappeared in the doorway carrying over his arm the thick vicuna coat of the Prince de Foix. . . . On entering the big room he sprang lightly on to one of the red plush benches which ran around its walls. . . . Between the tables and wall electric wires were stretched at a certain height; without the slightest hesitation Saint-Loup jumped nimbly over them like a steeplechaser taking a fence. . . . The proprietor and his staff stood fascinated, like race-goers in the enclosure. (II, p. 426)

> And when Saint-Loup, having to get past his friends, climbed on to the back of the bench behind them and ran along it, balancing himself like a tightrope walker, discreet applause broke from the body of the room. On coming to where I was sitting, he checked his momentum . . . and, stooping down, handed to me with an air of courtesy and submission the vicuna cloak which a moment later . . . without my having to make a single movement, he arranged as a light but warm shawl about my shoulders. (II, p. 427)

Compared to a racehorse on a classic frieze, Saint-Loup is rendered transparent to his heritage, becoming the container of all those past epochs of aristocratic behavior, as his ancestors come to fill in the outline through which we read the family in reading his figure, "as, through a work of art, the industrious, energetic force which has created it, and rendered the movements of that light-footed course which Robert had pursued along the wall, as intelligible and charming as those of horsemen on a marble frieze" (II, p. 429). Like the pottery of Combray, he is pictured so that the substance of another time may shine through. The figures are transparent containers for the qualities Marcel sees or remembers through them: Swann for his qualities of a Sunday afternoon, Gilberte for the impression of her eyes, the grandmother for the figuration of death, and Saint-Loup for his heritage. The sense of these primary figures in the layers of memory is akin to the persistence of the smell of tarragon and lilacs, of the sound of weeping.

The Proustian lyric of narration is reinforced, against the forgetting that is inherently possible in a simple linear reading, by an enduring doubleness; the thickening of texture in the transposed parts with their visible and sensitive overlay catches the sight, fixes the feeling, and allows the memory to persist, so that the slightest gesture or the most dramatic one (an old lady lifting her hand or a noble young man trampling down the symbols of luxury), the tiniest object or the greatest one (a sprig of some herb or some majestic spreading tree) can call forth all that art has transposed into the text.

Temporal Frames

So far I have discussed only spatial frames, borders, and superpositions of sights and memories upon each other. Yet, given his preoccupation with time, it is scarcely surprising if, among writers, Proust has an exceptionally strong and complicated relation to temporal frames.

The following paradigmatic passage turns about the repetition of one melodic sung phrase as it is posed against the imminent departure of Marcel's mother from the train station in Venice. To wait for the resolution of the passage is to miss the train, in all probability, but the measure of intensity with which the listener participates in the song inflicts a mental and corporeal paralysis upon him; the entire scene is set in a delay and a suspense that heightens the style and creates a perfect temporal frame about the subject focused upon, which has its own temporal unfolding at the center, playing in counterpart against the train's fixed point of departure, both held in place by the mental delay:

> And when the hour came at which, accompanied by all my belongings, she set off for the station, I ordered a drink to be brought out to me on the terrace overlooking the canal,

and settled down there to watch the sunset, while from a
boat that had stopped in front of the hotel a musician sang
O sole mio.

The sun continued to sink. My mother must be nearing
the station. Soon she would be gone, and I should be alone
in Venice, alone with the misery of knowing that I had dis-
tressed her, and without her presence to comfort me. The
hour of the train's departure was approaching. My irrevocable solitude was so near at hand that it seemed to me to
have begun already and to be complete. (III, pp. 666-67)

As with the famous little melody of the Vinteuil sonata, the
rhythm of the phrase in the song now replaces normal time, and
its words, normal language, holding the listener enthralled as this
reconstructed time passes differently from ordinary time. It is the
fixated attention which itself is important, rather than the song.
The double sadness of the moments thus spent within the song's
own universe depends partly on the unselective nature of the
fixation and partly on the meaning of the enchantment, which is
the realization of such irrevocable solitude.

The sun of the song is heard within the loneliness of the self—
"sol" along with "solitude"—so that the sinking of the sun and
the development of the song toward its resolution join with Marcel's own irresolution. The sudden disintegration of the universe
about the self occasioned by the realization of this solitude takes
place now in the very center of the Proustian canvas, as if the
world were to crumble back into its elements, denying the holistic arrangement once conceived of as available to perception. Only
the oddly obsessive repetitions of this passage will bind the parts
of Venice and the self together, as if in five successive stages of
the consciousness, each and all attached to three words alone:

For I felt myself to be alone; things had become alien to
me; I no longer had calm enough to break out of my throbbing heart and introduce into them a measure of stability.
The town that I saw before me had ceased to be Venice. Its

personality, its name, seemed to me to be mendacious fictions which I no longer had the will to impress upon its
stones. I saw the palaces reduced to their basic elements,
lifeless heaps of marble with nothing to choose between them,
and the water as a combination of hydrogen and oxygen,
eternal, blind, anterior and exterior to Venice, oblivious of
the Doges and of Turner. And yet this unremarkable place
. . . contracted me into myself until I was no more than a
throbbing heart and an attention strained to follow the development of *O sole mio*. (III, p. 227)

The only continuity seems that of the "throbbing heart" and the
melody, the only concentration that of the mind upon the song,
the only contraction that of the self into the unfolding movement, while all around represents dissolution, loss, and departure. The tension builds and the despair with it, in the impotence
of all but art:

. . . and in this lonely, unreal, icy, unfriendly setting in which
I was going to be left alone, the strains of *O sole mio*, rising
like a dirge for the Venice I had known, seemed to bear
witness to my misery. No doubt I ought to have ceased to
listen to it if I wished to be able to join my mother and take
the train with her; I ought to have made up my mind to
leave without losing another second. But this was precisely
what I was powerless to do; I remained motionless, inca-
pable not merely of rising, but even of deciding that I would
rise from my chair. My mind, in order not to have to consider the decision I had to take, was entirely occupied in
following the course of the successive phrases of *O sole mio*,
singing them to myself with the singer, anticipating each
surge of melody, soaring aloft with it, sinking down with it
once more. (III, p. 668)

The tension has risen to an unbearable pitch, with the listener's
unfolding realization of exactly what he is listening to, in this
fourth stage of the text's contrapuntal music: he is making him-

self late for the train, so that the melody *O sole mio* is weighted with melancholy, in this very awareness:

> I was well aware that in reality it was the resolution not to go that I was making by remaining there without stirring, but to say to myself: "I'm not going," which in that direct form was impossible, became possible in this indirect form: "I'm going to listen to one more phrase of *O sole mio*"; possible but infinitely painful, for the practical significance of this figurative language did not escape me and while I said to myself: "After all, I'm only listening to one more phrase," I knew that the words meant: "I shall remain by myself in Venice." And it was perhaps this melancholy, like a sort of numbing cold, that constituted the despairing but hypnotic charm of the song. (III, p. 669)

Now the powerlessness of the listener and the power of art combine to make one of the great passages in Proust, set in relief only by this buildup I am relating to a kind of temporal framing. Within the scene now at its zenith, opposites combine in a held picture, held by the arrest of the sun in its astonishment. And what is held is human emotion against the emptiness of culture and nature, desire and anguish against the grip of this memory forever, the commonplaces of even Venice against the poignancy of sensitive vision and great writing, as the fading light merges with the unfading bronze to triumph over the dust and ashes, in a realization as substantial as the Venetian palaces, in all their former glory, are unsubstantial in the face of human suffering, even self-inflicted, as the miraculous build-up of pain into art, through art:

> My mother must by now have reached the station. In a little while she would be gone. I was gripped by anguish at the sight of the Canal which had become diminutive now that the soul of Venice had fled from it, of that commonplace Rialto which was no longer the Rialto, and by the song of despair which *O sole mio* had become and which, bellowed

thus beside the insubstantial palaces, finally reduced them to dust and ashes, completing the ruin of Venice; I looked on at the slow realization of my distress, built up artistically, without haste, note by note, by the singer as he stood beneath the astonished gaze of the sun arrested in its course behind San Giorgio Maggiore, with the result that the fading light merged forever in my memory with the throb of my emotion and the bronze voice of the singer in an equivocal, unalterable, and poignant alloy. (III, p. 669)

But under this extraordinary arrest upon the surface, an active potentiality has developed, and in a perfectly unpredictable surge of movement and of one long sentence, the narrator draws upon all his reserves, rushing in what he calls a "hot haste," exactly the opposite of the cold numbness and the icy chill of the wasted Venice around him, to the station to catch the train and his mother. Suddenly then the scene of indecision and of temporal measure, built up into a highly intense presence over five successive stages, is distanced almost at the speed of light by the receding train, as through the windows the neighboring town of Padua and the slightly more distant Verona in turn make their farewells, like the receding edges of the picture.

Now objects and places and emotions are restored to themselves, cities to their fullness, and the solitude sensed both in the song and in the sun is temporarily overcome.

Inscription

The final inscription of time could take as its model a scene in *Le temps retrouvé* in which Marcel spends his whole day in bed by a window looking out on the leaves of the park's tall trees; here among the greenery filling the window he suddenly glimpses the church tower neatly framed in the rectangle of the window. This passage refers back to the earlier one of the steeples framed from a moving carriage, in order to repeat the frame; but this time the borders are unmoving as they are narrow, and the view

is stable. Now it is less a question of art and of mental repicturing than of reality; so the thought-out distinction between the
real and the figures casts a sharper light on both:

> Not a representation of the steeple, but the steeple itself,
> which, putting in visible form a distance of miles and of
> years, had come, intruding its discordant tone into the midst
> of the luminous verdure—a tone so colourless that it seemed
> little more than a preliminary sketch—and engraved itself
> upon my windowpane. And if I left my room for a moment,
> I saw at the end of the corridor, in a little sitting room
> which faced in another direction, what seemed to be a band
> of scarlet—for this room was hung with a plain silk, but a
> red one, ready to burst into flames if a ray of sun fell upon
> it. (III, p. 716)

The picture exemplifies Marcel's clinging to and then going
past the "real," denying it its figurative importance, until it is,
and as it is, framed by the human choice, accidental perhaps, or
perhaps purposeful: "my windowpane." Unlike the moving picture forms seen from the carriage, into which the steeples adjusted themselves one after the other, and also unlike the famous
picture of the sunset placing itself in the train window, analyzed
by Georges Poulet,[42] this insertion of the green and red of the
picture into the vision of the narrator abed is controlled by the
borders of the pane, and made, from an explicable outer object,
into a picture at once representative or real, and abstract. The
picture, for one instant, holds it all.

As for the abstraction itself, the deduction of general laws from
the individual phenomena, it is more and more the object of
Marcel's quest, whether it is considered spatially (like line and
border) or in a temporal mode (such as progress and decay over
the years). For the spatial mode, the geometrical spirit and the
painterly eye suffice; for the temporal mode, the narrator's philosophical and psychological observation are more than adequate.
But for both, does not this X-ray vision, whose penetration prevents the recognition of sight's aesthetic pleasure, threaten the

surface delight and even significance of what is perceived, felt, and conveyed?

> Just as a geometer, stripping things of their sensible quali-
> ties, sees only the linear substratum beneath them, so the
> stories that people told escaped me, for what interested me
> was not what they were trying to say but the manner in
> which they said it . . . or rather I was interested in what had
> always, because it gave me specific pleasure, been more par-
> ticularly the goal of my investigations: the point that was
> common to one being and the other. . . . So the apparent
> copiable charm of things and people escaped me, because I
> had not the ability to stop short there—I was like a surgeon
> who beneath the smooth surface of a woman's belly sees the
> internal disease which is devouring it. If I went to a dinner-
> party I did not see the guests: when I thought I was looking
> at them, I was in fact examining them with X-rays. (III, p.
> 738)

The set of psychological laws, like the search for lost time, appears to have replaced the passion for the fleeting surface of the formerly impassioning "real." When the real as seen and nar-rated once again regains its power to impassion, it is then that Marcel will rediscover the power of the superimposition of frame upon frame.

A delay in the text, separating the second part of *Le temps retrouvé* from the first, begins with another train ride, after many years spent in a sanatorium. This time passed as neutral, not curative and not described, leads to an intensely described scene of arrest, whose top frame is explicit, in both its re-membering of the pieces and its stoppage. The sudden monologue, set off by quotation marks, brands this passage as a highly dramatized one:

> It was, I remember, at a halt of the train in the middle of
> the countryside. The sun lit up half the trunk of a line of
> trees along the path of the rails. "Trees," I thought, "you

have nothing further to say to me, my numbed heart hears you no more. I am nonetheless right in the center of nature, and it is only with the chill of boredom that my eyes perceive the line separating your luminous forehead from your shadowy trunk. If ever I could have thought myself a poet, now I know I am one no longer. Perhaps in the new and sterile part of my life, humans can tell me what nature no longer does. But the years when I could perhaps have been capable of celebrating it will never return." (III, p. 855)

The passage is one of loss, and incapability, about just what matters in the length of the book, and about what, to all appearances, will never now be recaptured. Its halt, within the motion of the train and of memory; its doubt, so strongly signaled; and its drama, etched in the monologue presented as a dialogue in the text, "as with someone who might have been with me and who might have been capable of taking more pleasure than I did from the fiery reflections in the windows and the rosy transparency of the house." But this companion, imagined, lacks the same happiness in the sight as Marcel himself. He has both shown and been disappointed by himself and the other in himself, the reader of the sights as of the text.

The scene is all the stronger in its obvious contrast with the enthusiastic description of the sunset framing in the train window preceding it, so long ago. Not only have sights and humans now gone abstract and cold, but doubt has set in about the creative venture itself, in the light of this new perception about the relation of happiness and ardor to perception; the doubt traverses many temporal stages, and after the dialogued passage just quoted, the repetition in simply narrated form makes a desperate confession of emptiness:

... I knew that I knew myself to be worthless. If I really had the soul of an artist, surely I would be feeling pleasure at the sight of this curtain of trees lit by the setting sun. . . . A little later I had noticed with the same absence of emotion the glitter of gold and orange which the sun splashed upon

the windows of a house; and finally, as the evening ad-
vanced, I had seen another house which appeared to be built
out of a strange pink substance. But I had made these various observations with . . . absolute indifference. (III, pp.
886-87)

From this dryness or lack of feeling only the renewed doubling
or thickening of experience can cure, as in the rapid crescendo
of the three final and famous privileged moments of the book
where time is remembered and recaptured. The sudden and redeeming hope of these successive and cumulative moments is
introduced by a sentence of strong emotive and cognitive—we
might say, re-cognitive—impact. "But it is sometimes at just the
moment when everything seems lost to us that the signal arrives
which can save us; we have knocked on all the doors which lead
to nothing, and then we happen to knock unaware upon the only
one through which we can enter, and which we would have sought
in vain for a hundred years, and it opens" (III, p. 866). The three
incidents of the uneven paving stone, the crisp napkin, and the
sound of the spoon against the plate strike him like a vision,
inserted and dramatized; here the secret of the recognition, the
re-creation, and the recapturing is found, this happiness that was
lacking in the simple and one-layered perception.

Into these double experiences he inserts all the others, restor-
ing the depth that was momentarily lacking. The sound of the
spoon against the plate restores the train passage, as if a railman
had struck a hammer against a trainwheel, and the whole scene
is given anew. This is without the sense of loss, for when the salt
sea surges in the napkin felt crisply against his lips, bringing
blue-breasted mermaids, such an extraordinary return to a privileged image of childhood permits and prepares his sad observation that the true paradises are those we have lost. The essence
of things must be framed in the moment and then reframed
atemporally, in a space where the superposition of two moments
liberates man from the order of time, albeit temporarily. To the
painting the right colors must be given, and a succession of dif-

ferent materials: what is right for mornings at the sea, or after-noons in Venice, will be wrong for the depiction of Rivebelle evenings, "when, in the dining-room that opened on to the gar-den, the heat began to resolve into fragments and sink back into the ground, while a sunset glimmer still illumined the roses on the walls of the restaurant and the last watercolours of the day were still visible in the sky—this would be a new and distinct material, of a transparence and a sonority that were special, com-pact, cool after warmth, rose-pink" (III, p. 904). And this trans-parency recreates not just the afternoons of perception, but the former passage where, to the rosy glimmer upon the wall, he had been only indifferent.

In this spiritually and spatially aware life, where the moments are distinct and the tints are different, the signs of chance are seen as necessary givens for the world of art and the translator of them, the interpreter or artist who is its writer and its best reader. "Seize me as I pass, if you can, and try to solve the riddle of happiness which I set you" (III, p. 899). The sudden dialogue set into the text here reminds us of the interior dialogue in the passage of natural invitation, in the description of the trees: na-ture speaks within the prose poet here in the narrator's interior discourse with himself. In these inserts of natural and poetic drama within the narrative flow, the play of the framed passage acquires its fullest potency: the narrator, as reader of his own attitude toward the exterior and of the self, merges in his own creation of the self, receptive to the full and luminous moment of super-position.

And so the reader, who we are, initially seen in the little boy, with his lantern slides and his edition of Georges Sand, returns to read once more with those other eyes: now he reads in "the inner book of unknown symbols (they must have been symbols carved in relief, whose contours my attention, as it explored my unconscious, groped for and stumbled against and followed like a diver exploring the ocean-bed)" (III, p. 913), and with this reading no one can help. Reading is a solitary act of creation: none can create with us or collaborate in the reading. This conception of subjectivity at its summit, as it is placed in the reading of experience, determines the final painting, lonely, great, and doomed as anything but painting in its own borders, necessarily set.

Revelation and Restoration

A figure reveals another; by the end of the novel, the superpositions of art and life work in the opposite way, but still in slow motion. Instead of the grandmother in a funeral chariot as she is compared to Caravaggio's Medusa or to a guardian statue by the tomb, Carpaccio's St. Ursula is to reveal gradually the identity of the figure accompanying Marcel to Venice, and beyond, in his memory and ours.

This revelation, made of the past within the present ("A time has now come, when, remembering . . ."), is introduced by the notion of seeing, and initiated in an emotionally charged development within one sentence, painting an unforgettable scene, whose depth is rendered greater by the religious overtones: baptism, revelation, the Christ figure, the mother figure, and by the setting in the sanctuary of St. Mark's; its importance within the novel goes still further and depends in part upon the mosaic of contemplation, a topos that will return at the end of the novel:

> A time has now come when, remembering the baptistery of St. Mark's—contemplating the waters of the Jordan in which St. John immerses Christ, while the gondola awaited us at the landing-stage of the Piazzetta—it is no longer a matter of indifference to me that, beside me in that cool penumbra, there should have been a woman draped in her mourning with the respectful and enthusiastic fervour of the old woman in Carpaccio's St. Ursula in the Accademia, and that this woman, with her red cheeks and sad eyes and in her black veils, whom nothing can ever remove from the softly lit sanctuary of St. Mark's where I am always sure to

find her because she has her place reserved there as immutably as a mosaic, should be my mother. (III, p. 661)

This formal delay in the very long sentence leading up to the presence of the mother and assuring the relevance of the work of art as it is finally transposed into that one human figure, uses the gestures and some of the renowned monuments of classicism, and the memory it keeps. The mosaic here, with its preparation of the place for the mother so loved, suggests at once fragmentation, juxtaposition, and resolution. Upon this mosaic a soft lighting falls, and endures, protecting the figure at last revealed under the veil.

Nor is it unimportant—to echo the text—that what they are looking at together is a mosaic of Christ's baptism, and that Marcel's mother throws, at that moment, a shawl over his shoulders. Like Saint-Loup's bringing Marcel the vicuna coat to protect him from a cold draft, here the mother's action repeats that scene, suggestively, and her shawl refers also to the cloak in the Carpaccio painting itself, the referent or model in art for Albertine's Fortuny cloak, which is copied from it, and which represents it, like a trace of Venice transported to Paris, and now, in memory, retransported to Venice. The day before she was to leave him forever, she took this cloak on her ride with Marcel in the open carriage to Versailles. He had forgotten the coat, and now, in the scene before the baptismal mosaic, when his mother cloaks him, the gesture taking into itself all the strength of Saint-Loup's friendship in that former scene, she makes reparation for lost time, and also for the lost parts of vision, itself always a mosaic. Christ's baptism thus adds its significance of re-creation to the waters of Venice, suggesting implicitly that the mother may restore and renew this artist son, who would eventually want to save his own re-cognitions and revelations: "I had recognised it down to the last detail, and, that cloak having restored to me as I looked at it the eyes and the heart of the person who had set out that evening with Albertine for Versailles, I was overcome for a few moments by a vague feeling of desire and melancholy" (III, p. 662).

If the feeling is dissipated, the mosaic nevertheless remains, a work of art like the book and Time reconstructed, where remembrance is not lost but regained in the successive picturings and unveilings. What is protected by the mother's shawl, the friend's coat, and Albertine's cloak, is each time the same thing: the intense subjectivity, the very essence of feeling, that eventually leads to the creation of the mosaic of memory and of time. Françoise will make her own collage and mosaic of bits and pieces, her "boeuf à la mode," from fragments of meat, her repaired windowpanes with torn pages of newspaper, her dress from various scraps of material. Of such work as this, glorious and continuous, but no more so than her domestic creations, the narrator will build his book with means as humble as they are cosmic, less like the construction of a cathedral than of a vestment: "pinning an additional leaf on here or there."

For Françoise would always make do; we are called upon, in art as in life, to do no more, but we find in the long run that it is enough. Like patchwork, the novel is composed of stuck-on pieces, just as she stuck paper or material to what needed covering and fixing. This is the secret of the dressmaker, the cook, the *bricoleur*, but of the artist and writer as well, and of anyone constructing a life: the composition is simply made, of what is at hand, and the center piece is placed in focus by the framing borders.

Closure in Time

Like the smell of lilacs lingering and the sight of hawthorn blossoms enduring, all the memories in their transparent recall endure, dense in the mind through their spatial doubling and their temporal delay. One of the great final passages, brief in its sentences and almost hidden in the foliage of the paragraph in which it is so modestly inset, itself exemplifies the holding of the view, its concealment, and its final revelation:

The mind has landscapes which it is allowed to contemplate only for a certain time. I had lived my life like a painter climbing a road high above a lake, whose view is denied to him by a curtain of rocks and trees. Suddenly through a gap in the curtain he sees the lake, he has its expanse before him, he takes up his brushes. But already night is at hand, night when one can no longer paint, and on which the dawn will not rise. (III, p. 1092)

The generalization about mind and landscape, about contemplation and brevity, leads to an abrupt personal statement in which all of the narrator's life of vision and painting is encapsulated, a sentence placed visibly and emotionally upon the rise of a path. The view hidden by a natural framing curtain of rocks and trees is revealed only in a breach in the frame, through which, when Marcel sets his sights correctly, the whole expanse of vision lies before him and beneath him. As a painter this time he is able at last to take an overview upon the natural scene, in a fitting climax to all the previous superpositions and overlays, cloakings and revelations, in this sentence where the first person replaces the initial generalization. When the third person replaces the first person, before the generalization begins afresh, a distance is created once more, and the scene closes up again, as the "I" is replaced by the "he." The tripartite repetition at the end: "he sees / he has / he takes up" creates a rhythm whose excitement increases, until the complete stop in the fourth sentence on the level of the impersonal, "one can no longer paint," as the cosmic display meets the personal incapacity, with the inevitable fall of darkness over sight, coinciding with the generalizing "one" thrown over the subjective "I." These sentences are themselves covered over in the flow of the prose that surrounds them as if they were, as they are indeed, poetry. No show is made of them, and no paragraph signal sets them apart as marked, so that this frame, the quietest and the most telling of all, is perceived only inside, through the breach not in the typography but in the thought.

This passage is itself surrounded by a border blacker than the rest, dark in its metaphysical import, being mortal:

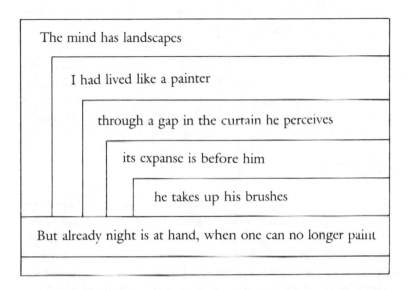

The mind has landscapes

I had lived like a painter

through a gap in the curtain he perceives

its expanse is before him

he takes up his brushes

But already night is at hand, when one can no longer paint

In this passage the painter is no longer other, Elstir or Carpaccio or Giotto, but is at last the narrator himself. What is seen is a natural sight—not related to human skill—and bordered by other natural elements, as a metaphor of a life in relation to a text. Life itself with its perceptions beyond the text is finally cropped off at the lower edge by death itself, so that the whole passage works on two levels: nature cropping off nature, twice, and life's end cropping off the edges of life and text, putting an end to it all.

And it is Proust's reader, who is Marcel's, but is more than those, as Proust wanted it, the reader of himself, who observes the cropping and the closure. As Proust says of those readers we become: "For it seemed to me that they would not be 'my' readers but the readers of their own selves, my book being merely a sort of magnifying glass like those which the optician at Combray used to offer his customers—it would be my book, but with its help I would furnish them with the means of reading what lay inside themselves" (III, p. 1089).

"But . . . was there still time and was I still in fit condition to undertake the task? . . . But my memory was old and tired" (III, p. 1089). These sentences of doubt precede and frame the painting's closing off, which fills in the circular outline of the great book, in which the doorbell is still sounding, the bell is still ringing, whose sound neither this nor any other memoried listener can alter or forget. Now finally casting off all other sounds and sights, the reader listening descends within the self where the signs heard and seen all endure with the past we bear, and to which we can possibly return, under what is forever surrounded, cloaked, and cropped off.

Art endures. Bergotte rises from his sickbed to look once more at Vermeer's "View of Delft," which he thought he knew by heart; the painting has worked as a quiet leitmotif throughout the novel, representing Swann's major aesthetic interest, and recurring periodically at different points as an understated test of the reality of art, and its imaginative power. As the Vinteuil sonata with its celebrated little phrase represents far more than itself for the narrator, so this picture represents and reveals for the artist included in this work of art his own test of reality, representation, and value.

And now, at the moment of Bergotte's death, it has come from The Hague to the Palais du Luxembourg, in Paris, where Swann had felt it essential to go to see it, as if for Bergotte. A critic has maintained that a little patch of yellow wall in that painting is of a beauty "sufficient to itself," and not remembering that specific part, Bergotte goes, ill to death, to stand before the painting, seeing for the first time in it some small figures painted in blue, the sand painted in pink, and the "precious matter" of the little yellow wall itself. Looking, even as he grows dizzier, at this "precious" spot, he judges his own writing by it, finding he should have made his language "precious in itself, like this little patch of yellow wall" (III, p. 185). The triple appearance of the relatively uncommon term *précieux*, "precious" in this small space of text, as minimal a space as the little patch of wall, and the repe-

tition of the "little patch of yellow wall" itself, marks the border
of his life as it passes into death, even as he repeats to himself,
like a talisman: "Little patch of wall with a sloping roof, little
patch of yellow wall." He has weighed that sight against his own
life, and given, finally, the latter for the former.

The obligations of art are of a different world, and these "unknown laws which we obeyed because we bore their precepts in
our hearts . . . those laws to which every profound work of the
intellect brings us nearer," explain that balance and that choice.
The final frame of Bergotte's own picture is placed there by the
work of art itself; this death focused through one small patch of
yellow composes a picture exceptionally revealing among the many
in Proust's novel. The revelation concerns not just the picture by
Vermeer, but that picture and its patch of wall as they are given
their most fitting sacrifice in Bergotte's death and lasting meditation. "They buried him, but all through that night of mourning, in the lighted shop-windows, his books, arranged three by
three, kept vigil like angels with outspread wings and seemed,
for him who was no more, the symbol of his resurrection" (III,
p. 186). No passage in Proust has a greater relevance to the great
sentences on mind and landscape, for in predicting the fall of
night, it predicts also the salvation by art which the dark border
might have seemed to interrupt.

Bateson argues that art participates in our quest for a funda-
mental integration of self and world: "For the attainment of grace,
the reasons of the heart must be integrated with the reasons of
reason" (SE, p. 129). And with those of art itself; here the narration, for all its own reasons, adds its own natural closure to
the sides of the painting where we all read ourselves, at nightfall,
and in time.

PERCEPTION AND VIRGINIA WOOLF

Nothing neat. Nothing that comes down with all its feet on the floor.
The Waves

Literary Measure

The frame is not only an exterior phenomenon, but may also be that upon which something is shaped, its informing and referential measuring device, its framework. Virginia Woolf's essay *Street Haunting*, which reads like a prose poem, has as focus and as formative frame just the length of one small pencil, providing the excuse for an excursion at twilight through the London streets, at once uneventful on the exterior and rich in interior events.[43]

"No one perhaps has ever felt passionately towards a lead pencil. But there are circumstances in which it can become supremely desirable to possess one; moments when we are set upon having an object, a purpose, and excuse for walking half across London between tea and dinner. As the foxhunter hunts in order that open spaces may be preserved from the builders, so when the desire comes upon us to go street rambling, the pencil does for a pretext" (SH, p. 1). The apparent triviality of the errand renders the landscape all the more appealing, in itself and as an escape from the everyday domestic scene, ironically deserted in honor of the tiny object upon which all else—for the moment—will be modeled. Written in an intensely lyric tone, the essay wanders along the dazzling streets of a London winter at dusk, when the windows just lit serve to frame the sights of the imagination, some projected, some arising in response to what is glimpsed, all in the joyful irresponsibility conferred by the oncoming darkness.

The essay owes part of its charm to the circling of the imagined picture, as it is rounded out and then closed off. The simplest object within acts as a container and concretion of sights. The China bowl on the mantelpiece seems to contain all the remembered scenes unfolding from it: a windy day, some intertwining vines and pillars in the courtyard of a country inn, an Englishman polite among the wrought-iron chairs, and the memory of the acquisition of the bowl itself. All these sights are interwoven and held by the objects around which they focus, all serving as the interior pattern for the exterior scenes among which the wanderer moves, forming them by the figure of wandering itself. The selective crystallization of an instant has already come about, and by its return in the conscience, it is doubly framed: "The moment was stabilized, stamped like a coin indelibly, among a million that slipped by imperceptibly" (SH, p. 4). Or then a brown stain upon a carpet brings back memories of Lloyd George, in anger at whom a cup of coffee was spilled there: these objects open out from the memory, inciting the imagination of such moments. The interior eye forms the scene, from the object out.

The thought of the pencil, on the other hand, brings to a point of converging focus the exterior scenes passing through the eye, meant only to graze the surface, not to penetrate it. The sight is not, says Woolf, intended to dwell; but a halt must be called here to the scenes pictured, to the idea of a lady measuring out tea for some visitor, to the clerks shuffling papers in the dim light of offices. For the observing eye can approve only the most superficial glance, skimming the catalogue of the sights offered to it, selected for inclusion: "the glossy brilliance of the motor omnibuses; the carnal splendor of the butchers' shops with their yellow flanks and their purple steaks; the blue and red bunches of flowers burning so bravely through the plate glass of the florist's windows" (SH, p. 8).

Yet the shortcomings of the unprofessional eye are real, in particular, its lack of practice at framing the trophies so subtly caught, in order to "bring out their more obscure angles and relationships." The latter is the role of the professional author; for amateur sight, untroubled by compositional criteria, unused to arranging, is in need of some measuring rod, no matter how small, on which and about which to fit and fix the gaze. A little rod about finger-length begins to lay its bar across the rapidity and abundance of the sights: "Really I must—really I must—that is it."

And so the writing and seeing self coincide, finally returning to the domestic objects with their accumulated and nonfictive aura of memory. After the illusion of assigning roles to others, costuming them—like a lady with pearls about her neck in a silk dress on the balustrade, or her counterimage, the dwarf with her beautiful feet—the mind returns to its own duties, bearing its own trophy from the wandering, making it the center of future attention amid the objects to which it has given a fresh view: "Here again is the usual door; here the chair turned as we left it and the china bowl and the brown ring on the carpet. And here— let us examine it tenderly, let us touch it with reverence—is the only spoil we have retrieved from all the treasures of the city, a lead pencil" (SH, p. 35). This most modest ruling rod works as a typically metaliterary interior frame, the tiny writing tool against which the scenes are held up and judged one by one, and by means of which all the perambulatory vision is sought out and preserved. An initial pretext, preceding the text, the minimal object leaves the maximum trace of personal inscription and perception, measuring the haunting value of literary wandering.

A View of the Picture: To the Lighthouse

But, whatever the reason may be, I find that scene is my natural way of marking the past. Always a scene has arranged itself: representative, enduring.

    "A Sketch of the Past," *Moments of Being*

PROTECTIVE SCENES

Several pictures of pictures in *To the Lighthouse*[44] provide their own perspective on enclosure. Mr. Bankes, wondering at Mrs. Ramsay's silent beauty, at the "swoop and fall of the spirit upon truth" which she exemplifies, has, he thinks to himself, to catch the 10:30 train at Euston; the hapless juxtaposition of those two concepts in the same sentence reveals the definite if droll limit on the sides of the portrait: beauty is edged in by time and practical considerations. Even if "one must remember the quivering thing, the living thing . . . and work it into the picture" (TL, p. 47), the picture is decidedly nervous, as the repetition declares: "He did not know. He did not know. He must go to his work" (TL, p. 48).

But that comic closure serves: Mr. Bankes has thereby formed his own self-portrait for us, in forming Mrs. Ramsay's, and it is to his unimaginative view that the more abstract picture made by Lily Briscoe will be initially presented. Lily shows him her picture with a singular purple shape, "just there," which is the trace upon her canvas of the subject, Mrs. Ramsay reading to little James. As opposed to the singular shape, Mr. Bankes thinks with the words of the generalizing onlooker: "Mother and child, objects of universal veneration." The picture, says Lily, is not meant to represent them, but to render them the tribute of "a shadow here and a light there." Her worry is not exterior reference, but rather interior coherence: how can she connect this mass on the right with the one on the left, without breaking the unity of the whole? But then she herself puts a closure to this scene, by taking "the canvas lightly off the easel," and closing her paintbox more firmly than is necessary. The click of closure seems "to surround in a circle forever" everything within her range of sight (TL, p. 83).

To these perspectives of framing in by closures practical, temporal, and spatial, the borders may be neat; they may, on the other hand, be interrupted by the slightest gesture, as for instance the edge of "an authenticated masterpiece by Michael Angelo" is interrupted by Mrs. Ramsay's shawl as she tosses it over the gilt frame. Being quite as genuine as it, she is the more authenticated by the insertion of the picture, becoming a Madonna touched by the Master's hand, as both frame and shawl outline her head "absurdly"—a hyperbolic to be read as supermotivated and superlative—as she raises her little boy's forehead toward her, to kiss him. This second Madonna scene may be compared to Madame Arnoux's dazzling portrait on Flaubert's ship in *Sentimental Education*, and referred back implicitly to the classic motif of protective mother and protected child, for "universal veneration," as Mr. Bankes would say.

Later, Mrs. Ramsay, seeing her husband's need to protect her, removes the green shawl from the picture frame to fold it about her shoulders and take his arm, as if by a substitute gesture: the picture is still protective and a work of natural art.

Yet a last scene for Mrs. Ramsay's interruptive, pictorial, and protective shawl pictures her winding it about the preserved skull of the boar which so frightens her little girl, shutting off the terror and making a circular curtain phrased like a reassuringly repetitive nursery song: "wound it round the skull, round and round and round . . ." (TL, p. 173). But at the same time Mrs. Ramsay reassures little James, before he goes to sleep, that the treasure is "quite unhurt. He made sure that the skull was still there under the shawl. But he wanted to ask her something more. Would they go to the Lighthouse tomorrow?" (TL, p. 173). As she is angry with them all for having aroused his hopes—since she must say no—she herself reaches for the protective object, misses it, and thereby sets a firm closure on this sequel to the Madonna scene, at the center of which a *vanitas* figures: "Then feeling for her shawl and remembering that she had wrapped it round the boar's skull, she got up, and pulled the window down another inch or two, and heard the wind, and got a breath of the perfectly indifferent chill night air and murmured good-night to Mildred and left the room and let the tongue of the door slowly lengthen in the lock and went out" (TL, p. 173). Signals of strong ending pervade this text of closure on all sides. On the side of human feeling: loss, and a sensation of chill; on the side of nature: the sound of wind, the breath of the frigid air, and the darkness; on the verbal side, a habitual message of closure, in the "good-night" said to the little girl, and a further suggestion, only adumbrated in the "tongue" of the door slowly lengthening prior to departure, of the text speaking its own closure; on the gestural side, Mrs. Ramsay's rising to her feet from the seated and more thoughtful position, and leaving the room, even repeated in her "going out" (TL, p. 173).

By the repetitions as in the departure, this scene is closed off; the three deliberately framed shawl scenes of protection and nurturing prepare the loss of Mrs. Ramsay herself, and her generative impulse.

In a second reading, this set of portraits, protective passages, and closures reframes itself in its very imperfection as compared with the clear edges of much former literary portraiture, of which Flaubert's picture of Madame Arnoux on shipboard, already referred to, stands as an example, framed as she is through the eyes of her admirer, posed in front of a sunlit background, set in high relief against the flat and full surroundings: a perfect and perfectly framed portrait. On the other hand, contemporary closure is often imperfect, by design, and imperfectly said: "It was only that she could never say what she felt. Was there no crumb on his coat? Nothing she could do for him? . . . Will you not tell me just for once that you love me? . . . But she could not do it; she could not say it." The knowledge, however, is no less certain: "She had not said it: yet he knew" (TL, p. 136).

What the reader must add to what is not said, in order to read it and to frame it, makes a double construction for the closure. The shawl that covered the frame and then covered Mrs. Ramsay's shoulders now covers—but cannot hide—the skull; and Mrs. Ramsay will die, always, in the middle section of the book, her death veiled over and left in ellipsis as the canvas has been. The loss, we remember, is inscribed only between brackets, inset deeply in text and memory for all its quiet; this is the inner frame for the picture. "Mr. Ramsay, stumbling along a passage one dark morning, stretched his arms out, but Mrs. Ramsay having died rather suddenly the night before, his arms, though stretched out, remained empty" (TL, p. 194).

James's question about the lighthouse, and what it is, is authentically answered only in the text itself. At the end of the novel, Lily Briscoe's canvas, also "authenticated" in its own way as the tribute she had wanted it to be, replaces or reframes the Michelangelo: even the Madonna scene, with the head outlined "absurdly" by the gilt frame, is itself replaced and kept. The text preserves, although the scenes are "already the past," and Mrs. Ramsay's cohering influence has departed. The work of art and vision she insisted upon endures.

Later, Mrs. Ramsay's heritage, protective and revealing, previously signified by the shawl, confers on Lily Briscoe the power to paint, inspires her sight, according to one possible interpretation by the reader of those junctures of shawl and canvas, of life and art, of love and vision.[45] "Mrs. Ramsay, Mrs. Ramsay," Lily will call, tears streaming down her face; like Marcel's sobs, at his recognition of the extent to which he depends upon his mother, the call has not ceased: it persists all the more strongly when protected and cloaked over, covered up by the life and other speech, both exposed and framed by the text.

MOMENTS AND MEMORIES

Great framers of the past as it lives, present to the time of the text and its reading, Proust and Woolf are not dissimilar in the form and substance of their loving preservation of the epiphanic and revelatory instant. This is their heritage for us, as we would preserve our own significant instants, even in our transience. In life lived as literature, afterward, as in living commentary upon it, the placing into words of the memory and the moment enhances being itself.

To read Woolf's own appreciation of James and Proust is already to go some way toward understanding at once why the three have been chosen here to represent modernist writing and in what ways, for all their similar concentration on "illumination and analysis," Woolf is in fact nearer to Proust than to James, whose world of extraordinary perceptions she finds expanded by Proust to a

> sympathy so great that it almost defeats its own object. . . . For one thing, Henry James himself, the American . . . was an obstacle never perfectly assimilated even by the juices of his own art. Proust, the product of the civilization which he describes, is so porous, so pliable, so perfectly receptive, that we realize him only as an envelope, thin but elastic, which stretches wider and wider and serves not to enforce a view but to enclose a world. His whole universe is steeped in the light of intelligence. . . .The commonest actions, such as going

up in an elevator or eating cake, instead of being discharged automaticaly, rake up in their progress a whole series of thoughts, sensations, ideas, memories which were apparently sleeping on the walls of the mind. (GR, pp. 123-24)

Closely resembling Proust's privileged moments, Woolf's moments of shock and revelation are caused by something coming forth to the perception from "behind the cotton wool of daily life. . . . It is or will become a revelation of some order; it is a token of some real thing behind appearances, and I make it real by putting it into words. It is only by putting it into words that I make it whole."[46] These epiphanic moments must compensate for the "nonbeing" of the other times which make up most of our day. (I am reminded of what the surrealist André Breton called "nul" moments, refusing even to describe them, rejecting their description in the classic novels, to the profit of the intense perceptions awaited, concentrated upon, and hoped for above all else.)

Such a moment is found in *Mrs. Dalloway*, when the noise of the door's hinges brings back memories not just in the text but of the life, that life so intensely lived in the summers of St. Ives and recalled in "A Sketch of the Past," from *Moments of Being*: "For so it had always seemed to her when, with a little squeak of the hinges, which she could hear now . . ." (quoted in MB, pp. 23-24), as bringing back the sounds of Talland House and its entrance gate, like a high beginning signal· "You entered Talland House by a large wooden gate, the sound of whose latch clicking comes back . . ." (MB, p. 111). Like Swann's announcement at that other gate—that double ring—this entrance signal is an example of strong sonorous framing.

So it is with each of the elements transposed into *To the Lighthouse* and *The Waves*: The brooch lost at Talland House by a guest and shouted by the town crier, becomes Minta's lost brooch in the former novel. The towel the nurse folded over the fender, so that Virginia would not be frightened by the sight of the fire, finds its response in Cam's wanting the shawl to be thrown over the boar's skull in *To the Lighthouse*. The memories of Thoby in the sailboat with Leslie Stephen, his eyes bluer than ever at the thought of having to prove himself, are transposed in the scene between James and his father in the boat itself sailing *To the Lighthouse*. As the waves gave their rhythm to St. Ives, so they continue to beat on the shore of the novel by that name. These are moments recalled, revealing, and then made doubly real by being put in the words of a text. Thereby, too, they are made whole and rescued from dispersion, that they may make reparation for the fragments of the collage and the nullity of the other moments. Each is cast in a fashion to prolong it, in the text and in the mind, like those scenes Woolf said she made of the past, so that it might endure. It is after all, what we might do—if we could—with our own past, as it is lived and read into our present.

The Waves: *Poetics of a Pattern*

'Like' and 'like' and 'like'—but what is the thing that lies beneath the semblance of the thing? . . . let me see the thing. There is a square; there is an oblong. The players take the square and place it upon the oblong. They place it very accurately: they make a perfect dwelling-place. Very little is left outside. The structure is now visible; what is inchoate is here stated: we are not so various or so mean; we have made oblongs and stood them upon squares. This is our triumph; this is our consolation.[47]
   The Waves

STROKE, TEXTURE, DESIGN

Might not the fragments of our perception be so saturated that they, like prose, would become a poem? "Prose must take over—has indeed, already taken over—some of the duties which were once discharged by poetry" (February 21, 1927).[48] Certainly *The Waves* became the "poet's book" Virginia Woolf wanted to write: "what I want now to do is to saturate every atom. I mean to eliminate all waste, deadness, superfluity: to give the moment whole; whatever it includes. Say that the moment is a combination of thought; sensation; the voice of the sea. . . . Why admit anything to literature that is not poetry—by which I mean saturated?" (WD, p. 138). In this "ecstatic book," as Woolf called it, against a background of black wave there are held up for our perception, in alternate glimpses, a green bar, a purple ball, a pale yellow slab, then a red sunset, and elsewhere, an expanse of green grass, a red carnation, and some lavender violets; inside, a window is reflected in the side of a green jar, near a brown cabinet, and on a green baize-covered table, the white napkins from which memory unfolds, and this book with it.

"Look." The shape, edge, and mass of things, their proportions and distortions, are presented in themselves as objects for a painter's eye, detached from specific reference as they are from use; with the removal of superfluity, the substance as meaning is stripped bare, within its visible borders.[49] What is perceived throughout this book is available aesthetically, to the senses, and to thought, rather than to direct representation:

> The room was gradually rising into view, like a thing that drowned many fathoms deep; shapes were taking on mass and edge. Here was the line of a picture frame; here the door of a cupboard; here, perhaps, most baffling, was a pool of glass; a mirror; giving another view of the room. And yellows and purples instead of being evenly framed ran, like paint to the tip of a brush, down into corners, or along rims—giving a false view of the proportions even of such ordinary objects as a plate, or a knife and fork. (W, I, p. 113)

From "such ordinary objects" is made a new painting; but the picture turns about, in its lines and sense, as we watch. To its high color corresponds a high and constantly shifting intricacy of nonreferential pattern, accompanied, threatened, and stifled by the bass continuo of the waves pounding upon the shore, like some darkly stamping beast: "so now, the sound of the sea, its great thunder of water, made all these little [brightnesses?], these intricacies, these lines and spirals, intersecting, obscuring, cutting each other into zigzags to shapes, forgotten; by its rise and fall, its smooth falling; its blackness; its perfect regularity and monotony and indifference" (W, I, p. 192). Indifference wins out over the bright intricacy, as the temporal pattern of the day will win out finally over the figures included within it.

Other designs rise against the dark: from the outset the aging children play and speak and see in formal and characteristic patterns, in an initial antiphonal chant opposing the three male to the three female voices, each of the latter representing an element; Jinny's fiery physicality, Rhoda's watery isolation, Susan's proximity to earthy and natural things. The beginning verbs alternate between seeing and hearing, in this aesthetically foregrounded world so sharply designed by and for the senses:

> "I see a ring," said Bernard . . .
> "I see a slab of pale yellow," said Susan . . .
> "I hear a sound," said Rhoda . . .
> "I see a globe," said Neville . . .
> "I see a crimson tassel," said Jinny . . .
> "I hear something stamping," said Louis . . .

The distinct rhythmic play of the individual voices against and with each other in counterpoint prepares the sustained interior narrative of each. The rhapsodic musings reveal the six lives in their most essential aspects, as well as their characteristic representations in the collective picture, those identifying traits and features, like Jinny's gesture of lifting her arm, Susan's workworn hands, Rhoda's dreaming eyes, Louis's self-consciousness, Neville's exactitude, Bernard's verbalizing. The antiphonal structure between the six characters works out on a larger scale the structure already apparent at the inception: I see / I see / I hear / I see / I see / I hear; the corresponding framing pattern of ten panels, with its classic borders, forms the text into a perceptual whole, while at the same time evolving through the cycle of the seasons, the lapse of one day, and the life of six characters, separately and together. " 'I do not believe in separation. I am not single,' says Bernard" (W, p. 67). Individual perception is given coherence by the collective. The consciously impersonal italicized interludes describe the rise and fall of one day as a metonymy for a whole life; during the first five, the sun rises, and during the last five, it sets among the breaking waves. These interludes are composed of waves and shore, of dawn and evening light, of birdsong and trees, and a quiet room; their recurring pattern set against the personal meditations[50] provides a densely textured balance.

The stress laid upon the centralizing or focusing and heavily patterned interludes serves the novelist's purpose as painter and poet, to shift attention between the narration with its personal engagement and the bordering design. *The Waves* was not to be read as a novel, said Virginia Woolf (W, II, p. 582). Her constant preoccupation here is never with plot and always with perception, whose crucial processes are a deep fascination with the various, the six-sided sight as opposed to the single one: the constant temptation to be absorbed by the object perceived with poetic concentration—that gift Woolf has and shares—is countered by the shifting sides of the high perception itself. "One might well be dazed in a trace if one looked with complete intensity at one thing: might well feel the whole mind sucked down a funnel; amazed at the existence of objects; whereas, when the light forever changed . . . then the mind was following wild gleams and likenesses; forever seeing resemblances and not knowing where the edge was" (W, I, p. 177).

A study of the holograph drafts makes clear her increased insistence upon the framing design.[51] Originally, only one of the ten interludes began with the sun's position in the sky, and the vivid picture of the land and seascape now to be read in every interlude was far less striking; in the final version, each interlude sums up the preceding one, commencing its attack in like fashion, with the sun and its position: "The sun was now . . . ," and with the color of the sky. The waves' strokes in their semiabstract horizontal pattern upon the picture are a stylized surface that suggests the folds from which the text develops, as from the folds of a handkerchief or a napkin (both of which enter the scene here), opening out with memories and closing up in a design their interrelating feeling and form.[52]

FOLDS AND OPENINGS

In the successive reworkings of a crucial passage, garden and sea, passivity and perception, representation and creation, the single and the collective life are seen as they are gathered into a unifying whole. The first draft and corrections read thus:

> mind
> However, the lonely person, man or woman, young or aged, for it ~~who would be thinking there, in the room, thinking~~ does not matter—the power that centralises, what ~~must else~~ is otherwise be lost, ~~gathering together~~ in its mind, not collecting . . . all that was said in the garden, but ~~some~~ fragments, ~~& then, setting to work to make them coherent; for the world now begin, Even~~ in ~~this pale dawn to~~ making a coherency of them, ~~would~~ now ~~drew the book to~~ opened ~~the book & wrote~~; thought; I am ~~here trying to~~ telling myself the story of the world from the beginning; ~~making from the after all,~~ I am ~~no longer~~ not ~~tossing on the waves~~ concerned with the single life; ~~I am~~ but ~~the thinker who compares; &,~~ am ~~now thinking it together to so that making unity; & in the hope that there will be when I have this scene~~ . . . But ~~what certainly~~ since they are all to be seen ~~at together then,~~ at the same moment; this is the beginning of the ~~story. The white fresh page has this on it.~~ (W, I, p. 6)

These unifying strokes, preserving folded or implicated pleats kept in the mind, like furrows of land and sea and thought, gather into the creased napkin "such fragments as time having broken the perfect vessel keeps safe" (W, I, p. 9). This last fragment, reworked to a fine edge, reappears in a coherent final text of gathering, whose focus fits a room and a unifying sight: "I am not concerned with the single life but with lives together. I am trying to find in the folds of the past such fragments as time preserves . . . there was a napkin, a flowerpot and a book. I am telling the story of the world from the beginning, and in a small room, whose windows were open" (W, II, p. 42). The room and the windows hold and join interior and exterior vision: the folds of the napkin or the creases of the tablecloth around which the six personalities will be knit in circular and privileged moments, simultaneously represent the waves "sinking and falling, many mothers, and again, many mothers, and behind them many more, endlessly sinking and falling." As the matrix image of the text, these nightgowned mothers hold up into the height of the crest, and depose upon the shore, a child. The mode is that of *generation*, the images those of opening and flow. The creases and folds of gown and wave gather up a series of implicated objects small and large: Susan's handkerchief, twisted and crumpled from her agony at seeing, framed through a hole in the hedge, Jinny kiss Louis, as well as the sheets of the dormitory beds opening out in the pages; yet the rich creases are also and still the lines of the sand shoals, lying under the sea, like a design on the freshly swept page.

The napkin unfolds or *explicates* into life a host of individual and collective memories, each of which, returning like a leitmotif along with the pounding of the waves, remains a constant center, Proustian and preserved. Gradually building its momentum, the image impresses itself on the reader's mind, throughout the draft versions: "The lady sits between the two long windows, writing. The gardeners sweep the leaves with giant brooms" (W, I, p. 15), and the sight so highlighted is shared: " 'I see the lady writing. I see the gardeners sweeping,' said Susan" (W, I, p. 17). Simple, the phrase returns at the center of memory and language, an image held transfixed in the text and recounted: " 'At Elvedon the gardeners swept and swept with their great brooms, and the woman sat at a table writing,' said Bernard" (W, I, p. 142). In these woods of Elvedon, life is seen mixed with other lives, haunted by the figure of a lady writing, "between two windows. And the solitary is no longer solitary" (W, I, p. 17). As a little crease in the napkin opening out into the woods forms the original trace, this "first writing on the first page," the phrase is able to gather the elements caught in the memory like a net, to intensify and to hold the images, "for otherwise they must perish. And then, when the phrase has been found, it must be spoken aloud, to somebody else" (W, I, p. 17). These are the stages of perception and creation, unfolding from the central image to set the whole in successive stages, opening out. The cohering power of sight and statement is made visible as it is framed in the borders of a little clearing of the forest at Elvedon: "Down below, through the depths of the leaves, the gardeners swept the lawns with great brooms. The lady sat writing. Transfixed, stopped dead, I thought, 'I cannot interfere with a single stroke of those brooms. They sweep and they sweep. Nor with the fixity of that woman writing.' It is strange that one cannot stop gardeners sweeping nor dislodge a woman. There they have remained all my life" (W, p. 241).

And then in the final chapter, an elderly Bernard now meditates upon the old, familiar, and simple image, rendered present by the gerundive, as the image makes a cohering interior knowledge, knowing at once its content and its limits: "And by some flick of a scent or a sound on a nerve, the old image—the gardeners sweeping, the lady writing—returned. I saw the figures beneath the beech trees at Elvedon. The gardeners swept; the lady at the table sat writing. But I now made the contribution of maturity to childhood's intuitions—satiety and doom, the sense of what is unescapable in our lot; death; the knowledge of limitations; how life is more obdurate than one had thought it" (W, pp. 268-69). Having endured throughout the life, as throughout this long text, the image must be passed on, "to somebody else." And so it has been.

THE COHERING PICTURE

In each of Virginia Woolf's novels, there falls to one character the task of forming the central coherence by taking and developing the group picture from different colors and shapes and substances, until the final composition is there to be understood: " 'I was this,' says Louis, 'Neville that, Rhoda different again, and Bernard too.' " (W, p. 126). By the multiple shifts in lighting and perspective, the substance of each character is displayed, half-abstract, for example, pure color or pure form, non-referential; "in violent patches, spaced by blank voids," these substances form a collective picture (W, p. 125). Their picture is made by Bernard, for "It is he who is the centre of these troops; he who presides and causes these contradictory waves to circle round him" (W, I, p. 344), like the six converging figures. To him is given the writer's responsibility of framing, from disparate images and from fragments of consciousness, a holistic perception; gathering the pattern, first for the farewell to Percival where the group about the dinner table forms a flower with seven sides, and then in the corresponding group dinner at Hampton Court, where their diminished and only six-sided flower is preserved: from the rising and falling of nature, sun, and time; from the swelling of the waves upon the shore and their break, with which this book will end.

The napkin preserves in its folds the framed moments around all the tables of memory, which are the gathering places of Woolf's tableaux, but which also serve as the conveners of the elements in memory: " 'I do not know altogether where I am,' said Bernard; 'which of the many little white tables with glasses and knives and forks this one is' " (W, I, p. 343). Past and future are linked as the table scene joins others, from *Mrs. Dalloway* and from *To the Lighthouse* in particular: these set scenes are the high moments of the text, accentuating not the abstract outer analytical description, but the unique and united moment: here, now, as the rhythm makes an expectant pause, the six friends await their hero, Percival, as the predicted center of their circle and of their picture. Each turn of the revolving restaurant door makes an empty framework under their collective gaze, centered on one focal point: "Things quiver as if not yet in being" (W, p. 118). Their world is made up of waiting, of their watching eyes, of the blankness of the white tablecloth like a page on which their collective story has not yet been completely written. Each person entering is defined negatively, by not being Percival, whereas each reiteration of the obsessive borders that will eventually contain his appearance increases the accumulating suspense: " 'The door opens, the door goes on opening,' said Neville, 'Yet he does not come.' " (W, p. 120). The shape of each glance returns to be caught and controlled by the door's outline: " 'He has not come,' says Neville. 'The door opens and he does not come' " (W, p. 121). Like the lighthouse beam pulsing its rhythm as the temporal indication for the dinner tableau in *To the Lighthouse*, the revolving of the door here gives form to the glances in the long delay, where the reader too awaits the entrance around which the scene has to focus, and which is empty in its revolving border.

At Percival's entrance, the antiphonal play of distinct voices greeting the hero echoes the beginning passage of perception in its distinctly patterned outline:

> "Now," said Neville, "my tree flowers. My heart rises. All oppression is relieved. All impediment is removed. The reign of chaos is over. . . ."
>
> "Here is Percival," said Jinny. "He has not dressed."
>
> "Here is Percival," said Bernard . . . "sitting together now we love each other and believe in our own endurance."
>
> "Now let us issue from the darkness of solitude," said Louis.
>
> "Now let us say, brutally and directly, what is in our minds," said Neville. "Our isolation, our preparation is over." (W, p. 124)

Bernard speaks for this assembly whose desire knits them together in their seeing, humanly disparate but with the same borders to their collective gaze at present: "some deep, some common emotion. . . . We have come together . . . to make one thing, not enduring—for what endures? but seen by many eyes spontaneously" (W, p. 127). The contradictory impulses working against the common borders are clear: the instant coherence is lasting and not lasting, is worked out in depth and yet perceived only upon the surface. For the figures remain separate and find their juncture only in this instant framing.

Rhoda summons the members of the collective circle to bear

witness to their own sharpening of senses, their original statements on vision recaptured now: " 'I see . . . I see . . . I hear.
. . .' 'Look,' said Rhoda; 'listen . . . look how the light becomes
richer, second by second, and bloom and ripeness lie everywhere;
and your eyes, as they range round this room with all its tables,
seem to push through curtains of colour, red, orange, umber,
and queer ambiguous tints' " (W, I, p. 135). A chain of steel
blue is described as joining them together in one whole, bound
in a firm and festive frame, like the more fragile globe of perception, that metaphor "whose walls are made of Percival."

The determination of the participants to hold on to the picture
allows the perception "globing" itself to gather up the text within
itself: it must be held up whole against the litter of crumbs and
the dissipation of fragments and fruit peelings, against the dullness of everyday living and the everyday people—who are not
Percival—visible to everyday perception. In one of the peaks of
lyric swell, like the sweep of some giant and mounting wave, the
voices fill their perfected picture with their own concerns, the
figures separate in their outlines:

> "Forests and far countries on the other side of the world,"
> said Rhoda, "are in it; seas and jungles . . ."
>
> "Happiness is in it," said Neville, "And the quiet of or-
> dinary things . . ."
>
> "Weekdays are in it," said Susan, "Monday, Tuesday,
> Wednesday: the horses going up to the fields, and the horses
> returning; the rooks rising and falling, and catching the elm
> trees in their net . . ."
>
> "What is to come is in it," said Bernard . . ."We too have
> made something that will join the innumerable congrega-
> tions of past time." (W, I, pp. 145-46)

The picture shows coherence, as it is contained.

EBB AND SHADOW

But into the picture "the shadow slants." The outline of their
collective picture loses its sharpness, until at last the chain breaks,

disorder returns, and the current of time and unhappiness flows faster even than before. What, asks Bernard, "does the central shadow hold?" The omnipresent and haunting curtain of death and darkness, hanging over the light upon the sea—this natural temporal frame constantly perceived in the italicized panels—will fall slowly and then more rapidly as the wave is felt to fall, over the six-sided personal construction globed and meant to have been preserved: "I have been all," says Bernard, "but no more."

The collective lament at Percival's going ("how may we signal to all time to come that we, who stand in the street, in the lamplight, loved Percival?") marks also the end of the miraculous cohesion in the group painting: " 'For ever,' said Louis, 'divided' " (W, p. 231). Bernard's globe of sensation should have held against division, until its truth is challenged: "The illusion is upon me that something adheres for a moment, has roundness, weight, depth, is completed. This, for the moment, seems to be my life" (W, p. 238). The others do not see the completed spectacle he has bordered, but only an elderly man, grey at the temples, unfolding his napkin, from whose folds the memories have been pulled forth. In a final phantom dinner party, he sums up their lives in a last framing monologue, becoming part of their picture (draft in the notebook, p. 757),[53] before the "general death," as Woolf first planned it. But the point of view suddenly switches toward the outside, where his one consciousness is reflected upon as if it were to have perished: "Now he is dead, the man I called Bernard."

The fate of Bernard's consciousness so pictured, in his personal sight, is that of the picture seen also from outside. For that reason, the emotional weight suspended from his personal losses and findings, of a train ticket as of a mood, rings with a special significance: " 'He has gone,' " said Neville, " 'Without a ticket. . . . Are we not all phrases in Bernard's story? . . . The train has gone without him, he has missed his train; he has lost his ticket. But it does not matter" (W, II, p. 474). When he is finally seen to have kept the other half, like a talisman retrieved, he is perceived to have gathered himself and his fragments of consciousness within individual borders, which do indeed matter for the whole issue of personal formulation: "I, Bernard." Formerly constituted only by his audience, for whom he has summed up settings and situations, he now takes on again, and completely, the burden of a consciousness individual and collective, in a simple but all the more effective statement of a cohesive picture: " 'Heaven be praised, I said, we need not whip this prose into poetry. The little language is enough' " (W, p. 263). And still later, the cohering moment regains its own sufficient frame: "The moment was all; the moment was enough."

FORMAL BORDERS

Around this personal meditation, the formal and natural borders for human perception remain strongly marked. As the slow rhythm of the ten panels of *The Waves* crosscuts against and interferes with the continuing narration and psychological development within, the sea continues to be heard, like a tragic chorus. The natural and descriptive borders of panels are closely linked in style and images, from the opening shot to the final break of the waves upon the shore in a single line. These meditations, as if emanating from some unspecified and impersonal voice, roll the few leitmotifs about like a small collection of pebbles, as the contours of the stated themes constantly intersect, sharing meanings and shifting lights in the forceful current of the descriptive passages. The *fall* of a wave becomes the fall of a leaf, of another sort of leaf or page, then the fall of the wind, whose *rise* is also the rise of both wave and sun; the intensely felt renewal in the conclusion is explicitly based on the rise and fall of water, of life, and of light, its force mounting wavelike until the final play on the word *break*, whose violence and yet obdurate hope the accumulated vigor enhances. Similarly, the *blade* of light, like a sharp and piercing ray of light, cuts and slices like a fan-shaped blade radiating from the central solar source, laid in broad strokes against the objects described. Cutting and separating, the blade connotes the sharpness of birdsong, the distinction of the notes, and the characters' aloneness within the monologues, each separate from the other, at the center of the search for things unbroken, for the wholeness of experience and the pictured moment.

The blades are also, originally, the shoulderblades of the woman who holds the lamp emitting the rays; but her outline becomes fainter and fainter as the border progressively loses its personal substance, to be made the formalized frame of sun and sea. Similarly, the gatherings of sheep *flock* together in *folds*, of shadow, *rolling* away or in, like the waves and the gathering night, while the dark itself washes in like the water, covering and discovering, *sweeping* in and over. The meanings too sweep and wash together, as perceptions are both clear and clouded, the outlines of objects both distinct and blurred, depending on the light and the perspective. Each frame composes a prose poem, quietly and unobtrusively: "this is poetry if we do not write it" (W, p. 196). Exalted in tone and formalized, each interrupts and interferes and intervenes, separating and bridging the monologue developments.

Description of description rarely suffices, and only the overall bridging can be suggested here. Briefly, the massing of waves, in their gradual deepening and darkening green hollows, together with the "shrill and sharp chorus" of the birds after each note sounds singly, form the continuo within the natural or framing sections of the text, where, in the interior narrative thus framed, each voice has its own monologue and then speaks in relation to others, as if responding to the birdsongs without. The birds, in harmony and then in singleness, in relation and in rivalry and in love, sang tremulously *"in the clear morning air . . . singing together as they chased each other, escaping, pursuing, pecking each other as they turned high in the air"* (W, pp. 73-74). The framing bird figures also set the *model* for human perception, for the sudden focus on one thing, on one object of concentration, as the attention of the group is called all at once to the singular thing like that of the friends focusing on the door through which Percival was to come, a passage marked with a violent clarity.

The sharp verbs themselves pierce into the border, as the birds plunge their beaks into the soft and amorphous body of the slug or the worm, cutting, like the blades of light, against all the profusion of the soft and the undefined. Again, following that border, the combined action of the group is severed like the song's contours, and gives them coherence, centering their gaze. The collective moments, outer and inner, confer intensity upon the formless, upon the shapeless to which they would give clearer form: *"They sang as if the song were urged out of them by the pressure of the morning. They sang as if the edge of being were sharpened and must cut, must split the softness of the blue-green light, the dampness of the wet earth; the fumes and steams of the greasy kitchen vapour; the hot breath of mutton and beef; the richness of pastry and fruit. . . . On all the sodden, the damp-spotted, the curled with wetness, they descended, dry-beaked, ruthless, abrupt"* (W, p. 109).

Now the correspondingly sharp objects, both exterior and interior, acquire definition and edge within the border, the sun falling in "sharp wedges," the plate gleaming like a frozen lake, the knife becoming an icy dagger: shapes that were unspecified take on hard outlines from the increasingly severe light, its pitiless clarity encouraging human severity, striking like the "flash of a falling blade," its glint dramatic in its disintegration of mass, its own waves pounding upon the house like the waves upon the shore. At evening, a flock of birds slices furrows in the twilight, while one sits solitary: the waves of light make a bravura traverse, like the image whose sight continually haunted Virginia Woolf: "a sudden flaunt and flash as if a fin cut the green glass of a lake." Each blade of grass or of light is perceived singly, and the glance focuses upon single spots of color: a brown cabinet, baize green the glint of a silver knife and fork, a lone green tree, a single spear of sun, and the side of one green jar, in which there wavers the window's reflection, as if in liquid response to the title. At the end, in the text penetrated by the waters as if by death itself, there falls a final sunset glow, redeeming mortality by the warmest colors: "A redness gathers on the roses, even on the pale rose by the bedroom window" (W, p. 296). Just so, within the heavy patterned borders, the single is gathered up within the mass, a

single birdsong into a crescendo of massed chorus and its reiteration, or from the rise of the wind to its summit force before its
subsiding. Within the overall pattern of rise and fall, leading from
dawn to sunset like the rise and diminution of a life or the rise
of a wave to its fall and break upon the shore—the verbal and
visual shifts, the distinctions and junctures of individual and group
voices, repeat in the inner human world the poetic frame outside.

Neither Bernard's narrative nor his will for coherence can hold
up against death. Against his acceptance of the waves rising in
himself, unyielding though he proves himself, there is set the
"omniscient epilogue" of the final line, set alone and standing for
the entire frame, retrospectively: *"The waves broke on the shore."*
His gesture of resistance is, of course, to no avail, as his will to
gathering is challenged and finally, naturally, vanquished by the
natural force with which Woolf equates the formal border and
asserts, in so doing, the final triumph of the authorial text over
the individual narration. Lyric, convincing, the text wins out, for
this final frame, however natural its reference, is the final tribute
to art.

There is little time, indeed, to complete the picture, whose
brushstrokes pick up, nevertheless, as each protective cover may
coincide with or produce a revelation at least momentary. The
reader now superposing one frame upon another, shawl upon
shawl, sight upon sight, and canvas upon canvas, has at least the
chance to construct, like Lily Briscoe, an individual picture that
can enclose "in a circle, forever," all there is before the eyes.

Yet at that moment, distance is recaptured, as space sets out a
picture and time stands still as if to keep it, seen from a high
viewing place chosen both in art and in life, far above the domestic and the natural scenes. Here, like Marcel, we seem all to
have lived our own lives as a painter, as if the picture, even the
one we know we constructed, were suddenly to be held out for
us by an age-old nurturing figure coming from the most ancient
time of life and of literature, held out already framed, beyond
fiction, both paged and true: "But for a moment I had sat on

the turf somewhere high above the flow of the sea and the sounds of the woods, had seen the house, the garden, and the waves breaking. The old nurse who turns the pages of the picture-book had stopped and had said, 'Look. This is the truth' " (W, p. 287).

VI / CONCLUSION:
CLOSING THE BORDER

Every literary description is a view. You might say that the
enunciator, before describing anything, is placed at the window,
less in order to see clearly then to base what is seen on the
frame itself: the window-edge makes the spectacle. To describe
is thus to place the empty frame which the realist author always
transports with him (more important than his easel), in front of
a collection or a continuum of objects inaccessible to language
without this maniacal operation . . . in order to speak about it,
the writer by an initial ritual, must first transform the "real" into
a painted object (framed) . . .
    ROLAND BARTHES, "The Model of Painting," *S/Z*

Each of the preceding essays, dealing with a different aspect of
the problems of and the attitudes toward framing, can be seen,
nevertheless, to turn around the same group of techniques for
putting the selected picture into relief: delays and pauses to surround, with temporal and spatial borders, the central focused
part, architectural surrounds to further mark them, repetitions
and drastic contrasts to call attention either to the borders or to
the dramatic quality of the scene pictured in them, an included
picture to develop by nonverbal means the significance of the
moral or psychological issues implied in the motifs thrown in
relief or an included observer to eye the picture from within it,
making an inner frame of vision useful (at times by its very deformation) for the reading from the outer border. The included
observer is metonymic for our own observation, and such parodies as Melville's *Pierre* and James's *The Sacred Fount* demonstrate the follies of pattern hunting and obsessive frame monger-
ing.
    The distance from the earlier tendency toward the isolation of

a picture or a scene as framed to stand out from the rest, or to stand still in the center of the narrative flux, to the later thrust toward the notion of the frame itself as the principal object of interest, represents the distance from premodernism to modernism at its height. From this point of view, to compare, for example, Jane Austen and Henry James is to compare a universe whose essential tidiness makes its own borders, further elaborated for specific moral assumptions and suggestions, with one in which the shifts of viewing stations and edging lines are themselves the spectacle, and have their own importance that depends on nothing outside, or even within. The walks and portraits of *Mansfield Park* and *Persuasion*, or again the play of the former and the overhearing in the latter are, in their complications, directed beyond themselves, toward the outcome. In the earlier late James, for instance, in *The Ambassadors*, the framing devices seem directed toward the pictorial, with the point of view only, as if by accident, corresponding to the borders of the aesthetic device (of the Luxembourg garden picture, the pastoral river picture, or the balcony pictures at apartment and hotel); *The Wings of the Dove* represents an intermediate step, the melodrama threatening the autonomy of the frame, while in the late James, particularly *The Golden Bowl*, the very utilization of the images, the psychological shifts, the alternations in viewpoint might be considered the occasions for more play with the frame, rather than the essential thing itself. In short, the focus turns to the focusing borders, the view to the view itself, and the frame turns out to be the Real Thing.

Modernism, as James represents it for us, was, and is (even in the era of Post-Modernism) this. Woolf's windowframe looking out on the lighthouse in the novel by the same name, and, in *The Waves*, her frame of nature replying to and overriding the human perceptions are more interesting in their reading than are the things and objects and perceptions framed;[1] Proust, the great moral ender for this modernism tale, while doing his own reframing as he does his—and our—own remembering, shows the fall of time as the final border, but its triumph in its own ironic perception. Proust's picture of the brush about to be taken up at nightfall, Woolf's of the canvas about to be completed,[2] James's of the bowl about to be broken and the price about to be paid, these border moments are their own investment and include within themselves their own reflective statement as their sufficient reason for standing in high relief against the rest of the text.

These importations of other genres into the genre of narration reflect earlier importations: Austen's pictures of Darcy in his house bring the suggestion of art, but not its real essence—for it is only what Darcy reveals of himself that counts, not that it is an art object, and the preparation of her play brings the preparation of what is planned and not realized as actual drama into the novel of the Park; in Hardy's repeatedly framed portraits of Jude and Tess against the harrow lines and fields and stones of their own landscapes, the pictorial takes second place to the moral, and the framing concern, to the strength of the character study; Poe, in bringing the picture of "The Oval Portrait" into his narration which entirely focuses on it, and Baudelaire, in reframing the picture poetically, go past the pictorial and the dramatic to reach a kind of poetry of melancholy, but the framed moments remain suggestive of what is implied by them. The mixing in of other genres by means of the framed moment remains an aesthetic one.

On the other hand, when James forces the reader's eye upon the borders bordering, the worlds of drama and art are included, draw our attention, but are less the whole story than the borders as such, being their own vector, picture, and drama. Woolf's late novels (poetic, as she wished) have some of the greatest lyrical passages anywhere, and the surest touch for the picturing of the picture—but the borders, italicized, bounded by architecture or nature, hold us beyond all else; Proust's musical repetitions and pauses and agonized delays, such as the Venice scene, are not, any more than are his paintings and portraits, just simple insertions, but they are beyond whatever they might mean, as his window views of Mademoiselle Vinteuil may well remain in our picturing memory past the details of the scene and their import.

All of that is included in the fall of the night of time and of the end of whatever project we might frame and focus on.

All the drama and picture and poetry of the scene is highly wrought into the narrative so that the genre distinction is already refused, and the frame, enlarged, includes within its metapoetic borders both the initial genre as ground and the included genre as figure. The new picture, though, is not to be a genre study any more than it is to be a character study or a study of plot. The study of frame is always a self-study of our reading habits as well as of the picture itself; by the sharp cropping of its sides, it knows its self-reflection to be at once finished and contained.[3]

It strikes me that it might all end with a picture.

NOTES

PREFACE

1. Virginia Woolf, *The Waves*, p. 263.

I

1. Henry James, *The Art of the Novel: Critical Prefaces*, ed. R. P. Blackmur.
2. My colleague Linda Nochlin has worked on this problem in relation to Manet.
3. *The Works of John Ruskin*, ed. E. T. Cook and Alexander Wedderburn, vol. 16, p. 187. Compare, from the same oddly attractive thinker and visionary: "Only, observe, true and vital direction does not mean that, without any defection or warp by antagonist force, we can fly, or walk, or creep at once to our mark; but that, whatever the antagonist force may be, we so know and mean our mark, that we shall at last precisely arrive at it, just as surely, and it may be in some cases more quickly, than if we have been unaffected by lateral or opposing force" (ibid., vol. 28, p. 442). For a brilliant discussion of Ruskin, see Jay Fellows, *Ruskin's Maze: Mastery and Madness in His Art*. The above is quoted in chapter 5, "Circumferential Considerations: Lines without Beginnings or Endings," p. 152. Virginia Woolf, who quotes with delight Ruskin's espousal of imperfection as a sign of greatness, condenses in one sentence the essence of his attraction for us: "for if anyone is able to make his readers feel that he is alive, wrong headed, intemperate, interesting, and lovable, that writer is Ruskin" ("Ruskin," in Virginia Woolf, *The Captain's Death Bed and Other Essays*, p. 50. Hereafter cited as CD).
4. José Maria de Hérédia, "Antoine et Cléôpâtre," *Penguin Book of French Verse*, ed. Anthony Hartley, p. 422.
5. Philippe Hamon, *Introduction au genre descriptif*, refers to the same sonnet as a remarkable example of inclusion
6. *The Note-books and Papers of Gerard Manley Hopkins*, ed. H. House, p. 249.

7. The simplest formal frame is obviously that of a poem, with its evident margins and centralizing lines. John Hollander's "Upon Apthorp House," in *Spectral Emanations*, p. 199, marks and gently mocks the firm outlines of formal verse:

> Within this narrow frame expect
> No marvels to remain erect
>
> . . . .
>
> How can the stately, white expanse
> Immured in my remembered glance
> Be folded up in the confines
> Of all these short and rigid lines?

8. The term "delay" is already found in James, as I will reiterate at the appropriate point. Joseph A. Kestner's *The Spatiality of the Novel* is a good reference work, particularly the chapter called "The Virtual," pp. 69-133, for this technique and others enabling the static presentation of the tableau or scene, as it is sometimes "bound" and sometimes "free," to use Shlovsky's terminology. (Kestner takes the term "virtual" from Proust's formulation about the relation of sculpture to characterization, and applies it to what he calls "spatial secondary illusion.") He is especially good at summarizing the Russian formalist approach, that of Tomashevsky and Tynianov as well as Shlovsky on superposition, parallelism, and contradiction, and comparing it to such concepts as Wölfflin's "closed" and "open" and the work of Genette and Todorov on description and "enchâssement" or "encadrement," on antithesis, gradation, and alternation, on the primary rhythm of the act and the secondary one of the rejection of the act.

In addition to authors less germane to the present text, Kestner discusses some of the visually framed or recessed passages of Austen's *Emma*, Hawthorne's *Marble Faun*, Flaubert's *Education sentimentale*, Hardy's *Mayor of Casterbridge* and *Jude* (above all its Gothic architecture), as well as James's *Portrait of a Lady*, using, even in the works we both discuss, passages other than the ones I have chosen. He argues that the recessed scene becomes "the background" for the larger work, whereas I find what I call the inset or included scene to be the figure read against the background of the larger or enframing one. My diagrams of the frames reflect that working inward toward the enclosed figure.

II

1. Georg Simmel, "The Handle," in *The Sociology of Georg Simmel*, Kurt H. Wolff, ed. and tr., pp. 116-24. Hereafter cited as GS.

2. One of the best ways to get a useful handle on Roger Fry's own aesthetic viewpoint (in *Vision and Design*, for example), is to set it at a certain distance, with the frame of, for example, Allen Mc-Laurin's *Virginia Woolf: The Echoes Enslaved*. Part one, "Roger Fry and Virginia Woolf," pp. 17-96, discusses Fry's theories of distance, appropriate to the discussion here, of Woolf and of others.

   Like Roger Fry, Charles Bouleau, in his *Charpentes: La géométrie secrète des peintres*, insists that "the limits make the thing visible." He describes the process of "after-framing," depicted in Paillot de Montabert's *Traité complet de la peinture* (1829), when the artist or the architect suppresses or adds parts to the surrounding borders after having finished the work (p. 47), and goes into some detail on the various effects of frames (the closed circle or tondo of Florence as opposed to the open frames of friezes in their musical rhythm, for example, pp. 31-48).In this optic fits Martin Heidegger's discussion, in his *Origin of the Work of Art*, of the "Gestell" in which the work of art sets itself; at the other stylistic and visual pole, Max Black's *Models and Metaphors* includes his study of the frame of literal words around the focused center.

3. Mehlis, in his "Aesthetic Problem of Distance," in Susanne K. Langer, *Reflections on Art*, pp. 79-80.

4. José Ortega y Gasset, in *Confessiones de "El Espectador,"* *Obras completas*, vol. 2, pp. 307-13. Quotation from p. 307.

5. Edward Bullough, in *The British Journal of Psychology*, 5 (1912), pp. 87-118; Monroe C. Beardsley, *Aesthetics*, pp. 192-93, 553.

6. Louis Marin, *Détruire la peinture*, p. 47. hereafter cited as DP.

7. Paul Claudel, *Introduction à la peinture hollandaise*, pp. 169-203.

8. Jacques Derrida, *La vérité en peinture*, p. 176.

9. J. J. Gibson, *Perception of the Visual World*. Hereafter cited as PV.

10. Karl Pribram, *Languages of the Brain*, p. 136, M.D. Vernon's *Psychology of Perception* provides more and relevant material on the phenomenon of perception. Anton Ehrenzweig's *Hidden Order of Art* makes an invaluable study of "Unconscious Scanning" (pp. 32, and ff.) and of "Enveloping Pictorial Space" (pp. 110 and ff.).

11. E. H. Gombrich, *The Sense of Order: A Study in the Psychology of Decorative Art*, p. 5.
12. Meyer Schapiro, "On Some Problems in the Semiotics of Visual Art," pp. 223-42. Hereafter cited as MS.
13. Rudolf Arnheim, *Art and Visual Perception*. Hereafter cited as AVP.
14. Youri Lotman, *The Structure of the Artistic Text*, especially chapter 1.
15. Victor Brombert, "Opening Signals in Narration," pp. 489-502; Edward Said, *Beginnings: Intention and Method*; Frank Kermode, *The Sense of an Ending*. In the special issue of *Nineteenth-Century Fiction* consecrated to "Narrative Endings" (vol. 33, no. 1, June 1978), there is rich material on closure, in particular by J. Hillis Miller, on "The Tying and Untying of the Thread," about Henry James's "The Figure in the Carpet," and by Kermode on "Sensing Endings," a summary piece on the issue. See also D. A. Miller, *Narrative and Its Discontents: Problems of Closure in the Traditional Novel*; and Barbara Herrnstein Smith, *Poetic Closure: A Study of How Poems End*. Gabriel Garcia Marquez, in an interview for the *Quinzaine littéraire*, 1-15 Jan. 1982, bears witness to the importance of the opening: "La première phrase pour moi est essentielle. . . . Elle doit englober tout le livre dans une boucle complète. Je peux passer des années à penser à une première phrase." This breaking into the text reminds me of the notion of creative attack that Adrian Stokes, in *The Invitation in Art*, p. 23, speaks of at such length and with such passion, that is, the moment in which the artist picks up his brush and starts work. Stokes compares this initial gesture to an attack on the nourishing breast or the undifferentiated or screen surface in the theories of Melanie Klein: upon this unmarked surface the artist makes a mark and a difference. The attack or opening is thus both violent and loving, always charged with emotion and aggression.

Boris Uspensky's chapter "The Structural Isomorphism of Verbal and Visual Art" (pp. 130-72, with its Conclusion), and particularly the parts called "The Frame of a Pictorial Text" (pp. 137-66), in his *Poetics of Composition: The Structure of the Artistic Text and Typology of a Compositional Form*, develops the ways in which estrangement (*ostranenie*) or the alienated viewpoint, and the technique of impeded form, permit the re-viewing of a picture or a text differently and afresh. In this sense, they are related to the internal/external relation of observer to visual object, and to the definition of the framing phenomenon as the point at which we perceive a shift "between a point of view internal to the narrative and a point of view external to the narrative" (p. 148). Uspensky's analysis of the ways in which the central "lifelike" figures are opposed to the background of conventionalized description, where the intensified semiotic quality points to itself as "a sign of a sign of represented reality" (pp. 162-63), reminds us of backgrounds and borders whose deliberately "unrealistic" repetitions point to their own conventions, their semiotically interesting differentiation from the figures holding the center of the stage, whom they surround and support.

16. The narration within the dramatic mode is differentiated by the changed voice of the narrator, thus distanced from the scene of the action. The stage audience sits transfixed in arrest and jbsorbed while the voice narrates precisely that which we cannot see: for example, the Queen Mab episode in *Romeo and Juliet*, which seems to have nothing or little to do with the plot. The insets can be expository, necessary to the plot, voluntary, or free in their function, and of the play-in-the-play sort; their relation to the frame is then of various kinds, but in every case the content is different from the content of the outer or framing text. "The Inset makes a disturbance of the surface; a part of the play, more or less sharply demarked, presents a plane which contrasts with the plane of its surround. It is a matter of relief (as in bas-relief), and the variation in the surface secured by the inset may be either by advance (or obtrusion) or by recession. Another mark of an Inset is that it produces a conflict, real or apparent, between what the audience sees and what it hears, a break in the fusion between picture and word" (B, p. 98). The contrasts between the inset and the frame are of three main sorts: between foreground and background, between advance and recession in time, and between narrative and drama. Using Jane Austen's *Persuasion* to illustrate how the inset might be seen to work in a novel, Berry points out the voice differentiation in a passage where Mrs. Croft suddenly speaks and describes an action, and the vibration between a foregrounded eight months in the present against a backgrounded eight years in the past: I take up the same detail later in my chapter on Austen, from a slightly different point of view. My use of insetting here, basically in the narrative mode, has to do with paintings and the arrest of action within a pictorial mode rather than with an offstage event pictured in words; but the same marking of the fore-

ground against the background is clear, and the term highly useful. Francis Berry, *The Shakespeare Inset: Word and Picture*. Hereafter cited as B.

17. Lucien Dällenbach, *Le récit spéculaire: Essai sur la mise-en-abyme*.

18. Philippe Hamon, *Poétique du récit*, p. 36. Hereafter cited as H.

19. See Barbara Johnson, "Poetry and Performative Language," in *Yale French Studies*, Mallarmé issue (1977), pp. 140-58. And see, for a general consideration, the work of Inez Hedges, on frames and their breaking as a surrealist process, *Language of Revolt: Dada and Surrealist Literature and Film*.

20. D. W. Winnicott, *Playing and Reality*. See also D. W. Winnicott, *The Maturational Process and the Facilitating Environment*, especially pp. 181ff., on the created transitional object as it is both created and found: "In health the infant creates what is in fact lying around waiting to be found. But in health the object is created, not found. . . . The object must be found in order to be created." The original form of Winnicott's theory is in his paper "Transitional Objects and Transitional Phenomena," *Collected Papers*.

21. Gregory Bateson, *Steps to an Ecology of Mind*. Hereafter cited as SE. The diagram is from p. 184.

22. Erving Goffman, *Frame Analysis*, is hereafter cited as FA.

23. Among the paradoxes of framing and containers, Douglas Hofstadter's *Gödel, Escher, Bach: An Eternal Golden Braid*, p. 167 and ff., offers some of the best. In the bottle on the beach, for example, the fact that it is sealed and contains a dry piece of paper is itself the frame message; how we should decipher the inner enframed message (whether a haiku, a call for help, or anything else) is only apparent in the outer frame, where the set of triggers or expectations for the decoding are set up. The size of that outer frame is to be taken into account, because the nested structure of a frame lets the observer "zoom in" and adapt the size of the subframe to the amount of detail desired. What is proper to the frame Hofstadter calls "self-engulfing," related to the classic phenomenon of mise-en-abyme. On which, see Dällenbach, *Le récit spéculaire*.

24. Eisenstein, "The Cinematographic Principle of the Ideogram," in *Film Form*, p. 4.

25. Henry James, preface to *The Awkward Age*, p. 10.

26. My "Moral-Reading, or Self-Containment with a Flaw," in the issue of *New Literary History* devoted to "Literature and/as Moral Philosophy" (vol. 15, 1983-84), pp. 209-15, deals with *"The Golden Bowl*

... as a great container for the issue of morality and of reading and questioning the question of moral-reading. But *The Golden Bowl*," as I point out there in relation to our issue there and here, "is crystal, has a flaw, and will be shattered, even as it contains the story, not just its own but also ours here. This last story is critical" p. 209, quite unlike the well-wrought urn, and Stevens's cold white porcelain bowl, in "The Poems of Our Climate," in *The Palm at the End of the Mind*, p. 158.

27. As examples of genre-changing, I shall mention only a few: Saint Amant's seventeenth-century poem "La Chambre du desbauché" makes a peculiar change in the rhythm of the perception, as the paintings upon the drunken dreamer's wall spell out their reeling lifelikeness in spittle and other traces of former residents; Théophile Gautier's nineteenth-century Mademoiselle de Maupin, disguised as "Theodore," plays Rosalind in *As You Like It* as would a Shakespearean boy actor playing a girl playing a boy, and thus reveals her startling femininity by way of pseudo and acted masculinity, so that the heavily inset play informs the epistolary novel. The insets are as interesting as, or more so than, the enframing poem and tale. The self-referring inset of one genre may occasionally undermine the validity of the enframing text of another: so in David Lodge's recent novel *Changing Places*, the exchange of jobs and wives leads to a final nonresolution of the mixup, as the final freeze frame, presented as in a film being made, changes the novel to film and the standard narrative line to a question, touching on all such novels.

III

1. Jane Austen: *Northanger Abbey* is hereafter cited as NA; *Pride and Prejudice* is hereafter cited as PP; *Mansfield Park* is hereafter cited as MP; and *Persuasion* is hereafter cited as P.

2. Charlotte Brontë, letter to G. H. Lewes, 1848, quoted in PP, preface, p. 7; Virginia Woolf, "Phases of Fiction" in *Granite and Rainbow*, p. 140, hereafter cited as GR.

3. A. Walton Litz, in his *Jane Austen: A Study of Her Development*, p. 8, clearly sets Austen's novels against a background of "eighteenth-century dialectic involving Reason and Feeling, Judgment and Fancy," in a classic debate. Robert Heilman, in his "E Pluribus Unum: Parts and Wholes in *Pride and Prejudice*," in *Jane Austen: Bicentenary Es-*

says, ed. John Halperin, p. 125, shows how she " 'outflanks' the two key positions and thus modifies them. . . . An *a priori* rightness and an *a priori* wrongness undergo the corrective of experience." In his preface for *Pride and Prejudice* (PP, n. 1), Tony Tanner makes a convincing analysis of this novel, originally called *First Impressions*, in its relation to the British empiricist tradition. Senses must be corrected by reason, and the whole crux of the matter of judgment and prejudgment. He quotes, in this context, Litz's view that the novel resembles a three-act play, its performance then leading to reflection and its extension in letter-writing.

Virginia Woolf's "satisfaction" with the novel illuminates in its turn our own with the work of both novelists, satisfaction taken in no trivial sense: "It may be the very idiosyncrasy of a writer that tires us of him. Jane Austen, who has so little that is peculiar, does not tire us, nor does she breed in us a desire for those writers whose method and style differ altogether from hers. Thus, instead of being urged as the last page is finished to start in search of something that contrasts and completes, we pause when we have read *Pride and Prejudice*. . . . We compare *Pride and Prejudice* to something else because, since satisfaction can be defined no further, all the mind can do is to make a likeness of the thing, and, by giving it another shape, cherish the illusion that it is explaining it, whereas it is, in fact, only looking at it afresh. . . . *Pride and Prejudice*, one says, has form . . . we have been aware of check and stimulus, of spectral architecture built up behind the animation and variety of the scene." ("Phases of Fiction" GR, pp. 116-17).

4. The book lies also in another mental realm entirely from *Pride and Prejudice*. Marvin Mudrick, in his *Jane Austen: Irony as Defense and Discovery*, maintains that *Mansfield Park* serves as the image of the Established Church and the rural conservatism on which the city's sophistication encroaches, and, more drastically, that in this novel Austen gives up the irony she had practised for so long, having engaged herself to affirm what Edmund and Fanny affirm. Litz makes a like observation: this work, he says, is the "counterstatement to *Pride and Prejudice*, all of whose virtues—irony, vitality, style—are transformed into the sins of *Mansfield Park*" (p. 112). For him this represents a "stylistic retreat from the exposed position of *Pride and Prejudice*." My opposite and exposed position on this matter is evident in the number of pages I devote to the novel.

5. For a description of the gardenscape and of the author's interest in the romantic and the picturesque, see Tanner's notes to *Mansfield Park*, and Litz's descriptions of the winding paths we must imagine. This shade and this wilderness seem to respond perfectly to what Jane Austen thought she had left out of *Pride and Prejudice*: "The work is rather too light, and bright, and sparkling, it wants shade, it wants to be stretched out here and there" (letter to Cassandra, quoted in PP, p. 39).

6. The term "key" refers to Erving Goffman's *Frame Analysis* (see chapter 1).

7. For Austen's own exposure to amateur theatricals, see the description by Litz, Jane Austen, pp. 118-19, and pp. 122-26.

8. In *Persuasion*, Virginia Woolf finds "a peculiar beauty and a peculiar dullness. . . . The writer is a little bored." And she laments, in believing that Austen would have changed greatly, that "the most perfect artist among women, the writer whose books are immortal died 'just as she was beginning to feel confident in her own success.'" (*The Common Reader*, p. 149).

9. Herman Melville, *Pierre; or, The Ambiguities*, hereafter cited as PA. These ambiguities intrigue: R. P. Blackmur, in his "Craft of Herman Melville: A Putative Statement," treats *Pierre* as a demonstration case of the breakdown of storytelling, and the heightening of the sense of the artificial. "Melville either refused or was unable to resort to the available conventions of his time as if they were real; he either preferred or was compelled to resort to most of the conventions he used for dramatic purposes not only as if they were unreal but also as if they were artificial" (p. 78). It is of course this artificial interest which makes the framing impulse so strong and its effect so strongly readable. In the atmosphere of "universal lurking insincerity," which *Pierre* is imbued with, the putative level is high, as Blackmur means it. "His work constantly said what it was doing or going to do and then, as a rule, stopped short" (p. 78). Even the descriptions are rather assertions than descriptions, and the whole case is a workbook in what, according to Blackmur, does not work (pp. 75-90). Also on *Pierre*, Lawrance Thompson, "God's Stony Heart," in *Melville's Quarrel with God*, pp. 247-96. See Alfred Kazin's chapter on Melville in *An American Procession*.

In his *American Jeremiad*, Sacvan Bercovitch shows how *Pierre's* treatment of the American Way unveils "ambiguity after ambiguity, until it ends in a solipsistic void, like a movie reel of the Puritan ritual run backward at top speed." To hold the ambiguities together, such conjunctive expressions in all their oddness, like "Chronometricals and Horologicals," never entail the necessity of choice, but rather an "ambiguous mutuality," worked through in all aspects of the work and its author, Melville and not-Melville, as Bercovitch shows him admiring and ridiculing Pierre. In the same way, the two heroines, light and dark, are aspects of the one ambivalent heroine, at once Pierre and not-Pierre. Even the interchange at the conclusion between the stone walls, weeping, and Pierre's stony face, dry—perhaps part of the possible influence Bercovitch sees in Melville's having read Hawthorne's story "The Great Stone Face"—shows this play of ambivalence, the double face of the single figure (pp. 28-30 and p. 196).

10. Thomas Hardy, *Jude the Obscure*. Hereafter cited as J.
11. Florence Emily Hardy's *Life of Thomas Hardy* (1962), quoted in Thomas Hardy, *Stories and Poems*, p. 107.
12. *Hardy's Notebooks*, ed. Florence Hardy, quoted in J I.M. Steward, *Thomas Hardy*, p. 12. See also the recent edition of *The Personal Notebooks of Thomas Hardy*, ed. Richard H. Taylor.
13. *Notebooks*, in Steward, *Hardy*, p. 15.
14. Quoted in J. Hillis Miller, *Thomas Hardy: Distance and Desire*. From Marcel Proust, *A la recherche du temps perdu*, vol. 3, p. 311.
15. Thomas Hardy, *The Return of the Native*. Hereafter cited as RN.
16. Thomas Hardy, *Tess of the D'Urbervilles*. Hereafter cited as T. Hardy's repetitions have nowhere been better analyzed than in Miller's *Fiction and Repetition*, whose preface (pp. 1-22, esp. pp. 1-2) cites Tess as a leading example of a story about repetition, where the act of writing already includes that tracing out of repeats, like the novel itself, which Hardy felt as a mark imprinted on his mind; analytical philosophy, says Hardy, cited by Miller, can never explain "why it was that upon this beautiful tissue . . . there should have been traced such a coarse pattern as it was doomed to receive." Miller interprets this as the metaphor assimilating "the real even to the act of writing about it. It defines both the novel and the events it presents as repetitions, as the outlining again of a pattern which already somewhere exists" (pp. 116-18, and 120).

Miller's interpretation of Walter Benjamin's emblem ("The Image of Proust," in *Illuminations*, pp. 203-17)—the sock as empty sack and also a gift filling the sack, as also, again, a sock, which is then also the emblem of Proust's recovery of himself ("From oneness to twoness, from figure to literal ground, the relation is continuously reversible. Each state of the object is both the literal ground of the other and the figure of it," p. 11)—will apply equally to Hardy, as Miller interprets him.

17. Virginia Woolf on Hardy, merciless, is also illuminating about his loneliness: "A laugh, a blush, half a dozen words of dialogue, and it is enough; the source of our delight is perennial. But Hardy has none of this concentration and completeness. His light does not fall directly upon the human heart. It passes over it and out on the darkness of the heath and upon the trees swaying in the storm. When we look back into the room the group by the fireside is dispersed. . . . Nor was Hardy any exception to the rule that the mind which is most capable of receiving impressions is very often the least capable of drawing conclusions." (*The Second Common Reader*, pp. 229-30). For a double frame of author upon author upon author, we might read Virginia Woolf quoting with approval Hardy's "correct" appraisal in his notebook of Henry James, "who has a ponderously warm manner of saying nothing in infinite sentences" (CD, p. 66).

18. L. M. Findlay's comments are instructive about the ways in which Hardy's architectural placing of figures responds to Rossetti's pictures, for example, Cytherea, in *Desperate Remedies* (1871), who, sitting by the window "like another Blessed Damozel," supplies an early version of Sue in *Jude* with her "detachment from the physical world" (p. 2). It was Rossetti's fascination with "emotional and mystical barriers" and balconies and windows (*La Donna della Finestra*, inspired by Dante), these obstacles separating the lovers, which became so resonant in Hardy's work. Already, Findlay points out, Pater's art criticism had in the mingling of sensual and spiritual, influenced the description of Eustachia Vye in the "Queen of the Air" chapter from *Return of the Native* (1878). Arabella's sensuality responds, says Findlay, to the allure of Rossetti's painting *Bocca Baciata*, and its replica *La Bionda del Balcone*, of *Venus Verticordia*, the *Blue Bower*, or *Lady Lilith*, whereas Lady Lilith's spiritualized counterpart, *Sibylla Palmifera*, and the related sonnets, "Soul's Beauty" and "Body's Beauty," show the Rossettian conflict which reminds us of the visible conflict in *Jude*.

In the following passage from the manuscript version, where Sue leans over the casement, Hardy suppresses such physical expressions as "close by him," "Her side, and her," "and her tears fell upon his arms," to leave the inaccessibility of the figure clear in the visible details: "Jude had reached the window which was quite a low one, so that she was visible down to her waist. She let go the casement-stay and put her hand upon his, her moonlit face regarding him wistfully. . . . Jude seized her hand and kissed it. . . . In a moment of impulse she bent over the sill, and laid her face upon his hair, weeping, and then imprinting a scarcely perceptible little kiss upon the top of his head, withdrawing quickly, so that he could not put his arms round her, as otherwise he unquestionably would have done. She shut the casement, and he returned to his cottage" (quoted in Findlay, "D. G. Rossetti and *Jude the Obscure*," pp. 1-11).

My colleague Gerhard Joseph has also worked on perspective and the framing impulse: "Tennyson's Optics: The Eagle's Gaze," pp. 420-28, and "Victorian Frames: The Windows and Mirrors of Browning, Tennyson, and Arnold," pp. 76-87.

IV

1. In Poe, *Complete Tales and Poems*, p. 644. Hereafter cited as CTP. Other quotations from Poe are found in *Edgar Allan Poe, Selected Writings*. Hereafter cited as PSW.

2. In Edgar Allan Poe, *Oeuvres choisies*, tr. Baudelaire, p. 552-56. Hereafter cited as OC.

3. Charles Baudelaire, *Oeuvres complètes*, ed. Claude Pichois, vol. 1, pp. 38-40.

4. The heavy eroticism underlying the text is meant to underlie my own close reading.

5. As for the airless and embedded nature of this and much Poe—a model author for the framing of text and commentary, one of the most intelligent studies of framing comes from Barbara Johnson, in her "Frame of Reference: Poe, Lacan, Derrida," in *The Critical Difference: Essays in the Contemporary Rhetoric of Reading*, pp. 110-46. Her chapter considers the way in which "any attempt to follow the path of the purloined letter is automatically purloined from itself," which is what, according to Johnson, it was always and already

saying. Literature is, says Stanley Fish, language "around which we have drawn a frame, a frame that indicates a decision to regard with a particular self-consciousness the resources language has always possessed" (quoted by Johnson, in ibid., p. 128, from "How Ordinary Is Ordinary Language?" *New Literary History*, vol. 5, no. 1, p. 52). Derrida's "parergonal" view is mentioned here, with its quotable quotation: "Frames are always framed: thus, by part of their content," with Johnson's comment: "The total inclusion of the 'frame' is both mandatory and impossible. The 'frame' thus becomes not the borderline between the inside and the outside, but precisely what subverts the applicability of the inside/outside polarity to the act of interpretation" (p. 128). Were I to continue the game, I should of course, comment upon the single quotation marks I have had to put (' ') or then, were I not already quoting, the double quotation marks (" ") surrounding the frame as it becomes part of the content of the critic's own sentence. Sima Godfrey, whose article "Baudelaire's Windows," (*L'Esprit créateur*, vol. 22, no. 4 [Winter 1982], pp. 83-100), discusses Baudelairean framing in one of its most interesting aspects, that of the inside/outside dialogue, contributes an unusually useful analysis of Baudelaire's sexualized treatment of the pen and paintbrush. In a forthcoming study ("Baudelaire and the Poetics of Nostalgia"), she quotes Baudelaire admiring Constantin Guys at work, muscular, and operating like a creator (and fathering), "faisant jaillir l'eau du verre au plafond, essuyant sa plume sur sa chemise, pressé, violent, actif . . . un feu, une ivresse de crayon," and, in parallel, Baudelaire's mother's letter describing two paintings his father had owned, a Saint Anthony with a cross at hand, and in profane imitation, a bacchante with a thyrsus instead of the cross, surrounded by cupids. Since the painting of Guys had absorbed the "arabesque lines," and since the hermaphroditic character of the thyrsus corresponds also to a statue of a hermaphrodite which the father possessed, the conjunction of the poem, the musician to whom it is dedicated (Franz Liszt), and Constantin Guys (the ejaculatory painter, as Baudelaire sees him), makes a net of reference difficult to cast off. The father figure, like the god causing honey and water to spurt forth in the imagination, is also the creator and the androgyne. In relation to Freud, to the figures of father and androgyne, see Leo Bersani's study, *Baudelaire and Freud*, essential reading for those interested in the lacks in Baudelaire, and in the reading of psychoanalytic theory with texts. Esther Rashkin has done an interesting piece on Usher and on the way the reader is haunted by the secret encoded in the text: "Spirals of Haunting: Reading the 'Unreadable' in *The Fall of the House of Usher*," read in manuscript.

6. In relation to this expression, and playing further on the contemplation of texts translated by authors themselves adept at framing, let me give a few examples of Poe's "Oval Portrait" as translated into Spanish by Julio Cortázar. The comparison is useful, for here the repetitions characteristic of Poe, instead of being elided, as they often are in Baudelaire, are stressed and restressed: the intensely "long, long" and devoted reading comes out: "Mucho, mucho leí . . . y intensamente, intensamente miré." As for the "life-likeliness," the result of which we have seen in Baudelaire, Cortázar gives only a "possibility of life" in the expression ("possibilidad de vida"), and for the "pallid" and the pall it casts, he retains the exact word: "la pálida tela," already strengthened in the next sentence by the rhyme "lívida" for the livid light that filters in, finding its echo in the conclusion, when the painter of the living death becomes himself pale unto death at the contemplation of the living portrait, "púsose pálido," even while crying out at Life itself, creator of death, for a properly melodramatic framing faithfully and unobsessively rendered. (Edgar Allan Poe, *Cuentos*, tr. Julio Cortázar vol. 1, pp. 71-74.)

7. The fact that the word "pâlir" exists in French, and could therefore have been used for "to grow pale," and the whole family of words, "appalled," "pall," and "pallor," entitles us to examine the choice of the substitution of the word "épouvanter," admittedly stronger, but without the essential suggestion of paleness. Here, as elsewhere, the text may be seen to profit from the lack it makes sensible to the obsessed and interested look.

8. Cited by Jonathan Culler, "Prolegomena to a Theory of Reading," pp. 58-66.

9. Yves le Dantec mentions two lines from Shelley in relation to the part of Baudelaire's "Un Fântome" called "Le Cadre," which lend their own hue to this rereading of a tale: "With hue like that when some great painter dips his pencil in the gloom of earthquake and eclipse," and which Baudelaire had occasion to translate. See the critical edition of *Les fleurs du mal*, ed. Crépet et Blin, pp. 361-62.

10. Monique Daubanton's essay, "L'ovale du portrait," on Poe's "Oval Portrait," pp. 102-10, is especially astute about the egg.
11. The reference is to Poe's tale by that name (PCT, pp. 711-19).
12. The Baudelaire poem is taken from the Crépet et Blin edition of *Les fleurs du mal*, pp. 84-87.
13. The black and luminous baroque yields this high contrast as a setting at once musical, verbal, and visual. In the light of the present reading, the variants of the poems given in the Corti edition of 1968 (n. 8, above) are instructive to the obsessed reader, for increasingly the poem becomes darker and denser. What is light becomes, rather, dreamy (I, line 11: "légère allure orientale" changed to "rêveuse . . . "), and what was only "somber" and luminous becomes "noire et pourtant lumineuse," in line with the oxymoronic quality of much of the poem (I, line 14). A simple "odeur de fourrure" finally gives off a supersensual "parfum de fourrure," more appropriate to the sense of the poem (II, line 14). At the same time there is an ominous and profound change from the glittering of ornament ("miroirs, pierres, métaux, dorure"), where mirrors and precious stones framed the exterior beauty, to "bijoux, meubles," and so on, associating the domestic to the glitter and weighing it down (III, line 4), while rendering more absract the naked beauty: "elle noyait . . . Son beau corps nu" becomes "elle noyait sa beauté" (III, lines 11-12). The latter change is significant, as it leads to the drowning-of-the-heart theme in the final segment, called "The Portrait," where the feeling of some "Harmonie du soir" looms large, as it does at the end, completely changed, to give, finally, the vow that the assassin, Time the painter, shall not kill with his "aile rude" the memory of the beauty, held as in a monstrance: "Celle qui fut mon plaisir et ma gloire!"
14. Or any of the avatars of Venus, the Majas, the Odalisques, and their successors.
15. The curtains bring in others from other texts, visual and verbal: those, red in color, from all the "Ladies at Their Toilet" and the "Ladies in Their Bath" of the Fontainebleau School, as if on theatrical display (see my *Eye in the Text: Essay's on Perception, Mannerist to Modern*). In these inclusions of display and involvement, as the ladies stare at the spectator and the labyrinth engulfs the reader, the images of both the reader and the read are manipulated by a mannerist hand.

16. Michael Riffaterre pointed out to me the matching of the hermaphrodite original with the French hermaphroditic term here, as the male and the female are joined by the hyphen. The equivalent English expression to the "brick" is phonetically apt.

17. "Le vierge, le vivace, et le bel aujourd'hui," Mallarmé's most celebrated sonnet. For an unusually fine analysis of the associative net of images connected with white in Mallarmé, see Micheline Tison-Braun, *Poétique du paysage: Essai sur le genre descriptif*, pp. 98-103.

V

1. In *The Novels and Tales* (New York Edition). Hereafter cited as NT.
2. *A Small Boy and Others*, p. 368.
3. Preface to *The Princess Casamassima*, in NT, vol. 5, p. xv.
4. Tzvetan Todorov, "Le secret du récit: Henry James," pp. 81-115.
5. Jean Perrot, "Enigme et fiction métalinguistique chez James," pp. 53-66.
6. Charles Anderson, *Person, Place, and Thing in Henry James' Novels*; Viola Hopkins Winner, *Henry James and the Visual Arts*. See also, on the problems of James's involvement with drama, scene, and story, Leo Benjamin Levy, *Versions of Melodrama: A Study of the Fiction and Drama of Henry James*, and Henry James, *The Scenic Art: Notes on Acting and the Drama, 1871-1901*, ed. Allan Wade.
7. Hereafter cited as EV.

Holland's sense of the visual is strong, his comments on each of the major novels considered here being clearly informed by this sense. On Veronese, in Milly's Venice, he has this to say: "When Densher agrees to stay in Venice, he agrees to perpetuate the fraud which is Milly's betrayal, fixing himself squarely in the picture at *The Supper in the House of Levi*, there to hear the call to repentance. Yet the same action, staying in the picture at Venice, fixes him squarely as the admiring young man with the wine jug, still sampling the sacred wine in *The Marriage Feast at Cana*" (p. 313). Holland's commentary is peculiarly enlightening, as it never simply *tells* us of what picture it is or is not in the text, but places his reader, as James's reader and the reader of the canvases, squarely in the center of the picture's style and substance. Of the novel, he says: "Like the rich color and gilt background of a Byzantine painting, like the hard and strong glasses of a mosaic, like the mannered art of the Bronzino painting, it is in the candor of its own confession 'dead, dead, dead.' As in the case of the pictures in Sir Luke's office, which were 'in particular framed and glazed,' so Milly is *framed* as well as glazed by the novel which takes her to use as the subject of its chilled embrace, and manages, in the eighth book, that 'her death shall have taken place.' She is betrayed by the very fiction that enshrines her" (p. 321). James's composition, claims Holland, is like that of Veronese. Art controls, too, the enchaining from novel to novel of the construction that James's fiction is: the Palladian church of *The Golden Bowl* and the exotic pagoda, as Holland points out, are more splendid versions of Gilbert Osmond's house in *Portrait of a Lady* with its "jealous apertures" and its "small high windows" (p. 337).

8. Leo Levy's *Versions of Melodrama* illustrates the crossing of genre lines.

9. Ruth Bernard Yeazell, *Language and Knowledge in the Late Novels of Henry James*. Quentin Anderson, *The American Henry James*.

10. Torgovnick, *Closure in the Novel*.

11. In Henry James, *The Aspern Papers and Other Stories*. This tale illustrates, above all, James's "innate preference for the represented subject over the real one" (p. 114). The problem of the "real" in the story is real; it is undone in two ways, outside and in. From outside the "reality" is questioned by the scorn of the "real" gentleman and lady for the actual droplets of rain on the umbrella.

12. In *Eight Tales*, ed. Morton Dauben Zabel, p. 166. Hereafter cited as ET. J. Hillis Miller analyzes the weaving in and out, the stitches and patterns and ambiguities of the difficult Jamesian figure as they are associated with the essential metaphor of the Figure of the Carpet. Miller, "The Problematic of Ending," pp. 3-7.

13. In *The Complete Tales of Henry James*, ed. Leon Edel, vol. 9. "The Third Person" serves as a Jamesian takeoff on James's intricacies of vision, as two elderly ladies look at each other close up through the opposite ends of the same pair of field glasses. In *"The Turn of the Screw" and Other Stories*. Hereafter cited as TS.

14. In *Eight Tales*, Van Wyck Brooks explores the image of the watcher caught within what is observed. Reading "In the Cage," says one critic, is like watching Henry James "watching through a knot-hole somebody who was watching somebody else through a knot-hole" ("Henry James and the Trapped Spectator," in L. C. Knights, *Explorations*, p. 183).

15. Many of the tales mentioned here, associated with "In the Cage," illustrate different forms of constraint: "Glasses," "Broken Wings," "The Author of Beltraffio," and "The Altar of the Dead." The repeated architectural framing of "The Author of Beltraffio" prepares those in *The Portrait of a Lady*, *The Wings of the Dove*, and *The Golden Bowl*.

16. This grisly tale is not considered one of James's masterpieces; witness F. R. Leavis, who calls it of a "significant badness," attributing this to its date: "that morbidly sentimental and extremely unpleasant tale which—it is, of course, late—also illustrates poor James' weary, civilized loneness of spirit" (F. R. Leavis, *The Great Tradition*, p. 181). Constance Fenimore Woolson is at the center of this tale, and at that of *The Wings of the Dove*, as surely as is Minny, his doomed cousin. (Edel, *Henry James: The Conquest of London*, p. 148). It has a peculiar fascination, like something at once overripe and underthought.

17. In Henry James, *The Complete Tales*; of this story, Virginia Woolf says: "Henry James has only to take the smallest of steps and he is over the border. His characters with their extreme fineness of perception are already half-way out of the body. There is nothing violent in their release" ("The Ghost Stories," in Leon Edel, ed., *Henry James: A Collection of Critical Essays*, p. 50).

18. Novels referred to include *The Tragic Muse*, hereafter cited as TM; *The Awkward Age*, hereafter cited as AA; *The Portrait of a Lady*, hereafter cited as PL.

19. Hereafter cited as SF

20. Hereafter cited as TS. See Shoshana Felman's "Turning of the Screw of Interpretation," pp. 94-207, on some twists within the text.

21. Virginia Woolf points out how impressive the silence is during, but especially at the end of, the story: it is exactly this silence that prepares and then installs the final chilling halt, of the heart and of the tale, as if a groove of deadly quiet were to be finely chiseled about the inner terror. "Everything," she says, "at Bly is so profoundly quiet. The twitter of birds at dawn, the far-away cries of children, faint footsteps in the distance stir it but leave it unbroken. It accumulates; it weights us down; it makes us strangely apprehensive of noise. At last the house and garden die out beneath it. 'I can hear again, as I write, the intense hush in which the sounds of evening dropped. The rooks stopped cawing in the golden sky, and the un-

friendly hour lost for the unspeakable minute all its voice.' It is unspeakable" (Virginia Woolf, GR, pp. 71-72).

22. Hereafter cited as A.

23. Percy Lubbock treats thoroughly this process of vision, the demonstration, in Strether's character, of what "autobiography cannot achieve"; it is enough to prove finally how far the intricate performance of one man's thought is beyond his own power to describe and record it.

24. *Letters of Henry James*, ed. Percy Lubbock, vol. 2, p. 253.

25. Seymour Chatman, *The Later Style of Henry James*, makes an intricate and invaluable analysis of the cognitive apparatus and "heavy ratiocination" of the Jamesian mind, "for ever learning, sensing, reflecting, contemplating, piecing things out, 'looking at things that hover'. . . ." The beginning of *The Ambassadors* (not "Strether" but "Strether's first question") is typical of the entire approach of James's "sensitive beings" in their precognitive stance, as they are always wondering, feeling, asking themselves, seeking, thinking of, going into the idea of, thrilling to, and encountering (examples from *The Wings of the Dove*): these are *recipient* forms and not active or performative. Strether, struck by things, is the object, and the verbs of performance are negated for him: "he couldn't yet measure." The analysis applies mainly to the late novels and can be roughly divided as follows: psychological nominalizations, obliquity, neutral determination, ellipsis, deixis, cleft sentences, hyperbole, colloquial elements, and metaphors (pp. 6-105). It is this style that so irritates the nonpartisans of the late James; see Leavis's remark on the "Altar of the Dead": "it is of course, late." Matthiessen points out that James himself preferred *The Ambassadors* for its "roundness of structure," its "architectural competence," describing his perfection of a "device for framing and for interpreting experience" (F. O. Matthiessen, *Henry James: The Major Phase*, pp. 22-29).

26. Viola Hunt points out the reason for the choice of Lambinet: The other better-known Barbizon painters, such as Millet, would have brought to the reader's mind a great blurring of colors in a mist, whereas the sharpness of line and color here is essential (Viola Hunt, "Visual Art Devices and Parallels in the Fiction of Henry James," pp. 561-74). Since the river scene is like scenes of Renoir, Monet, Manet, and yet filtered through the Jamesian consciousness, the Impressionism of the whole scene should itself be read against James's

essays of 1905: "New England: An Autumn Impression" with his reactions to an exhibit of the paintings of Manet, Degas, Monet, Whistler, and of other "rare recent hands." In Henry James, *The American Scene*, pp. 45-46. See also James on Impressionism in "The Impressionists" and "John Singer Sargent," in *The Painter's Eye: Notes and Essays in the Pictorial Arts*, ed. John L. Sweeney, pp. 114-15, 217-18, and 221.

27. Hereafter cited as WD. The prototype for this melodramatic story is not only in the early death of James's cousin Minny Temple, but also, as Edel points out, in the suicide of Constance Fenimore Woolson, who loved James "immensely," and who ended her life in Venice, to his great shock (see his letter to Margaret Brooke, the Ranee of Sarawak, January 28, 1894, quoted in Leon Edel, *Henry James: The Master*, p. 298; The Venetian setting is described on p. 440). James meditated at length upon the difficulties of presenting a dying heroine. The difficulties of reading James are amusingly described by Virginia Woolf in a letter to Lady Ottoline Morell: "I actually read through *The Wings of the Dove* last summer, and thought it such an amazing acrobatic feat, partly of his, partly of mine, that I now look upon myself and Henry James as partners in merit. I made it all out. But I felt very ill for some time afterwards" (*The Letters of Virginia Woolf*, vol. 2, p. 548). Of James, she admires the "inexhaustible sensibility," the artistic form "which, as it imposes its stamp, sets apart the object thus consecrated and makes it no longer part of ourselves" (Virginia Woolf, *Collected Essays*, ed. Leonard Woolf, vol. 1, p. 285).

28. Among James's exposures by portraits, this Bronzino is the most celebrated. Viola Hopkins Winner supposes it is his *Lucrezia and Bartolommeo Panciatichi*, in the Uffizi Gallery; she cites also: "pictorial notes" taken by Longueville in "Confidence"; Leonardo's *Last Supper* viewed by Charlotte Evans and her father in "Travelling Companions" as they are in turn viewed, a scene reminiscent of that in the National Gallery where Kate looks at Milly looking at Densher looking at a painting; Christopher Newman in the Salon Carré of the Louvre in *The American*; and Roderick Hudson's statue of *Eve* (Winner, "Art Devices and Parallels," in *Henry James and The Visual Arts*, pp. 70-93). Adeline Tinter reminds us ("The Museum World," p. 155) that there is already an ancestor portrait in "The Sense of the Past."

29. Hereafter cited as GB. Preface taken from NT, vol. 23. See *New Literary History* (Winter 1984) for my response to several essays on *The Golden Bowl*, in its issue on *Morality and Literature* ("Moral Reading, or Self-Containment with a Flaw," on the topic of the Bowl containing the whole story of how we read and judge).

   In his *Henry James: The Treacherous Years*, Leon Edel refers to the triangular relationship behind that in the novel: Elizabeth Boott, her rich father Francis, and her husband Frank Duveneck. In *Henry James: The Master*, Edel suggests Charlotte as a possible avatar of Mrs. Jack Gardner, now that James could bring into the open certain of his more troubling triangular scenes of childhood to resolve them. (Whereas in *The Ambassadors* the implicit triangle of Madame de Vionnet, Chad, and Strether, and in *The Wings of the Dove* that of Kate and Milly and Densher, had met no resolution, here, it is resolved, for the only time, and the adolescent who has been Daisy and Maisie, the telegraph girl, and finally Maggie, emerges from the pagoda or cage into life.)

   See in particular for *The Golden Bowl*, Philip Weinstein, *Henry James and the Requirements of the Imagination*, and Yeazell, *Language and Knowledge in the Late Novels of Henry James*. The latter book examines several of the passages found in these pages, from another point of view. Yeazell claims, for instance, that during the final scene we see only Maggie, as the Prince claims to: other readers see, however, the Prince, or only his back, or then, only the *language* of the scene itself; such is my case. Yeazell is especially sharp in her analysis of the metaphors, like that of the pagoda, as elaborate ways of escaping the self, of the *strain* sensed in the tone of the verbal collaboration between the characters, and of the ways of *disclosure* and infolding.

30. The "large unity" and "grace of intensity" in Matthiessen, *Henry James*, p. 22. Mannerism is discussed by many critics, for example, Viola Hunt, in her "Visual Art Devices and Parallels in the Fiction of Henry James," pp. 561-74. For further discussion, see F. O. Matthiessen, "James and the Plastic Arts," pp. 533-50; and Adeline Tintner, "The Spoils of Henry James," pp. 239-51. For Maggie's "original terror of life," see F. W. Dupee, *Henry James*, p. 268.

31. Virginia Woolf, *Collected Essays*, ed. Leonard Woolf, vol. 1, p. 285.

32. For a possible double source of the "golden bowl" proverb, see Edel, *Henry James: The Master*, p. 219, and F. O. Matthiessen, *Henry James*, p. 96. The other source is Ecclesiastes 12:6-7: "Or ever the

silver cord be loosed, or the golden bowl broken, or the pitcher be broken at the fountain, or the wheel be broken at the cistern: then shall the dust return to the earth as it was." (Might we not also think of this source when considering the cord Charlotte seems to wear about her neck, held by Adam, at the end? It is, after all, itself a silver, moneyed cord, silken as it appears.)

Edel reminds us of an actual golden bowl: at Lamb House in Rye, King George I spent the night after his ship put in to the Sussex coast, and attended the christening of a baby, making a gift to the child of a golden bowl. Hence perhaps the "tone of old gold as well as a grand style and capacity," for the novel begun in 1903. The theme of the bowl previously occurs in the *Portrait of a Lady*, in the scene with Osmond and the porcelain cup, prone to breakage, and used as metaphors of human fragility. Even the "hardest pots," says Madame Merle, have a small hole: " 'Please be careful of that precious cup.' 'It already has a small crack.' said Osmond dryly, as he put it down" (quoted by Adeline Tintner, "The Museum World," p. 144.

33. The name is not particularly uplifting; but in her essay "The Man of Letters," Edith Wharton explains the Assinghams' role as that of the reflecting consciousness, "full, rich, universally prehensile," and attributes to them a classic function: "the Assinghams and others, who, oddly, resuscitated from the classic drama . . . swoop and prey and report in *The Wings of the Dove, The Sacred Fount, The Golden Bowl*" (Edel, ed., *Critical Essays*, pp. 34-38).

34. By this period, James greatly appreciated Whistler, with whom his relations were complicated (see Edel, *Henry James: The Treacherous Years*, pp. 90 and ff.: "But on the whole" said James, "nothing that relates to Whistler is queerer than anything else"). James's maturing appreciation can be traced (for instance, in *The Painter's Eye: Notes and Essays on the Pictorial Arts*): he begins by believing that Whistler's productions are not even pictures, but "incidents of furniture or decoration" (in 1869, p. 12); he comments in 1877 and 1878, "I will not speak of Mr. Whistler's Nocturnes in 'Black and Gold' and in 'Blue and Silver,' of his 'Arrangements,' 'Harmonies,' and 'Impressions,' because I frankly confess they do not amuse me. The mildest judgment I have heard pronounced upon them is that they are like 'ghosts of Velasquezes'; with the harshest I will not darken my pages. It may be a narrow point of view, but to be interesting

it seems to me that a picture should have some relation to life as well as to painting. Mr. Whistler's experiments have no relation whatever to life; they have only a relation to painting." The comparison with James's own critics is instructive: they picture him as progressively having a less corporeal relation to his characters and a less intimate relation to life, as his cast of characters is reduced and "skeletonized" to the point of having none of the "ungraceful appendages" most of us trail along after us (a good part of this criticism—so with what can they love?). As James moves toward the period of *The Golden Bowl*, where he has "less to tell and more to say," (R. P. Blackmur, "In the Country of the Blue," p. 203), the realms divide sharply; by 1903, when he is writing that novel, his opinion on the relation of life to art and understanding has been drastically modified.

Of Whistler, in 1897, he says, feelingly, concerning the "exquisite image" of Henry Irving as Philip II (*Arrangement in Black No. 3*), "To pause before such a work is in fact to be held to the spot by just the highest operation of the charm one has sought there. . . . an art and taste so rare" that a stupid generation, used to "coarser notions," cannot possibly recognize therein, and in Whistler's work in general, "one of the finest of all distillations of the artistic intelligence" (p. 258). The word "intelligence" may well be the key to it all, as if the contemporary quarrel between the partisans of "representational" interpretations and the "non-representational" texts were to have been fought years ago.

35. This and the dialogue quoted just before it open the way for such takeoffs as the delightful "In Darkest James" of Frank Moore Colby; as an example of his descriptions of what goes on when James is "moving about in the mind" and keeping his clues to himself:

"If—" she sparkled.
"If!" he asked. He had lurched from the meaning a moment.
"I might—" she replied abundantly.
His eye had eaten the meaning. "Me!" he gloriously burst.
"Precisely," she thrilled. "How splendidly you *do* understand." (p. 44)

36. This "bridge scene" is one of the two major framing sequences that Matthiessen adduces as testimony to the importance of the visual sense in James ("James and the Plastic Arts," pp. 533-50), the other

being of course the Lambinet picture as it is transposed to the scene of *The Ambassadors*.

37. The light and dark of the setting here correspond to the light and dark heroines, to the clash of their moral and personal codes.

38. Matthiessen, *The Major Phase*, claims that Maggie has at the end gained the bowl with no crack (p. 95) and that she is paid in full by the "golden fruit." The interplay of *fruit* (Pater's "fruit of a multiplied, quickened consciousness") and bowl is instructive, and as ironic as the bowl motif itself, whose power of *containment* and *displacement* as it contaminates the contents is illustrated by Dupee, ed., *Henry James*, p. 266: "The psychic content is too great for its container of elegantly forged happenings: it all overflows and slops about and is magnificently wasted."

39. Marcel Proust, *A la recherche du temps perdu*, cited by volume I, II, or III. Translations: Moncrieff and Kilmartin, adapted in some cases.

40. See, for instance, Micheline Tison-Braun, *Poétique du paysage: Essai sur le genre descriptif*.

41. In such cases as the "discovery" of Morel by Charlus and Jupien in the brothel scene, the shock and the exposure are all the more intensified for the "finding" being false. Here in fact the "discovery" is in reality fake, a planted scene, for the Prince de Guermantes has left the room to be replaced by three women, in the center of whom Morel lies stretched out and colorless, inactive and supine, aware of Charlus watching him and watching Charlus in return, in a two-way vision the latter ignores.

   The scene is given as a prototypical spying scene, with half-open doors, in a "transparent room," the action reflected in mirrors; the odd vision is intensified by the magic emblems on the wall, and concentrated through the incantatory repetitions of the name of the one spied upon or victimized: "It was indeed Morel before his eyes, but, as if pagan mysteries and spells still worked, it was rather the shadow of Morel, Morel embalmed, not even Morel resuscitated as Lazarus, an apparition of Morel, a ghost of Morel, Morel coming back or evoked in this room" (II, p. 1080). The repeating name makes a *nominal border* for the scene, a false-innocent presentation of the victim in the center of the picture, hemmed in, his real "vice" replaced by a false death in this simulation of a scene, half-shown, with what it should reveal covered over by a repeated shadow, reflected.

42. Georges Poulet, *Proustian Space*, treats exactly the problem that I have here called superpositioning; he refuses that term in favor of "juxtaposition," and studies the transitions made between past perception and future perception ("a few trees as transition between what you knew and a land that lay before you"). He is particularly convincing in his descriptions of the image's displacement, or of its conjunction with another, of its oscillation or wavering as it tries to substitute itself for another image or place, "to take its place" (p. 10). His analysis of the framed view from the train window is instructive of how one can treat enframed pictures made from a moving vehicle. See Poulet, *Studies in Human Time*, pp. 319ff.

One of the best analyses of Proust's dramatic and descriptive structure is to be found in B. G. Rogers, *Proust's Narrative Techniques*; Rogers studies the scene of the three trees and its send-back to Combray ("C'était, je me le rappelle, à un arrêt de train . . ."), and the insertion of future and past scenes into the present fictional basis (for example, "Mais il est temps de . . ." and "Pour en revenir à" . . .).

Also, on Proust's frames, see John Lapp, "Proust's Windows to Reality," *Romantic Review*, vol. 67, no. 1 (January 1976); and Diana Festa-McCormick, "Proustian Canvasses in Itinerant Frames," *Symposium* (Spring 1982), pp. 14-29.

43. Virginia Woolf, *Street Haunting: A London Adventure*. Hereafter cited as SH.

44. Hereafter cited as TL. Eric Auerbach's analysis of one frame in this novel, by the measure of the stocking held up to little James's leg by Mrs. Ramsay as she thinks of the small boy in the lighthouse, is justly celebrated. In his *Mimesis: The Representation of Reality in Western Literature*, pp. 525-33.

45. About the shawl—which I take as one of the essential emblems of the framing impulse—a note in Avrom Fleishman's *Virginia Woolf: A Critical Reading* comments: "The shawl's prior career is also sketched in: Mrs. Ramsay first has it hung over a picture frame, perhaps to hide decay (47); this arrangement of the shawl then frames her own head when she sits before the picture (51); she later removes it and wears it in the garden (104-14); dressing for dinner, she allows the children to choose a shawl to go with her black dress (128); and with this (green?) emblem she attempts to hide the emblem of death (178)" (Fleishman, p. 119, n. 14).

Insofar as the shawl serves as covering—as well as redeeming—Maria DiBattista's commentary on Woolf's veiling as an act of dissimulation of the power of the feminine voice is itself powerful: she sees it as the ritual veiling "of the female divinity, whose power it is to authorize that the bare and sterile grounds of life be draped, as the boar's skull was draped in *To the Lighthouse* and as the deserted beach in *The Waves* is draped, by a protective covering. The veil masks the narrator whose power and whose will control the ensuing narrative" (DiBattista, *"The Waves*: The Epic of 'Anon,' " pp. 146-89, in *Virginia Woolf's Major Novels: The Fables of Anon*, p. 150). These narrative garments, she continues, are the strategies and ploys that permit the authoritative feminine speaking voice: "This strategy extends and deepens our sense of the traditional anonymity adopted by ominiscient narrators (as in the novels of Jane Austen or Henry James), and redefines it as a peculiarly feminine guise, while at the same time not so modestly claiming omniscience—traditionally the attribute of male gods—as within a woman's power as well" (p. 151).

46. *Moments of Being*, p. 72. Hereafter cited as MB. The indelible stamp set on one lived moment among others is paradigmatic of the specific instant of the text as an arrested view or sensation within the flow of the whole: "The moment was stabilized, stamped like a coin indelibly, among a million that slipped by imperceptibly" SH, p. 4. This is G. E. Moore's "state of consciousness" (*Principia Ethica*). The ways in which Woolf's "moments of being" connect back with Pater's "select moments of vivid sensation" as well as with Wordsworth's "spots of time," and the relations with Hardy that one might draw upon, are sketched out in the initial chapter of Perry Meisel's *Absent Father: Virginia Woolf and Walter Pater*, especially pp. 47-52.

47. Hereafter cited as W. See also the useful volume, *"The Waves": The Two Holograph Drafts*, inscribed and edited by J. W. Graham, from which some of the quotations here are taken. Hereafter cited as W, I or W, II.

48. Virginia Woolf, *A Writer's Diary*, ed. Leonard Woolf, hereafter cited as WD.

49. As for the view, it is that of a painter (see W. L. George, "A Painter's Literature," and Quentin Bell, on Virginia Woolf's "Painterly Vision," in *Virginia Woolf: The Critical Heritage*, ed. Robin Majum-

dar and Allen McLaurin, esp. pp. 82-83 and pp. 138-42, respectively). If Henry James wanted, as he said in his essay on Balzac, to return to the novel the art of the brush, Virginia Woolf wanted to achieve, as Quentin Bell says, the "simultaneous splash effect" of the painter as opposed to the linear railway sentence (*Critical Heritage*, p. 86). It is toward this effect that the buildup of repeating passages works, accumulating strength on top of each other, like superimposed waves. To take an example, in the repeating passages of Rhoda offering her violets, again and again, the repetition permits the development of emotion, as well as the formal framing of the gesture of the dream: "I will pick flowers; I will bind flowrs in one garland and clasp them and present them—Oh! to whom? . . . I will gather my flowers and present them—Oh! to whom? . . . I will bind my flowers in one garland and advancing with my hand outstretched will present them—Oh! to whom?" (W, I, p. 57). The lamentation is peculiarly devoid of self-pity, yet is the modest bearer of the fully sensed tragedy of the isolated figures in one of Virginia Woolf's most desolate mindscapes.

Repeatedly, Woolf's manuscripts and notebooks convince us of her visual grasp of character as of situation. In her notebook called, on its cover, "Notes for writing," and on its spine, "Reading and Writing," she draws her conception of the novel:

TO THE LIGHTHOUSE
All character—*not* a view of the world
Two blocks joined by a corridor

(From *To the Lighthouse: The Original Holograph Draft*, ed. Susan Dick, appendix, p. 11. Hereafter cited as TLH.) Lily's looking has in it that "still intensity of emotion," that determination not to be taken in by the insincerity of appearances, to "press straight on," and to "hold the scene—so—in a vise and let nothing come in and spoil it," which enable her to draw it all together, to gather it up "together to stretch her eyes to stretch her mind farther & farther," as Woolf notes in the margin of the manuscript (TLH, pp. 264-65, 365). "It drew things together," THL, p. 346; this could be taken as the motif of the entire work, and—if the ideal were to be realized—of that work for this one now being written, for which it would have served as the developing object.

Thus the flowers that are dropped, over and over, are gathered up by art, as the repeats (the waves breaking on the shore of *To the Lighthouse* as they are at once the characters within the novel and the prefigurations for *The Waves*) make into a picture that which was fragments. "She had let the flowers fall from her basket, Lily thought, screwing up her eyes and standing back as if to look at her picture, which she was not touching, however, with all her faculties in a trance, frozen over superficially but moving underneath with extreme speed. She let her flowers fall from her basket . . ." (TL, pp. 288-89); "We stop and pick up fragments. I am irremediably inconclusive," says Bernard (W, II, p. 569). Phrases compose our triumph, says *The Waves*, where "we pound upon the shore: we are not to be confined" (W, II, p. 693): in our own language returning, the picture is reborn in bright and childish, redemptive terms: "A man seeking only that little language, which lovers use, broken, severed words, like those a child uses, when it sees the tree, the cow, the table, the hat" (W, II, p. 721). But the very "held" nature of the art guarantees its self-enclosure: the language of prose, "little," in this book of which the author says she "would be glad if the following pages were read not as a novel" (W, II, p. 582 verso, originally "were not read as a novel"), provides that the text itself, like the pictures "staring" at Bernard from the walls of the National Gallery, is unreferential, speaking always only of itself. "Mercifully," says Bernard (W, II, p. 568), "the pictures make no reference; they do not nudge; they n do not point. The private, the particular, & the vanish."

50. The characters' stance is described as that of poetic speakers, self-consciously perceptive of their locutional acts, and speaking in what George T. Wright calls the "lyric present" ("I fall!" "I'll fill my glass again. I drink," or "I die! I faint, I fail."). This antirealist and timeless dimension is associated with gesture in a poem and contributes to the densification of certain passages, set apart as lyrically framed. On Virginia Woolf, and in particular on *The Waves* and its structure, no one has written a more valuable study than Allen McLaurin, whose *Virginia Woolf: The Echoes Enslaved*, already quoted, takes as a starting point the philosophical and aesthetic premises on which her work is based. He spends the necessary time on the the-

ories of Roger Fry about distancing and framing and shows how they relate to such typographical play as, in *Orlando*, the following statement: "For which reason we leave a great blank here, which must be taken to indicate that the space is filled to repletion," after which indeed there is a space and then the next paragraph, with no more reference to the foregoing. His chapters 8, "Space: On Hollowing out a Canvas" (pp. 85-96), and 10, "The Double Nature of Repetition: *The Waves*" (pp. 158-65), are particularly useful. He studies the way in which the mirror, copy of a copy, is taken up by Roger Fry, and by Woolf later in her repetitious structures, how the framing around Mrs. Ramsay's head works in *To the Lighthouse* as it is framed by the window for Lily and thus taken out of practical life and reserved for the realm of art (p. 195), and how the parentheses around the emptiness of the central section, in its bracketing, relates to the idea of the frame as calling the reader's attention to the "whole shape" of the novel. In relation to the highly formalized and italicized form of *The Waves*, Jean Guiget, in *Virginia Woolf and Her Works*, tr. by Jean Stewart (London: Hogarth Press, 1965), p. 300, refers us to O'Neill's commentaries on his masks ("soliloquies should be arbitrarily set in stylized form, that will be the exact expression of stylized mask symbol"); but when this was printed (Nov. 8, 1931, in the New York Herald-Tribune), *The Waves* had already been in print for over a month. It seems to me that a more appropriate analogy can be drawn with Woolf's own notion of a "rhythmical order" (in *A Room of One's Own*, p. 292, as the boy and girl get into the taxicab: "the sight was ordinary enough; what was strange was the rhythmical order with which my imagination had invested it.").

James Naremore, in *The World without a Self: Virginia Woolf and the Novel*, studies Woolf's "shade of formality," her "fairly mannered rhythm" and the "slightly ornamental imagery" in her more poetic moods reflecting the vibrations of what she called the "tremor of susceptibility" in the self (pp. 117, 119). The stylized and artificial language in the play-poem of *The Waves*, where the self-conscious role of Bernard (" 'On the outskirts of every agony sits some observant fellow who points' ") helps to "generate an aesthetic crisis and call into question" its own being (p. 175). The vagueness of her language, says Naremore, reflects "her basic misgivings about the ego and about the words which are its signs" (p. 189).

51. I have used the useful drafts in holograph edition: Virginia Woolf, *The Waves: The Two Holograph Drafts*, transcribed and edited by J. W. Graham.

52. The texture in *The Waves* is dense, to approximate the feeling of a prose poem: "One wave after another. No room" (WD, May 1, 1930, p. 136), or again: "a serious, mystical, poetical work," and an "abstract mystical eyeless work" (WD, pp. 280, 309). In her *Transparent Minds*, Dorrit Cohn likens *The Waves* to a prose poem also; she calls it a play-poem-novel, and mentions it at the end of her book, *in extremis*, as such (pp. 263-65).

53. Here, before our eyes, in the manuscript, we see, as if metonymically in a pattern representing the whole, even the references to what in particular vanishes for the larger sight, the wide perspective revealed beyond and by the framed picture holding still. "Life stand still here," says Mrs. Ramsay still (TLH, p. 240).

VI

1. The ingenious analysis made by Rosalind Krauss of the use of the grid in contemporary art is relevant here to the frame in its purest border state as Roger Fry tends to see it in his more formalist period; in its most self-involved and nonreferential status, at the limits of form itself. Impervious to language, as she says, it accords with the code of the avant-garde artist as to silence, the refusal of outside intrusion, and the referral for sole subject matter to the privileged and self-referring ground of the pictorial object and its organization: "The grid promotes this silence, expressing it moreover as a refusal of speech. The absolute stasis of the grid, its lack of hierarchy, of center, of inflection, emphasizes not only its antireferential character, but—more importantly—its hostility to narrative. This structure, impervious both to time and to incident, will not permit the projection of language into the domain of the visual, and the result is silence." And, on the other hand, "the grid's power lies in its capacity to figure forth the material ground of the pictorial object, simultaneously inscribing and depicting it, so that the image of the pictorial surface can be seen to be born out of the organization of pictorial matter." (In "The Originality of the Avant-Garde: A Post-Modernist Repetition," pp. 47-66.)

2. Lily's final line drawn down the middle of the canvas is the perfect minimal gesture, dividing and defining the two parts of the picture

in relation to each other. Roger Fry points out, in *Transformations: Critical and Speculative Essays on Art*, p. 3, that "in all cases our reaction to works of art is a reaction to a relation and not to sensations or objects or persons or events." He lays heavy emphasis on the unity of framed forms, on the mosaic of vision and the close texture of the text. As for the field set apart by the frame, here everything relates, in a "coherence with every other tone and colour throughout the field" (p. 52). In speaking of his attitude, J. K. Johnstone (*The Bloomsbury Group*, pp. 46, 60, 86, 366) reminds us that, for instance, in Fry's description of a Sung bowl and its curves, there is only the relation of the concave curves inside to the contours outside, of the thickness of the walls in precise relation to the matter and its resistance, whereas there is absolutely no "reference to actual life" or to the date of the production of the bowl. Referring us to A. C. Bradley's belief that poetry is "a world by itself, independent, complete, autonomous" (p. 60), Johnstone quotes Fry's claim, in the same vein as today's critics of poetry, that "the purpose of literature is the creation of structures which have for us the feeling of reality, and that these structures are self-contained, self-sufficing, and not to be valued by their references to what lies outside" (p. 60).

3. This final quotation is from p. 10, Woolf's "Notes for Stories" notebook, included as an appendix to TLH, p. 47.

BIBLIOGRAPHY

PRIMARY SOURCES: EDITIONS CONSULTED AND REFERRED TO

Austen, Jane. *Mansfield Park*. Harmondsworth: Penguin, 1966.
———. *Northanger Abbey*. Harmondsworth: Penguin, 1972.
———. *Persuasion*. Harmondsworth: Penguin, 1965.
———. *Pride and Prejudice*. Harmondsworth: Penguin, 1972.
Baudelaire, Charles. *Les fleurs du mal*, ed. Crépet et Blin. Paris: Corti, 1968.
———. *Oeuvres complètes*, ed. Claude Pichois, 2 vols. Paris: Ed. Pléiade, 1975.
Gautier, Théophile. *Mademoiselle de Maupin*. Harmondsworth: Penguin, 1981.
Hardy, Thomas. *Jude the Obscure*. Harmondsworth: Penguin, 1978.
———. *The Personal Notebooks of Thomas Hardy*, ed. Richard H. Taylor. New York: Columbia University Press, 1979.
———. *The Return of the Native*. New York: Signet, 1959.
———. *Stories and Poems*. London: Dent, Everyman's Library, 1979.
———. *Tess of the D'Urbervilles*. New York: Signet, 1980.
James, Henry. *The Ambassadors*. Harmondsworth: Penguin, 1973.
———. *The American Scene*. New York: Scribners, 1946.
———. *The Art of the Novel: Critical Prefaces*, ed. R. P. Blackmur. New York: Scribners, 1950.
———. *The Aspern Papers and Other Stories*. Harmondsworth: Penguin, 1976.
———. *The Awkward Age*. Harmondsworth: Penguin, 1978.
———. *The Complete Tales of Henry James*, ed. Leon Edel. London: Rupert Hart-Davis (vol. 9, 1892-98).
———. *Eight Tales*, ed. Morton Dauben Zabel. New York: Norton, 1969.
———. *The Golden Bowl*. Harmondsworth: Penguin, 1966.
———. *Letters of Henry James*, ed. Percy Lubbock, 2 vols. New York: Scribners, 1920.
———. *The Novels and Tales of Henry James* (The New York Edition). New York: Scribners, 1907-17.

James, Henry. *The Painter's Eye: Notes and Essays in the Pictorial Arts*, ed. John L. Sweeney. Cambridge: Harvard University Press, 1956.

―――. *The Portrait of a Lady*. Harmondsworth: Penguin, 1975.

―――. *The Princess Casamassima* (The New York Edition). Harmondsworth: Penguin, 1977.

―――. *The Sacred Fount*. New York: Grove Books, Black Cat Editions, 1979.

―――. *The Scenic Art: Notes on Acting and the Drama, 1871-1901*, ed. Allan Wade. New Brunswick: Rutgers University Press, 1948.

―――. *A Small Boy and Others*. London: Macmillan, 1913

―――. *The Tragic Muse*. Harmondsworth: Penguin, 1979.

―――. *"The Turn of the Screw" and Other Stories*. Harmondsworth: Penguin, 1969.

―――. *The Wings of the Dove*. New York: Signet, New American Library, 1964.

Melville, Herman. *Pierre; or, The Ambiguities*. New York: New American Library, Signet Classics, 1964.

Poe, Edgar Allan. *Complete Tales and Poems*. New York: Vintage, 1975.

―――. *Cuentos*, tr. Julio Cortázar. Puerto Rico: Editorial Universitaria, 1969.

―――. *Oeuvres choisies*, tr. Charles Baudelaire. Paris: Livre Club Diderot, Coll. "Filigrane," 1972, pp. 552-56 for the translation of Poe's "The Oval Portrait."

―――. *Selected Writings*. Harmondsworth: Penguin, 1967.

Proust, Marcel. *A la recherche du temps perdu*. Vols 1-3. Paris: Ed. Pléiade, 1956.

Woolf, Virginia. *The Captain's Death Bed and Other Essays*. New York: Harcourt Brace, 1950.

―――. *Collected Essays*, ed. Leonard Woolf. London: Chatto and Windus, 1966-69.

―――. *The Common Reader*. New York: Harcourt Brace, Harvest Books, 1953.

―――. *Granite and Rainbow*. New York: Harcourt Brace, 1975.

―――. *The Letters of Virginia Woolf*, ed. Nigel Nicolson and Joanne Trautmann, 4 vols. New York: Harcourt Brace Jovanovich, 1975-1978. London: Hogarth, 1976.

―――. *Moments of Being*, ed. Jeanne Schulkind. New York: Harcourt Brace, 1978.

———. *The Second Common Reader*. New York: Harcourt Brace, Harvest Books, 1960.

———. *Street Haunting: A London Adventure*. San Francisco: Westgate Press, 1930.

———. *To the Lighthouse*. New York: Harcourt Brace, 1978.

———. *To the Lighthouse: The Original Holograph Draft*, ed. Susan Dick. Toronto and Buffalo: The University of Toronto Press, 1982.

———. *The Waves*. New York: Harcourt Brace Jovanovich, Harvest Edition, 1978; first prt., 1931.

———. *"The Waves": The Two Holograph Drafts*, transcribed and ed. J. W. Graham. Toronto: The University of Toronto Press, with the University of Western Ontario, 1976.

———. *A Writer's Diary*, ed. Leonard Woolf. London: Hogarth Press, 1954.

OTHER AUTHORS QUOTED OR READ ON FRAMING

Claudel, Paul. *Introduction à la peinture hollandaise*. Paris: Ed. Pléiade, 1965.

Ortega y Gasset, José. *Confessiones de "El Espectador."* In *Obras completas*, 6th ed. Madrid: Revista de Occidente, 1963.

Heidegger, Martin. "The Origin of the Work of Art." In *Poetry, Language, Thought*, tr. Albert Hofstadter. New York: Harper Colophon Books, 1975, pp. 15-88.

Hérédia, José Maria de. In *The Penguin Book of French Verse*, ed. Anthony Hartley. Harmondsworth: Penguin, 1974.

Hollander, John. *Spectral Emanations*. New York: Atheneum, 1978.

The Note-books and Papers of Gerard Manley Hopkins, ed. H. House. New York: Oxford, 1959.

Marquez, Gabriel Garcia. Interview in *La Quinzaine littéraire*, Jan. 1-15, 1982.

The Works of John Ruskin, ed. E. T. Cook and Alexander Wedderburn. London: Library Edition, 1903-12.

The Works of William Shakespeare, gathered into one volume. New York: Oxford Unviersity Press, 1938.

Stevens, Wallace. *The Palm at the End of the Mind*. New York: Random House, 1972.

Wharton, Edith. "The Man of Letters." In Edel, ed., *Critical Essays*, pp. 34-35.

CRITICAL COMMENTARY

Anderson, Charles. *Person, Place, and Thing in Henry James' Novels*. Durham: Duke University Press, 1977.

Anderson, Quentin. *The American Henry James*. London: John Calder, 1958.

Arnheim, Rudolf. *Art and Visual Perception*. Berkeley and Los Angeles: University of California Press, 1969.

Auerbach, Eric. *Mimesis: The Representation of Reality in Western Literature*, tr. Willard Trask. Princeton: Princeton University Press, 1953.

Bateson, Gregory. *Steps to an Ecology of Mind*. New York: Ballantine Books, 1972.

Beardsley, Monroe C. *Aesthetics*. New York: Harcourt Brace, 1958.

Bercovitch, Sacvan. *The American Jeremiad*. Madison: University of Wisconsin Press, 1978.

Berry, Francis. *The Shakespeare Inset: Word and Picture*. London: Longmans, 1965.

Bersani, Leo. *Baudelaire and Freud*. Berkeley and Los Angeles: University of California Press, 1977; coll. Quantum Books, 1982.

Black, Max. *Models and Metaphors*. Ithaca: Cornell University Press, 1962.

Blackmur, R. P. "In the Country of the Blue." In Dupee, ed., *The Question of Henry James*.

————. "The Craft of Herman Melville: A Putative Statement." In *Melville: A Collection of Critical Essays*, ed. Richard Chase. Englewood Cliffs, N.J.: Prentice-Hall, 1962.

Blanchard, Marc Eli. *Description: Sign, Self, Desire: Critical Theory in the Wake of Semiotics*. Approaches to Semiotics, no. 43. The Hague: Mouton, 1980.

Bouleau, Charles. *Charpentes: La géométrie secrète des peintres*. Paris: Seuil, 1963.

Brombert, Victor. "Opening Signals in Narration." *New Literary History* (1979), pp. 489-502.

Bullough, Edward. In *The British Journal of Psychology*, 5 (1912), pp. 87-118.

Caws, Mary Ann. *The Eye in the Text: Essays on Perception, Mannerist to Modern*. Princeton: Princeton University Press, 1981.

————. "Moral-Reading, or Self-Containment with a Flaw." *New Literary History* (1983-84), pp. 209-15.

Chase, Richard, ed. *Melville: A Collection of Critical Essays*. Englewood Cliffs, N.J.: Prentice-Hall, 1962.

Chatman, Seymour. *The Later Style of Henry James*. Oxford: Blackwell, 1972.

Cohn, Dorrit. *Transparent Minds*. Princeton: Princeton University Press, 1978.

Colby, Frank Moore. "In Darkest James." In Dupee, ed., *The Question of Henry James*.

Culler, Jonathan. "Prolegomena to a Theory of Reading." In *The Reader in the Text*, ed. Susan R. Suleiman and Inge Crosman. Princeton: Princeton University Press, 1980.

Dällenbach, Lucien. *Le récit spéculaire: Essai sur la mise en abyme*. Paris: Seuil, 1977.

Daubanton, Monique. "L'ovale du portrait." *Poétique*, Paris, no. 37 (Feb. 1979), pp. 102-10.

Derrida, Jacques. *La dissémination*. Paris: Seuil, 1972.

———. *La vérité en peinture*. Paris: Flammarion, 1980.

DiBattista, Maria. *Virginia Woolf's Major Novels: The Fables of Anon*. New Haven: Yale University Press, 1972.

Dittmar, Linda. "Fashioning and Re-fashioning: Framing Narratives in the Novel and Film." *Mosaic*, 16 (1982), pp. 189-203.

Dupee, F. W. *Henry James*. London: William Sloane Associates, 1951.

———. ed. *The Question of Henry James*. New York: Octagon, 1973.

Edel, Leon. *Henry James; The Untried Years, 1843-1870*. Philadelphia: Lippincott, 1953.

———. *Henry James: The Conquest of London, 1870-1881*. Philadelphia: Lippincott, 1962.

———. *Henry James: The Middle Years, 1882-1895*. Philadelphia: Lippincott, 1962.

———. *Henry James: The Treacherous Years, 1896-1900*. Philadelphia: 1969.

———. *Henry James: The Master 1901-1916*. London: Rupert Hart-Davis, 1972.

———. ed. *Henry James: A Collection of Critical Essays*. Englewood Cliffs, N.J.: Prentice-Hall, 1963.

Ehrenzweig, Anton. *The Hidden Order of Art*. Berkeley and Los Angeles: University of California Press, 1967.

Eisenstein, Sergei. "The Cinematic Principle of Ideograms." In *Film Form*, tr. Jay Leyda. New York: Harcourt, Brace and World, 1949.

Fellows, Jay. *Ruskin's Maze: Mastery and Madness in His Art.* Princeton: Princeton University Press, 1981.

Felman, Shoshana. "Turning the Screw of Interpretation." *Yale French Studies*, "Psychoanalysis and Literature" issue, nos. 55/56 (1977), pp. 94-207.

Findlay, L. M. "D. G. Rossetti and *Jude the Obscure.*" *The Pre-Raphaelite Review* (now *The Journal of Pre-Raphaelite Studies*), vol. 2, no. 1 (1978), pp. 1-11.

Fleishman, Avrom. *Virginia Woolf: A Critical Reading.* Baltimore: The Johns Hopkins University Press, 1975.

Fry, Roger. *Transformations: Critical and Speculative Essays on Art.* London: Chatto and Windus, 1926.

———. *Vision and Design.* London and New York: Oxford University Press, 1944.

Genette, Gérard. *Figures.* Paris: Seuil. Esp. "Ordre," vol. 3 (1972), pp. 77-122.

Gibson, J. J. *Perception of the Visual World.* Boston: Houghton Mifflin, 1950.

Godfrey, Sima. "Baudelaire's Windows." *L'Esprit créateur*, vol. 22, no. 4 (Winter 1982).

Goffman, Erving. *Frame Analysis.* New York: Harper, 1974.

Gombrich, E. H. *The Sense of Order: A Study in the Psychology of Decorative Art.* London: Phaidon, 1979.

Halperin, John, ed. *Jane Austen: Bicentenary Essays.* Cambridge: Cambridge University Press, 1975.

Hamon, Philippe. *Introduction au genre descriptif.* Paris: Seuil, 1982.

———, with Wayne Booth and Wolfgang Iser. *Poétique du récit.* Paris: Seuil, Coll. Points, 1979.

Hedges, Inez. *Language of Revolt: Dada and Surrealist Literature and Film.* Durham, N.C.: Duke University Press, 1982.

Hofstadter, Douglas, *Gödel, Escher, Bach: An Eternal Golden Braid.* New York: Vintage, 1980.

Holland, Lawrence Bedwell. *Expense of Vision: Essays on the Craft of Henry James.* Baltimore: The Johns Hopkins University Press, 1982.

Hunt, Viola. "Visual Art Devices and Parallels in the Fiction of Henry James." *PMLA*, 76 (1961), pp. 561-74.

Johnson, Barbara. *The Critical Difference: Essays in the Contemporary Rhetoric of Reading.* Baltimore: The Johns Hopkins University Press, 1981.

Johnstone, J. K. *The Bloomsbury Group*. London: Secker and Warburg, 1954.

Joseph, Gerhard. "Tennyson's Optics: The Eagle's Gaze." *PMLA*, 92 (1977), pp. 420-28.

———. "Victorian Frames: The Windows and Mirrors of Browning, Tennyson, and Arnold." *Victorian Poetry*, 16 (1978), pp. 76-87.

Kazin, Alfred. *An American Procession*. New York: Knopf, 1984.

Kenin, Richard, and Wintle, Justin. *The Dictionary of Biographical Quotation*. New York: Knopf, 1978.

Kermode, Frank. *The Sense of an Ending*. London and New York: Oxford University Press, 1966.

———. "Sensing Endings." *Nineteenth-Century Fiction*, vol. 33, no. 1 (June 1978), pp. 144-58.

Kestner, Joseph A. *Spatiality in the Novel*. Detroit: Wayne State University Press, 1978.

Knights, L. C. *Explorations*. New York: George Stewart, 1947.

Krauss, Rosalind. "The Originality of the Avant-Garde: A Post-Modernist Repetition." *October* (Fall 1981), pp. 47-66.

Leavis, F. R. *The Great Tradition*. Harmondsworth: Penguin, 1948.

Levy, Leo Benjamin. *Versions of Melodrama: A Study of the Fiction and Drama of Henry James*. Berkeley and Los Angeles: University of California Press, 1957.

Litz, A. Walton. *Jane Austen: A Study of Her Development*. London: Chatto and Windus, 1965.

Lotman, Youri. *The Structure of the Artistic Text*. Ann Arbor: Michigan Slavic Contributions, 1977.

Lowin, Joseph. "The Frames of Lorenzaccio." *French Review*, vol. 53, no. 2 (1980), pp. 190-98.

Lubbock, Percy. *The Craft of Fiction*. New York: Viking, 1921.

Majumdar, Robin, and Allen McLaurin, eds. *Virginia Woolf: The Critical Heritage*. London: Routledge and Kegan Paul, 1975.

Marin, Louis. *Détruire la peinture*. Paris: Ed. Galilée, 1977.

Matthiessen, F. O. *Henry James: The Major Phase*. London: Oxford University Press, 1944.

———. "James and the Plastic Arts." *Kenyon Review*, 6 (Autumn 1943), pp. 533-50.

———. *The James Family*. New York: Knopf, 1947.

McLaurin, Allen. *Virginia Woolf: The Echoes Enslaved*. Cambridge: Cambridge University Press, 1973.

Mehlis, Georg. "Aesthetic Problem of Distance." In Susanne K. Langer, *Reflections on Art.* Baltimore: The Johns Hopkins University Press, 1958.

Meisel, Perry. *The Absent Father: Virginia Woolf and Walter Pater.* New Haven: Yale University Press, 1980.

Melchiori, Giorgio. *The Tightrope Walkers: Essays on Mannerism in Modern English Literature.* Westport: Greenwood Press, 1974.

Miller, D. A. *Narrative and Its Discontents: Problems of Closure in the Traditional Novel.* Princeton: Princeton University Press, 1982.

Miller, J. Hillis. *Fiction and Repetition.* Cambridge: Harvard University Press, 1982.

————. "The Problematics of Ending." *Nineteenth-Century Fiction,* vol. 33, no. 1 (1978), pp. 3-7.

————. *Thomas Hardy: Distance and Desire.* Cambridge: Harvard University Press, 1970.

Mudrick, Marvin. *Jane Austen: Irony as Defense and Discovery.* Berkeley and Los Angeles: University of California Press, 1968.

Naremore, James. *The World without a Self: Virginia Woolf and the Novel.* New Haven and London: Yale University Press, 1973.

Perrot, Jean. "Enigme et fiction métalinguistique chez James." *Poétique,* no. 45 (Feb. 1981), pp. 53-66.

Poulet, Georges. *Proustian Space.* Baltimore: The Johns Hopkins University Press, 1977.

————. *Studies in Human Time.* New York: Harper, 1956.

Pribam, Karl. *Languages of the Brain.* Englewood Cliffs, N.J.: Prentice-Hall, 1971.

Reed, Arden. "Abysmal Influence." *Glyph,* 4 (1978), pp. 189-206.

Rogers, B. G. *Proust's Narrative Techniques.* Geneva: Droz, 1965.

Rosenthal, Michael. *Virginia Woolf.* London: Routledge and Kegan Paul, 1979.

Said, Edward. *Beginnings: Intention and Method.* New York: Basic Books, 1975.

Schapiro, Meyer. "On Some Problems in the Semiotics of Visual Art." *Semiotica,* 1 (1969), pp. 223-42.

Simmel, Georg. *The Sociology of Georg Simmel,* ed. and tr. Kurt H. Wolff. New York: Crowell-Collier, 1964.

Smith, Barbara Herrnstein. *Poetic Closure: A Study of How Poems End.* Chicago: University of Chicago Press, 1968.

Steward, J.I.M. *Thomas Hardy.* London: Allen Lange, 1971.

Stokes, Adrian. *The Invitation in Art*. London: Tavistock, 1965.

Tanner, Tony, ed. *Henry James: Modern Judgments*. London: Macmillan, 1968.

Thompson, Lawrance. *Melville's Quarrel with God*. Princeton: Princeton University Press, 1952.

Tintner, Adeline. "The Museum World." In Edel, ed., *Critical Essays*.

———. "The Spoils of Henry James." *PMLA*, 61 (1946), pp. 239-51.

Tison-Braun, Micheline. *Poétique du paysage: Essai sur le genre descriptif*. Paris: Nizet, 1980.

Todorov, Tzvetan. "Le secret du récit: Henry James." In *Novelles recherches sur le récit*. Paris: Seuil, Coll. Points, 1978. Pp. 81-115.

Torgovnick, Marianna. *Closure in the Novel*. Princeton: Princeton University Press, 1982.

Uspensky, Boris. *A Poetics of Composition: The Structure of the Artistic Text and Typology of a Compositional Form*. Berkeley and Los Angeles: University of California Press, 1973.

Vernon, M. D. *Psychology of Perception*. Harmondsworth: Penguin, 1962.

Weinstein, Philip. *Henry James and the Requirements of the Imagination*. Cambridge: Harvard University Press, 1971.

Winner, Viola Hopkins. *Henry James and the Visual Arts*. Charlottesville: University Press of Viriginia, 1970.

Winnicott, D. W. *Collected Papers: Through Paediatrics to Psychoanalysis*. New York: Basic Books, 1958.

———. *The Maturational Process and the Facilitating Environment*. New York: International Universities Press, 1965.

———. *Playing and Reality*. London: Methuen, 1982.

Yeazell, Ruth Bernard. *Language and Knowledge in the Late Novels of Henry James*. Chicago: University of Chicago Press, 1976.

INDEX

Library of Congress Cataloging in Publication Data

Caws, Mary Ann.
  Reading frames in modern fiction.

  Bibliography: p.
  Includes index.
  1. Fiction—Technique. 2. Discourse analysis, Narrative. I. Title.
  PN3355.C37 1984   809.3'923   84-16092
  ISBN 0-691-06625-6 (alk. paper)

Mary Ann Caws is Distinguished Professor of French and
Comparative Literature at Hunter College and in the Graduate School
of City University of New York. She is the author of many books,
among which are *The Inner Theatre of Recent French Poetry* (Princeton,
1972), *The Presence of René Char* (Princeton, 1976), and *The Eye in
the Text* (Princeton, 1981).